*Touring the
Shenandoah
Valley
Backroads*

OTHER TITLES IN JOHN F. BLAIR'S *TOURING THE BACKROADS*™ SERIES

Touring the Backroads of North Carolina's Upper Coast by Daniel W. Barefoot
Touring the Backroads of North Carolina's Lower Coast by Daniel W. Barefoot
Touring North Carolina's Revolutionary War Sites by Daniel W. Barefoot
Touring the Backroads of North and South Georgia by Victoria and Frank Logue
Touring the Coastal Georgia Backroads by Nancy Rhyne
Touring the Coastal South Carolina Backroads by Nancy Rhyne
Touring the Middle Tennessee Backroads by Robert Brandt
Touring the East Tennessee Backroads by Carolyn Sakowski
Touring the Western North Carolina Backroads by Carolyn Sakowski
Touring the Carolinas' Civil War Sites by Clint Johnson

Touring South Carolina's Revolutionary War Sites by Daniel W. Barefoot
*August 1999

Touring Virginia's and West Virginia's Civil War Sites by Clint Johnson
*September 1999

Touring the Shenandoah Valley Backroads

Andrea Sutcliffe

John F. Blair
Publisher
Winston-Salem,
North Carolina

BOOK DESIGN BY DEBRA LONG HAMPTON
PHOTOGRAPHS BY THE AUTHOR

*The paper in this book meets the guidelines
for permanence and durability of the
Committee on Production Guidelines for
Book Longevity of the Council on Library Resources.*

Photographs on front cover clockwise from top left—
*State Arboretum of Virginia from The White Post to Millwood to Berryville Tour
A typical Shenandoah Valley scene from The White Post to Millwood to Berryville Tour
Abram's Delight in Winchester from The Middletown to Winchester Tour
Natural Chimneys in Mount Solon from The Harrisonburg to Port Republic Tour
The Shenandoah River from The Massanutten Mountain–Page Valley Tour
Southern Virginia College in Buena Vista from The Natural Bridge to Lexington Tour*

Library of Congress Cataloging-in-Publication Data
Sutcliffe, Andrea.
Touring the Shenandoah Valley backroads / Andrea Sutcliffe.
p.   cm.
Includes bibliographical references and index.
ISBN 0-89587-181-5 (alk. paper)
1. Shenandoah River Valley (Va. and W. Va.) Tours. 2. Automobile travel—Shenandoah
River Valley (Va. and W. Va.)—Guidebooks.
I. Title.
F232.S5S88   1999
917.55'90443—dc21   99-23894

*T*o my father,
Edward A. Johnson,
whose idea of a good backroad
is one with grass growing down the middle

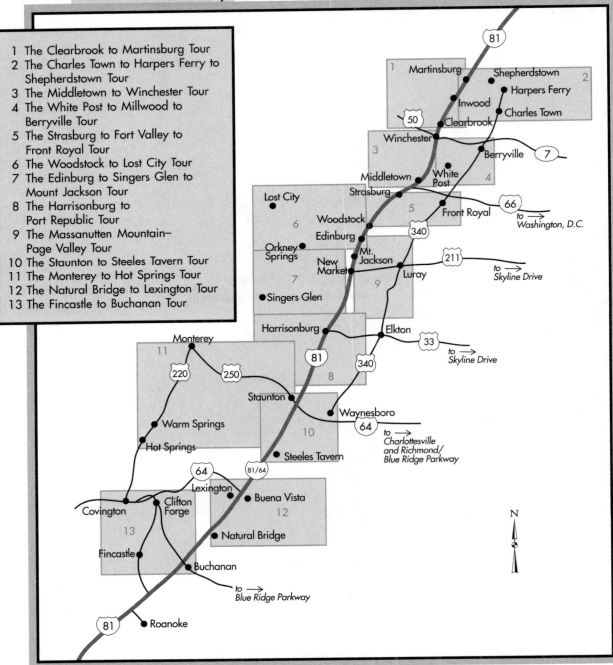

The Shenandoah Valley

1 The Clearbrook to Martinsburg Tour
2 The Charles Town to Harpers Ferry to Shepherdstown Tour
3 The Middletown to Winchester Tour
4 The White Post to Millwood to Berryville Tour
5 The Strasburg to Fort Valley to Front Royal Tour
6 The Woodstock to Lost City Tour
7 The Edinburg to Singers Glen to Mount Jackson Tour
8 The Harrisonburg to Port Republic Tour
9 The Massanutten Mountain–Page Valley Tour
10 The Staunton to Steeles Tavern Tour
11 The Monterey to Hot Springs Tour
12 The Natural Bridge to Lexington Tour
13 The Fincastle to Buchanan Tour

Contents

Preface

People are often surprised to learn how closely the history of the Shenandoah Valley ties in with the early history of the United States. As far back as the 1730s, German, Swiss, and Scots-Irish immigrant families began settling this area. Most came from the north, traveling through Pennsylvania and Maryland down an old north-south Indian trail that came to be known as the Great Wagon Road—today's U.S. 11. Over the next century, many stayed here, but many more continued their journey west through the Cumberland Gap.

In the 1750s, Valley settlers endured the horrors of the vicious random attacks that characterized the French and Indian War. During that same period, George Washington began his military and political career in Winchester. Twenty years later, Valley men volunteered in great numbers to fight in the American Revolution. Several became well-known generals in the Continental Army.

By the 1800s, the Valley's agricultural richness helped meet the growing nation's food needs. One of its sons, Cyrus McCormick, invented a machine that sparked a worldwide revolution in agriculture.

In 1862, the Shenandoah Valley's importance in the Civil War became evident in the many crucial battles fought here, led by Valley resident Stonewall Jackson.

For a while in the late 1800s and early 1900s, industry took hold in places, often to the detriment of the Valley's natural resources. Today, the forests and rivers have recovered considerably, and industrial development in the Valley is limited mainly to light manufacturing. The overall feel of the region is again one of small towns, orchards, farmland, and forested wilderness areas.

As in the other volumes in this series, the goal of this book is to bring history to life for backroads travelers by pointing out significant places and events along the way. The past rests here in layers, many of which are still visible if you look closely enough. In many spots, with just a little imagination, you can mentally transport yourself back in time 100 years or more.

Almost everywhere on these tours, you'll see homes, churches, and buildings that date to the 1700s and 1800s. Most are still in use. Many log homes have long been covered with clapboard siding or stucco, but their limestone foundations reveal the antiquity of their construction. The placement of chimneys in many of these old homes gives a clue to the ancestry of their builders: end chimneys were preferred by the British, while central chimneys were the style of the Germans. On these roads, you'll see many old mills, barns, and outbuildings—especially old stone or log springhouses and smokehouses. So long as these structures are preserved by caring owners, it is hard to forget that people once got by—not really that long ago—without refrigerators and supermarkets.

Now for a word about the research. In some locales, historical records were quite good. Historian John W. Wayland, who wrote many books on the area in the first half of the 20th century, and Samuel Kercheval, who in the early 1800s established himself as the Valley's first historian, provided a good base for my initial research. At the local level, recorded histories have been produced largely through the efforts of area citizens working alone or with historical societies to capture the stories of the past. Some of those accounts appear to be more complete and accurate than others. Sometimes, it was difficult to determine which account of a historical event was the correct one. In those cases, I tried to find additional information and then made a judgment call. More times than I cared to, however, I had to add caveats like "According to local legend" and "So the story goes." My overall purpose was to create a general guide describing points of interest and local lore for travelers, not an academic history of the Valley.

I routed the tours with history in mind, while also considering the scenic beauty of the drive and the time required to stay within the limits of a day trip. I could not include every town and historic site in the Shenandoah Valley and so had to make some hard decisions. Often, if a historic building or site was too far off a tour's main route, or could not be seen from the road, I chose to leave it out. If you are interested in a more detailed history of any part of the Valley, please refer to the bibliography for suggested books, or contact one of the many county historical societies listed in the appendix.

My father, a tireless backroads traveler, is well known in our family for saying, "Never go back the way you came." In designing these tours, I followed his advice. Most take the form of a circle that ends not far from where it began. But if your mind is agile enough to reverse directions, you may want to try, perhaps on another day, going back the way you came. I can guarantee that you will experience a totally different view and see things you missed the first time.

Interstate 81, which runs the length of the Valley and beyond, serves as the jumping-off point for all the tours. They are arranged geographically from north to south, for a total distance on I-81 of about 200 miles from Martinsburg, West Virginia, to just north of Roanoke. Many of the tours end near the start of the next one, which will allow travelers to connect two or more tours in an area, if they have the time and the inclination. Most roads are paved and well-maintained U.S., state, and county roads. In a few instances, the tours include short stretches of gravel roads, but you won't need a four-wheel-drive vehicle for any of them except perhaps on snowy winter days.

Driving instructions appear in italics. To give an idea of distances to turns and tour stops, mileages are given in tenths of a mile. Please keep in mind that these are approximate and that odometer readings vary from car to car.

Many of the small museums and attractions mentioned are staffed by volunteers and have limited hours of operation. Some are closed during the winter months. For those reasons, it's a good idea to call ahead to confirm opening and closing times. Addresses and phone numbers are listed in the appendix. The Shenandoah Valley Tourist Association and local visitor centers (also listed in the appendix) will be happy to provide information about food, lodging, and commercial attractions (such as the many beautiful caverns in the area), which are not covered in this book.

Most people visit the Shenandoah Valley in the summer or fall. But touring these backroads in winter or spring has its rewards as well. In the late fall and winter, when the leaves are off the trees, you'll be able to see things that are hidden at other times of the year. In early spring, the forests are dappled with the delicate white flowers of dogwood trees. By May and June, the pink blooms of mountain laurel and rhododendron add bursts of color to the just-greening woods. Whenever you visit, you'll be surprised at the scenic mountain landscapes and the unspoiled wilderness that can be found not far from places like Washington, D.C., Baltimore, Richmond, and Norfolk.

I could not have written this book without the help of staff members, librarians, and volunteers at the following places: the Shenandoah County Library, the Rockingham County Library, the Harrisonburg–Rockingham County Historical Society, the Society of Port Republic Preservationists, the Rockbridge Public Library, the Roanoke Public Library, the Augusta County Public Library, the Handley Library in Winchester, the Martinsburg Public Library, the James Madison University Library, the Rockbridge Historical Society, the Strasburg Museum, the Jefferson County Museum, the Bath Historical Society, and the Library of Congress. Thanks also go to Carolyn Sakowski at John F. Blair, Publisher, for giving me the chance to do this book. Steve Kirk, Blair's editor, was truly the reader's advocate on this book, making sure that my directions and descriptions were clear; thanks, Steve. I also appreciate the efforts of friends who test-drove tours, especially Austine and Tom Eversole and Jane and Fred Kruck. But the person who deserves the most thanks is my husband, Ed Sutcliffe, who cheerfully helped me double- and sometimes triple-check each tour's directions. His love, support, and good humor held fast no matter how many times I asked him to turn around to check a sign or pull off the road, usually on a moment's notice.

Touring the Shenandoah Valley Backroads

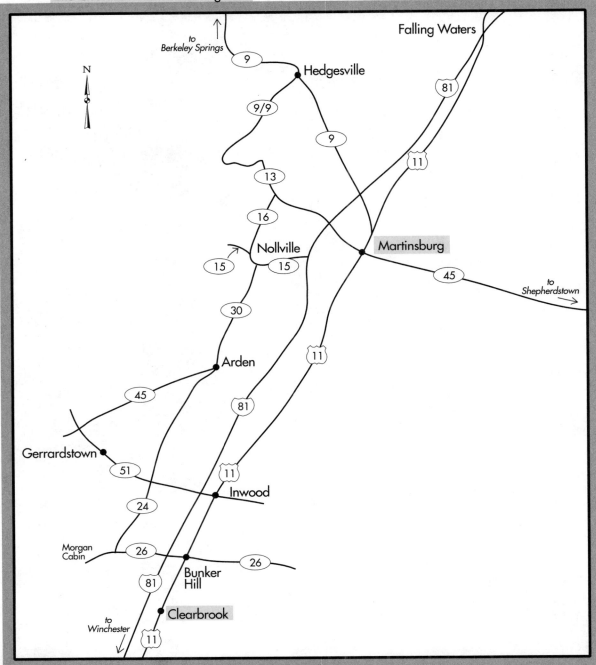

The Clearbrook to Martinsburg Tour

The Clearbrook to Martinsburg Tour

To begin the tour, take Exit 317 off I-81 just north of Winchester. Turn right on U.S. 11 North, known in this neck of the woods as the Martinsburg Turnpike. In about 1.5 miles, you'll enter the village of **Stephenson**, where a Civil War battle took place on June 15, 1863 (when the community was known as Stephenson's Depot). In another 0.5 mile, look on the right side of the road for a large stone historical marker. It describes how Confederate general Edward "Allegheny Ed" Johnson's troops, in a dawn attack, surprised Union general Robert H. Milroy's men, who were retreating from Winchester. The Southerners were able to capture the Union wagon train and take 2,300 prisoners. Johnson's army then moved on to Pennsylvania, where it was defeated two weeks later in the Battle of Gettysburg.

Continue 1.5 miles to the community of **Clearbrook**. As you approach the town, look for a gas station and convenience store on the left. Turn left just after the store on to Route 672 (Hopewell Road). Drive 0.8 mile after passing over I-81. A sign on the left at Waverly Road reads "Waverly Farm Jerseys." Just beyond the farm sign, turn left at the next driveway. It leads to a beautiful old two-story limestone building known as Hopewell Meeting, built by early Quaker settlers in 1759.

Alexander Ross came to Pennsylvania from Ireland as an indentured servant around 1693. (Many settlers paid for their ocean passage by agreeing to a period of servitude to the person who financed their journey.) Ten years later, when he was about 21, he earned his freedom. For many years, he worked as a carpenter. But when the colony of Virginia began to encourage settlement in the Shenandoah Valley in the early 1730s, Ross,

This tour begins north of Winchester on U.S. 11 in an area of early Quaker settlement. It passes a Civil War battle site at Stephenson and stops to visit a 1700s Quaker stone church, Hopewell Meeting, near Clearbrook, once the center of a thriving woolen industry in this area. From there, it crosses into West Virginia and heads west, passing another early settlement, Bunker Hill. It pauses at the restored log cabin of one of the area's first settlers and then winds through picturesque apple- and peach-orchard country along Apple Pie Ridge, visiting the historic towns of Gerrardstown and Hedgesville before entering the final stop on the tour, Martinsburg. Martinsburg is full of historic homes and buildings, many dating back to the time of its founding during the Revolutionary War.

If time permits, this tour is easily combined with the next one, which begins in Shepherdstown, just 7 miles east of Martinsburg.

Total mileage:
Approximately 52 miles

Defining the Shenandoah Valley

Although definitions vary, the Shenandoah Valley is generally considered to run from the West Virginia counties of Berkeley and Jefferson, where the Shenandoah River joins the Potomac River at Harpers Ferry, to south of Lexington, Virginia. It is part of the larger Valley of Virginia, which stretches from the Potomac to the eastern part of Tennessee. Strictly speaking, however, the Shenandoah Valley—as defined by the Shenandoah River and its affluents—is the area that extends from Harpers Ferry to south of Staunton.

Because the Shenandoah River runs north to south, residents have long referred to the northern part of the Valley as the "lower Valley" and the southern part as the "upper Valley." Geographically, it makes sense, but it can still get confusing. If you hear a longtime resident say he's heading "up the Valley," he's probably going south, not north.

a devout Quaker, and Morgan Bryan, an Irish Presbyterian, applied for a land grant. Between 1730 and 1732, they were granted a total of 120,000 acres in the northern Valley. Ultimately, they brought 70 families from around Chester, Pennsylvania, to settle here. Ross kept a 2,400-acre tract for himself and built a home, Waverly. Bryan's group settled near Bunker Hill. (Bryan's granddaughter, Rebecca, later married Daniel Boone.)

Quaker settlements in the area grew throughout the 1700s. By around 1800, the Quakers had established 17 meetings, or churches, in the Shenandoah Valley and neighboring Hampshire County, now part of West Virginia.

Hopewell Meeting still has an active Quaker congregation. It is said to be the oldest religious structure in continuous use in the Shenandoah Valley. Hopewell Meeting had its beginnings as a log structure built not long after settlers arrived in 1734. It was enlarged in 1788 and 1789 and at one time had a partition down the middle to allow for services by both Orthodox and original Quakers.

You passed the road to Alexander Ross's home, Waverly, before turning into Hopewell. From the meeting house, look south down the hill past the cemetery to see Waverly's dark rooftop and brick chimney. Ross built the home between 1735 and 1748. His descendants sold it and the surrounding 500 acres in 1826 to George Fayette Washington, a great-nephew of the

Hopewell Meeting

president (he was the grandson of Charles Washington, who was George Washington's youngest brother). It is believed that George Fayette Washington gave the house its current name. The home stayed in the Washington family until 1923.

As the years passed, the number of Quakers in the Valley gradually diminished. Some people moved away because of their opposition to both war and slavery (many were persecuted for their pro-Union stance during the Civil War). Others—including Dolley Todd Payne, who became Mrs. James Madison—married outside the faith and were no longer allowed to be members of the church.

To continue the tour, retrace your route to U.S. 11 and turn left. Before you turn, look to the right for the small log building that houses the Clearbrook Woolen Company. The current establishment is a fabric and blanket shop, but its name reflects the area's history as a spinning and weaving center from 1771 to 1971.

The original Clearbrook Woolen Company moved here in 1930, after a fire destroyed its predecessor, the Brucetown Woolen Mill (formerly known as the Pine Grove Woolen Factory and the Jobe Woolen Mill). Of all the mills in the northern part of the Valley, the Clearbrook Woolen Mill was probably the oldest and certainly the last to shut down. By the time it closed in 1971, the demand for domestic wool had shrunk drastically, the result of cheaper foreign wool and the popularity of synthetic fabrics.

Continue north on U.S. 11 for 3.1 miles to the West Virginia state line. From there, it is another 1.7 miles to an old red-brick mansion on the left, Edgewood Manor, in **Bunker Hill**. Now a bed-and-breakfast, Edgewood Manor was completed in 1839 by General Elisha Boyd for his son, John Boyd. This is the same General Boyd who built the mansion known as Boydville in Martinsburg (described later in this tour). Boyd operated two mills, a brick plant, and a cooper's shop at Edgewood in the 1820s.

Bunker Hill was the scene of much destruction during the Civil War. John Boyd's son, John Jr., was captured at Edgewood by Union soldiers and charged with being a spy. Stonewall Jackson once camped on the home's lawn. The tall monument at Edgewood's entrance drive commemorates Confederate general James Johnston Pettigrew of North Carolina, who was wounded at Falling Waters, north of Martinsburg, while retreating from

Guns at Hopewell Meeting

In the 1700s, the surrounding mountains were home to many species of wild animals. As Valley historian John Wayland noted, "In the early days Friends [Quakers] going to or from Hopewell were occasionally chased by wolves, and the men carried their rifles to the meeting house and stacked them in a corner. They were for defense against the wolves, not the Indians. The latter were not hostile to the Friends."

Although most Shenandoah Valley residents lived in constant fear of Indian attack throughout the 1750s and 1760s, the Indians respected the Quakers and left them alone. The Quakers had gained a reputation in Pennsylvania for treating Indians fairly, even offering to pay for the land they settled—a gesture the Indians appreciated but weren't sure how to handle, since the concept of private property was foreign to them.

Gettysburg. Pettigrew died at Edgewood before he could reach Winchester for medical treatment.

From Edgewood, drive another 0.2 mile on U.S. 11 to the blinking yellow light in Bunker Hill. Turn right at the light on to Route 26, which passes through the Mill Creek Historic District. As many as 10 mills operated in this area from the 1730s to the 1900s.

Less than 1 mile down Route 26 is an old stone building that was once the Bunker Hill Flour Mill. The mill was built around 1800 on the site of an earlier mill dating to the 1730s. Its waterwheel and race can still be seen. An old one-room schoolhouse is located across the road from the mill.

Turn around at the mill and drive back to U.S. 11. Cross it and continue west on Route 26. Just down the road on the right is a large brick building that houses Bunker Hill Antiques, a popular shopping stop. Just past the antique shop is Christ Episcopal Church, established in 1740 by Morgan Morgan (see below), Dr. John Briscoe, and Jacob Hite. It is thought to be one of the oldest churches in the Valley. Built in 1851, the present structure is the third church on this site. Many early settlers, including Morgan Morgan, are buried in its cemetery.

Continue down Route 26 to the stop sign at the intersection with Route 24. Stay straight past the stop sign. In about 0.5 mile, look to the left to see a clapboard-covered cabin with a West Virginia historical marker. This is Morgan Cabin, which was rebuilt in 1976 from many of the original logs of a cabin constructed by Morgan Morgan. A Welshman who came here from Pennsylvania in 1728, Morgan initially built a crude cabin for his family near this spot. About four years later, he completed the larger cabin that has been restored and stands here today. It is thought to be the first settler's house in what is now West Virginia. The clapboard exterior was added later to protect the original logs, which can still be seen from the inside. The cabin is open on Sunday afternoons from May through August.

Morgan's sons and grandsons fought in the Revolutionary War. His grandson James was an army chaplain who was killed execution-style at this cabin by British Tories, who cruelly forced his wife and children to watch.

The old stone-and-clapboard house across and down the road was built in 1761 by Zackquill Morgan, one of Colonel Morgan's sons and the founder of Morgantown, West Virginia.

Bunker Hill Flour Mill

Morgan Cabin

Turn around at Morgan Cabin and retrace Route 26 to the stop sign at Route 24 (Godmiller Road). Turn left. This lovely stretch of rolling road takes you past thousands of acres of apple and peach orchards. Great North Mountain is to the left.

In about 2.5 miles, you'll see a large white apple storage building on the left near an intersection. At the stop sign, turn left on Route 51. (Note that it may not be marked as such. West Virginia backroads often lack road signs, so look for the landmarks mentioned here.)

After about 0.5 mile, you'll pass a lovely old home on the left. This is Marshy Dell, a two-story log home dating to the late 1700s.

Proceed into the charming little village of **Gerrardstown**. Laid out by David Gerard in 1784, Gerrardstown is noted for being home to the first Baptist church west of the Blue Ridge. The village seems locked in the 19th century. Many of its original homes are still occupied, including the lovely stone house on the right in the heart of the village.

Just past the little general store on the left, turn left on Virginia Line Road and go several hundred feet to see the Gerard House. It was built by John Hays for John Gerard, an itinerant Baptist minister and the father of the village's founder, in 1743. It is listed on the National Register of Historic Places. The first floor is a crafts shop operated by the owners of a bed-and-breakfast housed in a turn-of-the-century Victorian home on the tree-filled property.

Return to Route 51 and turn left. A picturesque old brick home, Prospect Hill, is on the left after about 0.5 mile. Built in 1795 by William Wilson, this Federal-style house is now a bed-and-breakfast inn and the centerpiece of a working farm. In the 1750s, in the last Indian attack in this part of the Shenandoah Valley, the Kelly family was attacked and murdered at its log cabin here.

Continue north on Route 51 until it intersects Route 45. Turn right on Route 45. Here, high atop Great North Mountain's Apple Pie Ridge, a marker notes that the John Mills Tavern stood at this spot (known as Pack Horse Road at Mills Gap) in 1769. There is a parking area on the right where you can pull over to view the valley below.

After 4.4 miles, you'll come to a stop sign. Ignore the signs to stay on Route 45 East and instead go straight to the second stop sign and the intersection with Route 30. Again, note that the road may not be marked. Turn left. You will pass

Gerard House

Pendleton House

Bella Vista

Mount Zion Episcopal Church

many interesting old homes and rolling hills covered with apple and peach orchards as far as the eye can see—a gorgeous sight in the spring when the trees are in bloom.

After a little less than 2 miles, you'll see, on the left, a white stucco home with a massive stone chimney. This house was constructed in 1775 by Philip Pendleton and is thought to be one of the largest log structures ever built in Berkeley County. The original logs have long been covered with stucco. This treatment, fairly common in the Valley in the 1800s, preserved the log structure, helped insulate it, and gave it a more modern appearance.

About 1.3 miles past the Pendleton House, turn left at the stop sign on to Route 15; it may not be marked as such. After less than 0.5 mile, the road passes a farm complex on the left called Bella Vista, also known as the Frederick Seibert House. This home, built in 1807, has beautifully manicured grounds. On a pond near the road are several old stone buildings that once served as Seibert's distillery and tavern.

Just past Bella Vista, turn right on to Route 16 (Thatcher Road). Route 16 ends at a stop sign after 2.2 miles. Turn left. In 1 mile, the road passes an old white frame church. Veer to the left to stay on Route 6, which will take you up and then down Great North Mountain through a thick forest. As the road ends its descent of the mountain, look for the sign that says, "1-lane bridge ahead." Turn right on to Route 9/Route 99, the road just before the bridge. Note that Route 9/ Route 99 may not be marked. The bridge, located on Back Creek, is interesting because it was built with railroad rails. This Great North Mountain gap was named for John Park, who obtained a grant from Lord Fairfax in 1756 for property located nearby.

Route 9/Route 99 will take you to the old settlement of **Hedgesville***, about 4 miles away, where it meets Route 9, Hedgesville's main street. Turn right.* (If you turn left here and drive 1.4 miles, you'll see the old Snodgrass Tavern, said to have been visited by George Washington and his stepdaughter Patsy on their way to the baths in Berkeley Springs. The old tavern, which dates to the 1740s, is on the right past a concrete bridge.)

Hedgesville is on the edge of a well-traveled gap of Great North Mountain. Many old homes line its shaded streets. The town was founded in 1830, but settlers lived in the area for nearly 100 years before that. This was the site of Fort Hedges, one of the many stockade forts built along the mountains during the French and Indian War in the 1750s. The picture-pretty Mount Zion Episcopal Church, built in 1817 on land donated by Josiah Hedges, is on the left side of Route 9 after the turn.

Drive east on Route 9 to the city of **Martinsburg**, *about 5 miles away.* The road changes from a sleepy country backroad to a busy industrial and commercial highway on the way into town. The L. Norman Dillon Farm Museum is located on the right at the traffic light where Route 9 meets Ridge Road. This private museum is open on weekend afternoons; the emphasis is on farm equipment and farming techniques of the 1800s and 1900s. L. Norman Dillon, a lifelong farmer, began the museum to preserve the area's agricultural heritage.

Continue straight through several more intersections, following the signs for Route 9 East and U.S. 11 South. As you enter Martinsburg, you'll see an old brick firehouse—the Westphal Hose Company—straight ahead. Stay straight. The road curves to the left at the next light and becomes West Queen Street. Turn right at the next traffic light on to Race Street and drive about 0.2 mile. Turn right on Boyd Street. At the end of this residential street, you'll come to the grounds of Aspen Hall, now operated as an inn. Quaker settlers built a stone structure here around 1750; George Washington reportedly attended a wedding there in 1761. The first section of the present house was completed in 1788 by Edward Beeson II, one of Martinsburg's early leaders. Additions were built in the 1790s and in 1905.

Aspen Hall

Berkeley Springs Side Trip

The historic town of Berkeley Springs is a 20-minute drive west of Hedgesville on Route 9. Historians say that for hundreds of years before Europeans arrived on the continent, the springs' mineral waters were well known to Indian tribes as far away as the Great Lakes and the Carolinas. George Washington first visited the springs on a surveying expedition in 1748. They later became a favorite retreat of his; he even bought land and built a cabin here. The springs' days as a resort began in the late 1700s. They continue to this day at Berkeley Springs State Park, which invites modern-day visitors to "take the baths."

Ten miles south of Berkeley Springs is Cacapon State Park. The park offers picnic areas, golf, fishing, hiking, tennis, volleyball, swimming, and nature programs.

DOWNTOWN MARTINSBURG

1 Belle Boyd House
2 B & O Railroad Station and Roundhouse
3 Apollo Theater
4 Adam Stephen House
5 Triple Brick House
6 Old Stone House

7 Crawford Woolen Company
8 Dunn Woolen Company
9 Boarman House/Martinsburg Convention & Visitors Center
10 Berkeley County Courthouse

Return to Race Street, turn left, and cross Queen Street. The old red-brick house on the right at the corner is the Belle Boyd House. Now the home of the Berkeley County Historical Society and the Berkeley County Historic Landmarks Commission, this 1853 Greek Revival house was the childhood home of Civil War spy Belle Boyd.

As described in The Strasburg to Fort Valley to Front Royal Tour (pages 81–82), Belle Boyd began her covert career when, as a girl of 16, she shot a Union soldier in her parents' home at 500 South Queen Street here in Martinsburg; that house no longer stands. The headstrong Belle had a few adventures while living in this house on Race Street as well, including an episode in which she rode her pony into the house, miffed that her father wouldn't let her attend a dinner party he was giving.

The Belle Boyd House contains a museum devoted to Berkeley County's history. The museum offers exhibits about early Indian settlements, the Civil War in this part of the Shenandoah Valley, Belle Boyd, and other topics of local interest. The house's genealogy and history library contains copies of county records and early newspapers. The Belle Boyd House is also home to the Ben Boyd Bookstore, which features books, historical society publications, and history-related memorabilia. The house is open Monday through Saturday year-round except Thanksgiving and the last two weeks in December.

Belle Boyd House

Just past the Belle Boyd House, follow Race Street as it curves to the right into a large parking area facing several abandoned railroad buildings. These structures, which include a 16-sided roundhouse, were once part of a busy passenger and freight center for the B & O Railroad. The first trains were running between here and Harpers Ferry by 1842. Today, Amtrak trains serve commuters and other passengers from a new station thoughtfully designed to look as if it has always been here. The new station is attached to the 150-year-old B & O hotel and station house. Plans are in the works to restore the other historic railroad structures.

During the Civil War, Martinsburg was important to both sides because of its railroad and its strategic location near the Potomac River. The town changed hands at least 30 times during the war. In 1861, to prevent the Union from using the railroad to transport troops and supplies, Confederate general Stonewall Jackson destroyed everything but the station house. His efforts included wrecking many miles of track and disabling 35 locomotives. Later, when Jackson realized how useful the locomotives could be in the war effort, he fitted them with broad tires, hooked them to teams of horses, and dragged them south down the Valley Pike to Strasburg to be repaired and put to military use.

Old Roundhouse, Martinsburg Train Station

After much rebuilding in the late 1860s, the rails became important to Martinsburg once more, allowing its growth as a packing and distribution center for the area's many apple orchards. In 1885, another rail line, this one from Pennsylvania, was extended south to Martinsburg, making the town a major rail junction and sparking a period of rapid industrial growth.

Martinsburg has long been a crossroads. Around 1713, its location on the north-south Indian trail (which later became the Valley Turnpike and today's U.S. 11) made it a stopover for Tuscarora Indians heading north after they were driven out of the Carolinas. By the 1730s, British, Scots-Irish, and German settlers began coming into the area from eastern Virginia and Pennsylvania.

Adam Stephen, a Scotsman, laid out the town in the years before the Revolution. As was the custom, he wanted to name the town after himself, but he feared it would be confused with the Shenandoah Valley town of Stephensburg (since renamed Stephens City), south of Winchester. Instead, he named it after his friend Thomas Bryan Martin, who was a colonel and a nephew of Lord Fairfax. In 1758, Martin and George Washington served as Frederick County's representatives in the Virginia House of Burgesses. Martinsburg became the county seat when Berkeley County was created from Frederick County in 1772; at that time, it was still part of Virginia.

Before the Revolution, Martin, who was a British subject, was named justice of the peace of Frederick County. After the war, Virginia's first governor, Patrick Henry, reappointed him to the same office. But Martin refused to serve, probably thinking, according to one historian, that "a set of half-civilized and poorly armed inhabitants of a wild country would not give more than pastime to England's powerful armies and fleets."

From the railroad station parking lot, turn right on Martin Street. Go to the end of the block and turn left on Spring Street. The Apollo Theater, on the corner of Martin and Spring, has been used as a vaudeville, concert, and movie theater since 1913. It now operates as a community theater.

Drive three blocks to John Street and turn left. Continue past the stop sign at Water Street and drive across the railroad tracks to the parklike area on the left. Park in the grassy area and walk up the paved drive to two restored historic buildings—the Adam Stephen House and the Triple Brick Building.

This area is the original part of town, built along the banks of Tuscarora Creek. Adam Stephen, Martinsburg's founder and a Revolutionary War general, purchased 255 acres in the area in 1770 and later sold lots and developed the town. He built the lovely limestone house that bears his name between 1774 and 1789. Abandoned for many years, the house was donated to the city in 1959, and a major restoration effort was completed in the 1990s. The house is furnished as it might have been in the late 1700s to the early 1800s.

Triple Brick Building

Directly across from the Adam Stephen House is the Triple Brick Building, so called because it once housed three apartments. Now a museum, it was built in 1874 by a later owner of the Adam Stephen House as temporary housing for railroad workers. Exhibits include fossils, artifacts of early Indian and colonial life, military uniforms, early surveying equipment, railroad items, and quilts.

Adam Stephen House

The house and museum are open on weekend afternoons from May through October.

Adam Stephen was born in Scotland and earned a degree from King's College in Aberdeen in 1740. He first came to America as a surgeon on a merchant ship. In 1748, he gave up life at sea and returned to America. He lived first in Maryland and later moved to Fredericksburg, Virginia, where he practiced medicine until 1754, when he joined the militia and accompanied George Washington on his first expedition to Fort Duquesne. The following year, he served with General Braddock, Washington, and two other future Revolutionary War major generals (and future friends and neighbors), Charles Lee and Horatio Gates, on the ill-fated return trip to Fort Duquesne.

Stephen was promoted to the rank of major general in 1777 and distinguished himself in the battles at Trenton, Princeton, and Brandywine. At Germantown, however—a big defeat for Washington—General Stephen was charged with being intoxicated. Even though his inebriation was never pointed to as the reason for the Continental Army's defeat, he was court-martialed and dismissed from duty. He died in Martinsburg in 1791. His tomb lies beneath the monument honoring him, which is located in the 600 block of South Queen Street at Boydville (see next page).

Return to your car and drive back to John Street. Go one block to Water Street and turn left. On the corner is the Old Stone House. One of the city's earliest residences, it was probably built before 1779.

Go one block to East Stephen Street, turn right, and drive five blocks. Near the intersection with Church Street are the main buildings of the Blue Ridge Outlet Center, a group of restored red-brick factories that once housed Martinsburg's woolen mills.

Old Stone House

In the 1890s, William Henry Crawford came to this area from New York and established several mills. One was the Crawford Woolen Company (later known as the Berkeley Woolen Company), and another was the Martinsburg

Old Crawford Woolen
Company Mill

Crawford's elegant home on
South Queen Street

Worsted and Cassimere Company (later known as the Dunn Woolen Company). Today, these names denote the various buildings of the outlet center.

Crawford built an elegant home at 505 South Queen Street, a private residence today. He evidently lived beyond his means; he had to file for bankruptcy protection in 1912. He died of cirrhosis of the liver in 1914 at the young age of 47, having lost everything. The woolen mills were taken over by new owners and were operated until the late 1940s and early 1950s. During the first half of the 20th century, they provided wool blankets for the military in both world wars and upholstery fabric for the major

Boydville Side Trip

Boydville, another historic house in Martinsburg, is just a few blocks from the downtown area at 601 South Queen Street. A maple-lined drive leads past 10 acres of parklike grounds to the stone house, which is now operated as an inn. The house was built in 1812 by General Elisha Boyd, who fought in the War of 1812. After General Boyd's death in 1841, his daughter inherited the house. Her husband was Charles James Faulkner, who served as minister to France and on Stonewall Jackson's staff. Famous visitors to the home are said to have included Henry Clay, Belle Boyd, and Stonewall Jackson.

automakers. As happened elsewhere, the introduction of synthetics resulted in a decreased demand for wool, and the woolen industry here suffered.

Martinsburg's downtown has been called "a little encyclopedia of small-town architecture from the late 18th to mid-20th century" by the *Washington Post*. The city has designated seven historic districts. A walking tour of five of them is available at the Martinsburg–Berkeley County Convention and Visitors Bureau, located in the Boarman House at 208 South Queen Street. *To get there, continue past the outlet center to the stop sign at Raleigh Street and turn right. Go two blocks to West King Street; turn right at the traffic light and drive four blocks to Queen Street.*

To the left on Queen Street is the yellow-domed Berkeley County Courthouse, completed in 1856 on the site of an earlier courthouse. Belle Boyd was held here after one of her many arrests for spying for the Confederacy.

Across the street from the courthouse is the Martinsburg Public Library. Directly across from the library is the Boarman House, a brick building that is one of the oldest in the downtown area. Built in 1802, it houses the Boarman Arts Center as well as the visitor bureau.

Berkeley County Courthouse

The downtown area has several interesting shops, buildings, and churches. For a taste of times past, don't miss the old-fashioned soda fountain at Patterson's Drug Store, located at 134 South Queen Street.

The tour ends in Martinsburg. Follow the signs from the downtown area to I-81. If you'd like to continue exploring the area, Route 9 East will take you to Shepherdstown and then to Harpers Ferry, while Route 45 East will lead you to Charles Town. For more about these three historic towns, see the next tour.

Civil War Side Trip

U.S. 11 North continues to Hagerstown, Maryland, and the nearby Antietam battlefield. On the way, about 6 miles north of Martinsburg near the intersection with Route 4, is Falling Waters. This is where some historians say the first Civil War battle in the Shenandoah Valley was fought. On July 1, 1861, the Confederates fought a brief battle—lasting perhaps 45 minutes—under a relatively unknown officer, Thomas Jonathan Jackson, soon to become better known as "Stonewall."

Two years later, on July 13, 1863, Confederate troops retreating from Gettysburg crossed the Potomac here.

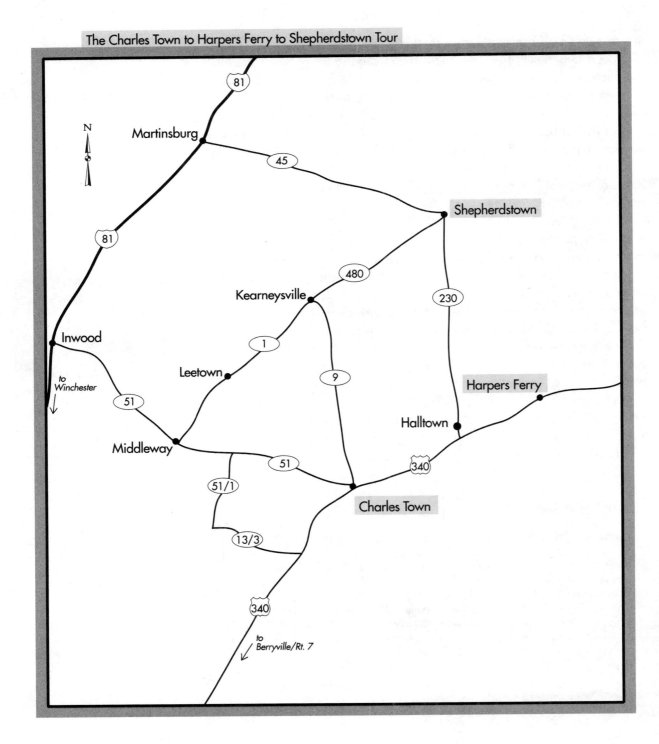

The Charles Town to Harpers Ferry to Shepherdstown Tour

The Charles Town to Harpers Ferry to Shepherdstown Tour

To begin the tour, take Exit 5 off I-81 south of Martinsburg. Turn on to Route 51 East at the stop sign at the end of the ramp. Follow Route 51 as it turns right at a traffic light, then left at the next traffic light. Continue straight on Route 51. In about 4 miles, you'll cross a bridge over Opequon Creek. This creek forms the boundary between Berkeley and Jefferson Counties, the two West Virginia counties in the Shenandoah Valley.

On the right just across the bridge is the entrance to Priest Field Pastoral, owned by the Catholic Church. There were few Catholic settlers in the Valley—most settlers were Quakers, Lutherans, Mennonites, Baptists, and Episcopalians. The story of how the Catholic Church came to own property in Middleway, West Virginia, is one of the Valley's enduring legends, with many variations.

The tale begins around 1794 with a Lutheran settler of Dutch descent named Adam Livingston. In those days, the road you are presently traveling was a main east-west route. The village of **Middleway** (originally called Smithfield) had developed around Smith Tavern, built about 1740, and was a popular stop for travelers. One night, Adam Livingston took one of those travelers into his home. The man became ill later that night and, fearing the worst, asked his host to call for a priest. Livingston refused, saying that no priest lived nearby, and that even if one had, he certainly wouldn't have a priest in his home. The stranger died that night and was buried quickly and without ceremony.

Shortly thereafter, a string of bizarre events began. One account says

This tour covers the northern top of the Shenandoah Valley, visiting the historic towns of Charles Town, Harpers Ferry, and Shepherdstown in West Virginia's Jefferson County. This area was Washington country for many years—the first president and many members of his family bought land and built homes here. As president, George Washington was instrumental in establishing a federal armory at Harpers Ferry, which decades later became the scene of a pivotal event that foreshadowed the Civil War.

The tour begins off I-81 at Inwood and passes through Middleway, Charles Town, Harpers Ferry, Halltown, Shepherdstown, and Leetown before returning to I-81 at Inwood. Most of Harpers Ferry is a National Historical Park, and several interesting museums are housed in the town's restored buildings. The National Park Service suggests allowing three hours to see everything; if you plan to hike along the scenic C & O Canal, expect to spend most of a day. The neighborhoods, museums, shops, and restaurants of Shepherdstown and Charles Town are also inviting, so you may want to split this tour over two days, in case you're tempted to spend much of your time out of the car.

Total mileage:
Approximately 60 miles

Monument to Adam Livingston in Middleway

that horses were heard running around the house at night, that flaming logs left the fireplace and danced about the kitchen, and that Livingston's farm animals died, his barn burned, and his money vanished. But the strangest occurrence of all was the sound of scissors clipping away day and night—scissors that left small holes in all the clothes, linens, and rugs in the house. Even visitors claimed they left the house with holes in their clothes. For many years afterward, the town was known as Wizard Clip because of the mysterious snipping that went on there.

Finally, in desperation, Livingston traveled to Shepherdstown, where a priest, Father Dennis Cahill, listened to his story and was persuaded to come to his house. The priest eventually said Mass in the house, and the strange occurrences stopped soon afterward. Amazed and grateful, Livingston converted to Catholicism. In 1802, he deeded 34 acres of his property to the Catholic Church on the condition that a chapel be built there.

Livingston later moved to Pennsylvania, selling all his land except for the field along Opequon Creek he had offered to the church. It wasn't until many years after his death that the church finally built the small frame structure that became known as Priest's Field Chapel. In 1978, the Catholic Church established a retreat and conference center here. In 1984, it erected a monument to Adam Livingston on the grounds.

Why Virginia Split

West Virginia came about when Virginia's westernmost counties refused to join the Confederacy with the rest of Virginia in 1861. Residents of the trans-Allegheny area (and even the Shenandoah Valley) had long believed their political and economic interests were not fairly represented in Richmond, where the state assembly was controlled by well-to-do plantation owners, lawyers, and businessmen on the east side of the Blue Ridge. There were few large farms west of the Blue Ridge, and relatively few slave owners.

West Virginia became a state, on the Union side, in 1863. Probably because of their strategic value to the North, the two panhandle counties of Berkeley and Jefferson were made part of the new state, even though many, if not most, of their residents sided with the Confederate cause. For years after the war, the story goes, many residents of Jefferson County continued to insist they lived in Virginia, not West Virginia.

Continue straight on Route 51 East for 4 miles past the bridge. Look for a West Virginia state historical marker on the right side of the road and prepare to turn right just beyond it. This is Route 51/Route 1 (O'Sullivan Road), although it may not be marked as such. Note that West Virginia road markers can be confusing and are often nonexistent, so be sure to follow the mileages and landmarks in this tour.

Cedar Lawn

The historical marker notes that Cedar Lawn, built by a great-nephew of George Washington, is down the road. George's older brother, Samuel, once owned nearly 4,000 acres in this area; his home, Harewood, built around 1770, is on the right a short distance up Route 51, past where you just turned. Harewood was the location of Dolley Payne Todd's wedding to future president James Madison in 1794. By that time, Harewood had passed to Samuel's son, George Steptoe Washington, who was married to Dolley's sister, Lucy. Both women were dismissed from the Quaker faith for marrying "out of meeting."

You'll pass Richwood Hall, an old brick mansion dating from the 1820s, after 0.8 mile on Route 51/Route 1, and then you'll see Cedar Lawn on the right 0.5 mile later. Cedar Lawn was not the first house on this property; Samuel Washington's oldest son (actually a stepson) and his wife, Mildred Berry, built a log-and-plank home named Berry Hill here in 1780. In 1825, their son, John Thornton Augustine Washington, constructed the brick house that stands today. One of his 13 children, Benjamin Franklin Washington, was a local lawyer who caught gold-rush fever in 1849. He organized an expedition of 80 Jefferson County citizens who hoped to get rich quick in California. No fortunes were made, but Washington stayed on and later became the first editor of the *San Francisco Examiner*.

George Washington became familiar with this part of the Shenandoah Valley while he was a young man surveying for Lord Fairfax in the late 1740s. His first-ever purchase of land, at the age of 18, was several hundred acres of fertile farmland near Bullskin Run, located a short distance southwest of Cedar Lawn near Summit Point. He encouraged his oldest half-brother, Lawrence, who owned Mount Vernon at the time, to buy land in this area. Lawrence purchased several thousand acres before dying of tuberculosis a few years later, at which time the land passed to his other brothers.

To see two more Washington family homes, continue until the road you are on

The Blakeley–Mount Vernon Connection

George Washington inherited Mount Vernon from his brother Lawrence because Lawrence died and his children did not survive childhood. When George died without fathering children, Mount Vernon (upon Martha Washington's death) went to a nephew, Bushrod Washington, a United States Supreme Court justice who was the eldest son of John Augustine Washington, the president's brother. Bushrod also died without children, and thus Mount Vernon passed to his brother, John Augustine Washington II, the builder of Blakeley. One of John's two sons, John Augustine Washington III, was born at Blakeley in 1821 and died during the Civil War while serving as aide-de-camp to General Robert E. Lee.

ends at a stop sign. Even though it may not be marked as such, the intersecting road is Route 13. Turn right. After less than 0.5 mile, turn left on to Route 13/ Route 3 (Huyett Road). In less than 1 mile, you'll pass Claymont Court Children's School on the left. Just past the school are Blakeley (on the right) and Claymont Court (up the hill on the left).

Blakeley, which is partly hidden from view by a grove of beautiful old oak trees, was built around 1820 by John Augustine Washington II, one of three grandsons of George Washington's brother John Augustine Washington. It is said that John built a more modest house here than he might have, since he was in line to inherit Mount Vernon. That great estate came into his possession in 1829.

Across the street from Blakeley is Claymont Court, a large home built by Bushrod Corbin Washington around 1820. This grandson of John Augustine Washington was active in local politics and represented the county in the Virginia assembly. At present, Claymont Court is owned by a private educational organization specializing in environmental issues.

Continue past Claymont Court on Route 13/Route 3 until you reach a stop sign. Turn right, then make an immediate left on to U.S. 340 North. After 3.2 miles on U.S. 340, take the exit marked "North 340/West 51/Charles Town/ Harpers Ferry." At the end of the ramp, turn left, following the signs for Route 51 West. This road becomes East Washington Street, Charles Town's main street.

Charles Town is worth a stop for its excellent Jefferson County Museum and for a walk or drive around its downtown area and peaceful tree-lined neighborhoods. The town was laid out on 80 acres by Charles Washington, brother of the president, who inherited it from their brother Lawrence. Charles gave the main street his family name and christened the four major cross streets after himself and his brothers—Samuel, George, and Lawrence. He probably named Mildred Street for his wife, although the name may have honored his younger sister, who died in infancy.

Today, Charles Town is probably best known for its year-around horse races at the modern track you'll pass on your way to the downtown area. Except for the Civil War years, horse racing has been a favorite pastime in this area since the town's founding. After the war, horse racing returned to Charles Town, but all bets were off, thanks to West Virginia's ban on gambling. It wasn't until 1933 that betting on horse races became legal again.

After you pass the racetrack, look on the left for the gray-brick home at 417 East Washington Street; it now operates as a bed-and-breakfast. Built in 1839 by a Dr. Stribling, the home was used as a headquarters by Union general Philip Sheridan. He and General Grant met here to make plans for dealing with Confederate general Stonewall Jackson in the Shenandoah Valley.

After another two blocks, you'll see Charles Town Presbyterian Church on the right after the traffic light. This church was used as a hospital by both sides during the Civil War.

Next door is the Jefferson County Library; the Jefferson County Museum is in the back of this building, with an entrance around the corner on Samuel Street. Open daily except Sunday from April to December, the museum focuses on the history of the county from early Indian times through World War II. It contains attractive displays on daily life in the 1700s and 1800s, as well as exhibits on the Washington family, the Civil War, and John Brown's raid on the federal armory at nearby Harpers Ferry. One of the museum's most popular items is the metal frame of the cot that Brown, who was wounded in the raid, used to rest on during his treason trial.

Andrew Hunter House

The restaurant on the corner of East Washington and Samuel Streets, across from the museum and library, was once the home of Andrew Hunter, one of the two state prosecutors in the Brown trial.

Happy Retreat

Charles Washington's Home

After inheriting the land on which he would later lay out a town, Charles Washington—George's youngest brother—and his wife moved here from Fredericksburg, Virginia, around 1780 and built a log home called Happy Retreat. The house has been greatly enlarged over the past 200-plus years and is still occupied today. Charles also had an office in town, from which he sold land.

To see Happy Retreat, turn left off Washington Street on to George Street (which runs next to the courthouse), drive several blocks to Blakeley Street, and turn right. Happy Retreat is the large white house on the hill at the end of the street.

The impressive Jefferson County Courthouse, still in use today, is at the other end of the block. It was built in 1837 to replace an 1803 structure. Jefferson County, named for Thomas Jefferson, was created in 1801. The courthouse was reduced to a shell after suffering heavy Confederate attacks during the Civil War and has undergone significant restoration and renovation since.

The courthouse was the setting for two of the three treason trials to take place in the United States prior to the 1940s. The more famous was the trial of John Brown in October 1859. The other took place in 1922 and involved three men whose actions while leading striking coal miners in Logan County, West Virginia, led to treason and murder charges.

Jefferson County Courthouse

The trial of John Brown (see the story of his famous raid later in this tour, page 25) lasted only three days, and the jury returned a guilty verdict after less than an hour of deliberation. The trial was widely covered by newspapers all over the country and drew many spectators, including John Wilkes Booth, who assassinated President Lincoln six years later. Brown was sentenced to hang at a gallows constructed on a nearby field; the hanging took place December 2, 1859. Pieces of wood thought to have been part of the gallows are on display in the John Brown Museum in Harpers Ferry. A state historical marker notes the gallows site, now occupied by the Gibson-Todd House at 515 South Samuel Street, just five blocks south of the library and museum. To help keep order during the hanging, some 1,500 troops, including a cadet corps from Virginia Military Institute, were called in. One of the corps commandants was a professor at V.M.I., Major Thomas J. Jackson, later known as "Stonewall."

Like most of the Shenandoah Valley, Charles Town and the surrounding area suffered terrible damage only a few years later during the Civil War. One of the several skirmishes in the region took place near Summit Point, about 7 miles west of the present tour stop.

It was near that same spot that British general Braddock's troops camped in 1755 on their way to fight at Fort Duquesne, near what is now Pittsburgh, during the French and Indian War. Not a popular man with his troops, Braddock was said to have insisted that a well be dug, even though springs were located nearby. Three young captains who later distinguished themselves in the American Revolution were with Braddock at his defeat at Fort Duquesne. All three—Charles Lee, Horatio Gates, and Adam Stephen (who founded Martinsburg)—were British-born, all were wounded in that battle, and all later sided with the colonists during the Revolution. In a strange twist of fate, all three were promoted to major general, were subsequently court-martialed, and ended up living near Charles Town after the war. For their stories—and their famous toast to one another—see the Leetown portion of this tour.

The next stop on the tour is **Harpers Ferry**. *To get there, turn around and head back down Washington Street the way you came into town. You are on U.S. 340 North; follow the signs for Harpers Ferry past several shopping centers, then follow the signs to the Harpers Ferry National Historical Park entrance, which is on the right at a traffic light. If you want to just drive through the town (be aware that no parking is available), turn left instead of right at the park entrance traffic light, following the signs for Bolivar and Harpers Ferry. The road winds through the two towns and the historical park, then continues to the visitor center and back out to U.S. 340.*

The historic sections of Harpers Ferry have been carefully restored by the National Park Service and are worth at least a two- or three-hour stop. You could easily spend a day or more seeing everything recommended in the National Park Service brochure, which you can pick up at the visitor center. If you enjoy hiking, you can walk the C & O Canal Towpath, which runs along the Potomac River, or part of the Appalachian Trail, which runs along the Blue Ridge through here. The national headquarters of the Appalachian Trail Conference is in Harpers Ferry.

If you park at Harpers Ferry National Historical Park, you'll pay a five-dollar entry fee, which includes parking, transportation to and from the town, and entry into all the museums. Shuttle buses run every few minutes up and down the 2-mile scenic road into the historic area.

Harpers Ferry sits perched below a cliff at the confluence of the Potomac and Shenandoah Rivers, one of the prettiest settings in the Valley. In 1783, before there was a town here, Thomas Jefferson passed through the area on his way to serve in the Continental Congress in Philadelphia. He later wrote about the site in his only book, *Notes on the State of Virginia*: "The passage of the Patowmac through the Blue ridge is perhaps one of the most stupendous scenes in nature. You stand on a very high point of land. On your

View from Jefferson's Rock

Jefferson Rock

*The Potomac River at
Harpers Ferry*

right up comes the Shenandoah, having ranged along the foot of the mountain an hundred miles to seek a vent. On your left approaches the Patowmac, in quest of a passage also. In the moment of their junction they rush together against the mountain, rend it asunder, and pass off to sea. . . . This scene is worth a voyage across the Atlantic."

If you are willing to walk a steep but short path (part of the Appalachian Trail) up from town, you can view this scene from the place he did, at a point above the Shenandoah called Jefferson's Rock. The view, although beautiful, may not seem quite as dramatic to modern eyes as it did to Jefferson's. In fact, even John Quincy Adams, who came here in the early 1800s, wrote that he thought Jefferson had overstated the scene.

Harpers Ferry was settled in the early 1730s by a man from Pennsylvania, Peter Stephens, who operated a ferry service here. In 1747, a Philadelphia architect and millwright named Robert Harper passed through the area on his way to Winchester to build a meeting house for a Quaker congregation. He recognized the business potential of the site and ended up buying land, building a gristmill, and taking over the ferry service.

Harper House, which Harper completed in 1782, is one of the oldest surviving buildings in town. Harper died that same year and never lived in the house. It served as the town tavern until 1803; among its guests were

George Washington and Thomas Jefferson. Harper House is on the walkway up to Jefferson Rock.

Harper House

In 1794, the federal government authorized the establishment of several armories for the manufacture and storage of guns and ammunition. At the time, the young nation was concerned about a possible future conflict with Britain. President Washington, remembering the area from his days as a surveyor, selected Harpers Ferry as the site for one of the armories, since it offered ready access to all the necessary resources for gunmaking: reliable water power, a source of iron ore, and abundant timber for making the charcoal to power furnaces and forges. Construction on the armory began in 1799. By the mid-1800s, more than 10,000 muskets, rifles, and pistols were being made here each year.

The town continued to grow as many other types of businesses were drawn by the availability of water power and the various transportation options. By the 1830s, the town had stagecoach service, toll roads, the Chesapeake and Ohio Canal, and the Baltimore and Ohio Railroad. By the late 1850s, the armory shops employed some 400 people.

Harpers Ferry drew the attention of the nation on October 16, 1859, when John Brown—an ardent abolitionist—and his 21-man "army of liberation" entered the federal armory area, took several hostages, and occupied the armory's fire-engine house, now referred to as "John Brown's Fort." Brown's goal was to capture the thousands of weapons stored in the armory and launch a slave revolt that he hoped would result in the abolition of slavery in the United States. But his plan was deeply flawed. A day and a half later, the "fort" was stormed by 90 United States marines sent from the Washington Navy Yard under the command of United States Army colonel Robert E. Lee. Brown was wounded in the attack and arrested; two of his sons died in the siege. Brown was tried and hanged in nearby Charles Town that December. Historians believe that his actions drew increased attention to the issue of racial equality and moved the country closer to civil war.

John Brown's Fort

The Civil War destroyed Harpers Ferry. The town changed hands eight times over the course of the war, and both sides participated in the raids and destruction that occurred. In September 1862, General Stonewall Jackson, following General Lee's orders (for a change, the story goes), carried out the first invasion of the North here, resulting in the surrender of 12,500 Union soldiers, the largest Confederate capture of the war. The scene of that battle, now known as Schoolhouse Ridge Battlefield, is located above the town. The battlefield was turned over to the National Park Service in 1998 by the Civil War Trust, which purchased the property from private owners. It is now part of Harpers Ferry National Historical Park. In 1864, Harpers Ferry served as the base for Union general Philip Sheridan's campaign of destruction in the Shenandoah Valley—known locally as "The Burning."

Because of the destruction, most Harpers Ferry citizens moved away during the war, and most of them never came back. The town's strategic location on the two rivers, a great advantage for business and industry, also proved to be its greatest long-term problem, as severe flooding periodically destroyed buildings and discouraged rebuilding and resettlement. The National Park Service took over the lower section of the town in 1944 and began restoring the buildings to their 1860 appearance.

Leave Harpers Ferry the way you came in; turn left from the visitor center parking lot on to U.S. 340, as if you were heading back to Charles Town. Continue south for 1.6 miles and take the Route 230 North exit, to the right. This road soon enters Halltown on its way to Shepherdstown.

Halltown is a reminder of the once-thriving paper industry in the Harpers Ferry area. A paperboard factory dominates the town, which was named for John H. Hall, an inventor. Hall owned a rifle factory in Harpers Ferry and developed the idea of using interchangeable parts, which allowed for machine production of rifles.

Turn right at the stop sign to stay on Route 230 through Halltown. The several new housing developments that will soon come into view are beginning to transform the rural feel of this area.

West of Halltown (but not on this tour) is another Washington family home, Beallair, a private residence today. Thomas Beall of Georgetown built the stone portion of the house sometime in the late 1700s on land owned by his father. Beall's daughter married George Corbin Washington, a grandnephew of the president. Their son, Lewis William Washington, moved into the house in 1840.

Lewis Washington was literally dragged into John Brown's raid at Harpers Ferry. Brown, who wanted a hostage with a well-known name, sent a band of men to take Lewis Washington and two patriotic heirlooms that had been gifts to George Washington: a sword from Frederick the Great of Prussia and a pistol from Lafayette of France. Brown's men broke into Beallair late on the night of October 16 and awakened Colonel Washington, who turned over the heirlooms and accompanied the raiders to Harpers Ferry. Brown is said to have worn the sword during his siege. Colonel Washington survived unscathed.

Shenandoah Street, Harpers Ferry National Historical Park

The Halltown area was also home to William Darke, who lived at Duffields. Darke fought with Braddock at Fort Duquesne during the French and Indian War. He served as a general during the American Revolution and was later a delegate to the Virginia Constitutional Convention in 1788. One day, according to local lore, he and James Stephenson of Martinsburg decided to settle a score by having a duel. Stephenson, a small man, came ready to fight with a small, slim rapier. Darke, who was tall and beefy, arrived carrying a very large sword. The onlookers began to chuckle at the contrast in size, and their laughter was soon shared by the would-be duelists. They decided to call off the fight and reportedly became fast friends.

Continue north for 6 miles past Halltown until you reach a stop sign where another road merges with Route 230. Continue north for 2 miles to Shepherdstown. Follow Route 230 North as it turns right on to Princess Street, then go two blocks and turn left on German Street at the stop sign. German Street is the town's main street.

Shepherdstown is one of the Valley's oldest towns. Some historians believe there were settlers in this area by 1717. Around 1730, people began to come here from Pennsylvania in search of fertile farmland. They crossed the Potomac about a mile south at Pack Horse Ford, one of the few places the river could be forded without benefit of a bridge or ferry. Thomas Shepherd arrived in 1732, bought land, and laid out the town, which was officially chartered in 1762. The early settlers were mostly of German descent, and they called their village Mecklenburg, probably after their home in Germany.

Congressional records from 1790 indicate that George Washington considered this town as one of three possible sites along the Potomac for the new United States capital, which was being planned at the time. The

Winchester newspaper actively promoted the site, arguing that its western location was at the geographic center of the new and growing nation.

In 1798, the citizens changed the name to Shepherd's Town to honor the community's founder. In the 1800s, this was a busy river port. With easy access to the C & O Canal, merchants and farmers could ship their wares east to Washington and west to Cumberland. Their main exports were flour and cement.

No Civil War engagements took place here, but several of the town's buildings served as makeshift hospitals for the many soldiers wounded in the Battle of Antietam, fought just a few miles away.

Today, Shepherdstown is a small college town with well-preserved 18th- and 19th-century homes, churches, and buildings, many of which have been turned into galleries, shops, and restaurants. For a complete walking tour of the town, pick up a free pamphlet at the visitor center, located at 102 East German Street.

Probably the most impressive building in town is McMurran Hall, at the corner of German and King Streets, now part of Shepherd College. It served as the Jefferson County Courthouse in the years that Shepherdstown was the county seat, between 1865 and 1872. In 1873, the building was sold to

The old Jefferson County Courthouse, now part of Shepherd College

the college, which had been established two years earlier. On this piece of land stood Thomas Shepherd's first house.

Across the street from McMurran Hall is the town library, housed in a quaint-looking 1800 building that originally served as the town's market house and later as the town hall, the jail, the courthouse, and the fire hall. In the 1760s, the town whipping post stood near here.

Shepherdstown Library

Several local hotels and taverns have had long histories. The Entler Hotel, at the corner of German and Princess Streets, dates back to 1793. It is now home to the Historic Shepherdstown Commission, which operates a museum that is open weekends from April through October. A section of the museum is devoted to the town's most famous resident, James Rumsey, and his inventions. Rumsey invented what many believe was the first successful steamboat, which he demonstrated on the Potomac River here in December 1787.

Rumsey was born in Cecil County, Maryland, in 1743 and moved to what is now Berkeley Springs, West Virginia, in 1782. There, he ran an inn and a store and built summer cabins for the visitors to the warm-springs resort—including one for George Washington.

Washington had long been interested in making Virginia's rivers navigable. He put Rumsey in charge of the Potowmack Navigation Company, which tried unsuccessfully to build canals in the Great and Little Falls area, near what is now Washington, D.C. Rumsey quit in frustration after a year on the job.

In 1782, Rumsey moved to Shepherdstown to be closer to a navigable part of the Potomac. He spent the next several years developing a steam system that could propel a boat using a jet of water. He soon became known around town as "Crazy Rumsey." On December 3, 1787, he loaded the craft with two tons of rock and eight of the town's ladies, then navigated up and down the river for two hours in front of an audience that included Revolutionary War generals Horatio Gates and William Darke. (The site of his demonstration is commemorated on the bluff above the river at the end of Mill Street; turn right into the town park to view the river and see the James Rumsey Monument. After crossing High Street on your way to the monument, you'll pass another interesting piece of Shepherdstown's past— the gristmill that Thomas Shepherd built in 1738, now a private home. Its

Rumsey Monument

The Little House

40-foot wheel is said to be the oldest and largest cast-iron overshot waterwheel in the world.)

George Washington kept up with Rumsey's progress and provided support and encouragement. In the meantime, John Fitch, a clockmaker from Connecticut, was experimenting with a steam engine that powered a paddle wheel, which he successfully demonstrated in Philadelphia in August 1787. After a long fight with Rumsey—who claimed Fitch had spied on him in Shepherdstown—Fitch received a United States patent for his steamboat in August 1791.

In 1788, Rumsey gained financial backing for further research from the American Philosophical Society in Philadelphia, which in turn founded the Rumseian Society. The Rumseian Society provided funds to send Rumsey to England to obtain European patents and gain financial support. Benjamin Franklin was the society's first president.

Rumsey arrived in London in 1788 and spent the next four years building and promoting a 100-foot steamboat. During that time, he became friends with a young American artist living there, Robert Fulton. Just as things were going well for Rumsey, he suffered a stroke while presenting his research to a London society in December 1792. He died the following day. His latest prototype was successfully demonstrated on the Thames not long after his death, but his vision of steam navigation perished with him. His nemesis, John Fitch, never was able to develop an economical version of his steam engine; Fitch died in 1798. Coincidentally or not, Rumsey's friend Robert Fulton abandoned his failing career as a painter and turned to engineering around 1794. In 1808, Fulton launched the *Clermont*, the first commercially operated steam-powered paddleboat, on the Hudson River in New York.

The Rumseian Society is still around. Based in Shepherdstown, it works to "set the record straight," according to its brochure, to see that Rumsey's contributions to steamboat navigation are recognized. A half-scale model of his first successful boat is on display at the Rumsey Steamboat Museum, located behind the Entler Hotel on East German Street.

Also located behind the Entler Hotel, facing Princess Street, is a charming little building called "The Little House." It's a furnished scale model of a two-story house about 10 feet square. It was built by home economics students at Shepherd College in 1928.

To continue the tour, drive west on German Street and turn left on Route 480 South (Duke Street), following the signs toward Kearneysville. In less than 1 mile, you'll pass Morgan Grove Park, on the left. Here is where Daniel Morgan assembled his Riflemen (some 93 Virginia volunteers) on July 17, 1775, to begin their famous beeline march to Cambridge, Massachusetts, where they became the first Southern unit to join General Washington's troops. The men made the 600-mile journey in 26 days, and Washington reportedly met them with tears of gratitude. In 1825, two of the surviving Riflemen fulfilled a pledge made by the group 50 years earlier to meet here once more, on the silver anniversary of their departure.

Continue on Route 480 South for nearly 5 miles to the traffic light in Kearneysville. Stay straight through the light, crossing Route 9. The road is now marked Route 1, heading toward Leetown.

Morgan Grove Park

A state historical marker at the intersection in **Kearneysville** notes that the house of Revolutionary War general Horatio Gates—Traveler's Rest—is 0.5 mile southwest. Although Gates is credited with leading the Continental Army to victory at the Battle of Saratoga, he charged when he should have retreated at the Battle of Camden in South Carolina, an action that led to his court-martial and suspension. He regained his command in 1782, later retired to his home here, and stayed until 1790, when he moved to New York.

In about 3 miles, you'll reach **Leetown**. After entering the town, you'll see a state historical marker titled "The Bower." It says that General Adam Stephen, who founded Martinsburg, lived here from 1754 until 1772. The mansion now on the property was built by Stephen's grandson, Adam Stephen Dandridge, in 1805. The Dandridge family still owns the house, which is located west of Leetown.

Continue 1 mile to a state historical marker on the right. This one commemorates Rio Prato, General Charles Lee's home. The limestone house, still occupied today, is hidden behind the trees and shrubbery just beyond the historical marker. The village that grew up here later became known as Leetown in General Lee's honor.

Lee was born in Wales and came to America in 1756 as an officer in the British army. (He was not related to the famous Lee family of Virginia.) He quit his commission and joined the American forces after the Battle of Lexington in 1775, the same year he bought this house and its surrounding acreage. Lee's fellow Revolutionary War general Horatio Gates told him about the property and encouraged him to buy it.

Lee retired here a bitter man, having been court-martialed and suspended from the Continental Army after retreating at the Battle of Monmouth in 1778. When Washington reprimanded him for failing to follow orders, Lee exploded with an angry response. Some historians think his retreat was intended to embarrass Washington. Historians trace Lee's resentment of Washington to the time when Washington was named to command the Continental Army; Lee believed he was better qualified for the job.

He lived a hermitlike life after his dismissal, sharing his house (which was unusual in that it had no interior walls) with his dogs. After the war, Washington wrote him a letter stating that he was coming through the area and would like to see Lee as a friend once more. When Washington arrived, the house was empty, and a sign on the door read, "No meat cook'd here today."

Lee's few friends included two neighbors, General Horatio Gates and

Rio Prato

General Adam Stephen, both of whom had also been booted out of the Continental Army. The story goes that the three old soldiers would gather at Rio Prato and toast each other as follows: "To Major General Charles Lee, who was cashiered from the Continental Army because, when he should have advanced, he retreated; to Major General Horatio Gates, who was cashiered because, when he should have retreated, he advanced; and to Major General Adam Stephen, who was cashiered because, when he might have advanced or retreated, he did neither." (It is said Stephen was drunk at the critical moment.)

Lee moved to Philadelphia in 1782 and died shortly after his arrival. His will specified that he not "be buried in any church or churchyard, or within a mile of any Presbyterian or Anabaptist meeting house. For since I have resided in this country I have kept so much bad company when living that I do not choose to continue it when dead." Against his wishes, he was buried with full military honors in Philadelphia's Christ Church graveyard.

Continue about 3.5 miles to the intersection with Route 51, where the tour ends. Turn right on to Route 51 West at the stop sign. In 4.8 miles, turn right on U.S. 11 North at the traffic light, then go a short distance and turn left at the next traffic light back on to Route 51 West, which will take you to the I-81 exit at Inwood, where you began.

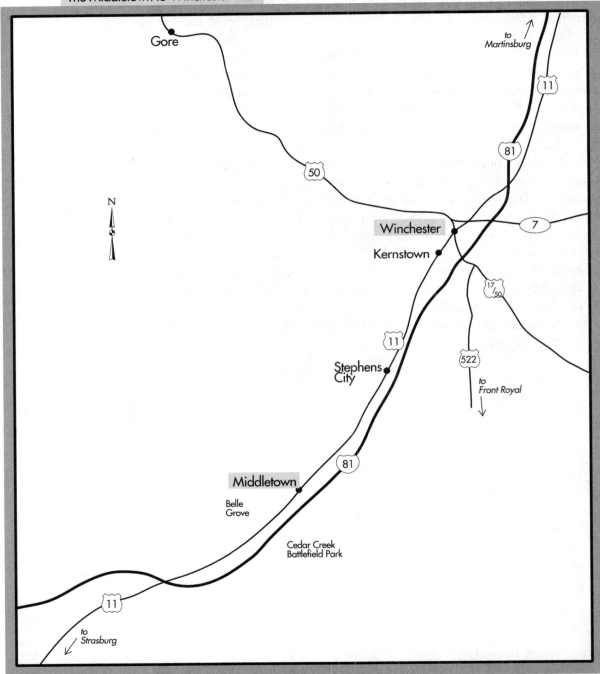

The Middletown to Winchester Tour

The Middletown to Winchester Tour

This tour begins in Middletown, just north of Strasburg, at historic Belle Grove mansion and the nearby Civil War battlefield of Cedar Creek. Passing the Wayside Inn, it heads north on the old Valley Pike (U.S. 11) toward Winchester, passing through the early settlements of Stephens City and Kernstown. Many Civil War engagements took place along this road and in Winchester. The tour ends in Winchester with a walking tour of the historic district and directions to Glen Burnie, a brick mansion built by the family of Winchester's founder in the late 1700s. The Winchester area was once home to the young George Washington, polar explorer Richard E. Byrd, novelist Willa Cather, and country-and-western singer Patsy Cline.

Total mileage:
Approximately 20 miles

To begin the tour, take Exit 298 off I-81 (marked Strasburg/Route 11) and turn on to U.S. 11 North toward Winchester. In 2 miles, you'll see signs on the left for Belle Grove.

Belle Grove is a 1797 mansion built by the grandson of the early Shenandoah Valley settler Jost Hite. The home and grounds are open daily for tours from April through October and on weekends at other times of the year. The Battle of Cedar Creek was fought all around this house in 1864; Cedar Creek Battlefield Park is just up U.S. 11 past Belle Grove's entrance.

Jost Hite was one of the first settlers in the Shenandoah Valley, arriving here from Pennsylvania in 1731 or 1732. He brought with him 16 families, including his five sons and three daughters and their families. One of Hite's sons-in-law was Jacob Bowman, whose many descendants live in the Valley today.

Hite was originally from Benfeld, a small town on the Rhine River south of Strasbourg in Alsace. He settled in Kingston, New York, in 1711. Around 1716, he moved to Pennsylvania. Fifteen years later, he secured two land grants totaling 140,000 acres in Virginia and moved to the area around Winchester.

Hite was one of thousands of settlers from Pennsylvania to follow the Indian Trail—later known as the Pennsylvania Road, the Great Wagon Road, the Valley Pike, and U.S. Route 11—into the Shenandoah Valley, and from there to points south and west. The Royal colony of Virginia encouraged these early settlers, offering generous grants of land with few strings attached. It even dropped the requirement of mandatory Church of England attendance, which gave Quakers, Mennonites, and Lutherans in Pennsylvania further incentive to come here. But the colony's motives were largely self-serving. Virginians on the eastern side of the Blue Ridge referred to the Valley as "the Back Country" and considered it useful primarily as a buffer zone—a place where increased settlement would help protect them from Indian attacks.

Belle Grove, administered by the National Trust for Historic Preservation and still a working farm, has been restored to its early-1800s appearance. It was built by Major Isaac Hite, Jr., a Revolutionary War officer whose first wife was Nelly Madison, the sister of President James Madison. It is said that James Madison and his bride, Dolley, spent their wedding night in an earlier house on this property after their marriage at Harewood, near Charles Town, in 1794.

Knowing of his brother-in-law's plan to build Belle Grove, Madison wrote to his friend Thomas Jefferson for design advice. Although no written record exists to indicate any response from Jefferson, the emphasis on symmetry and a few other touches at Belle Grove have led some to believe that Jefferson offered ideas for the house.

Belle Grove

Belle Grove's exterior was built from locally quarried limestone. The front portion of the house features "dressed" limestone—that is, limestone blocks that were chiseled smooth to form a flat surface, which was considered at the time to present an appearance superior to the rough natural stone. This effect cost one-third more to achieve, so it was done only on the front of the house. Undoubtedly, the extra work impressed early visitors, but the effect is lost today—to the modern eye, the stones look like concrete blocks.

Isaac Hite attended the College of William and Mary but dropped out to take part in the Revolutionary War. Phi Beta Kappa was founded at William and Mary in December 1776, and Hite was the first person to be taken into that organization by its charter members. He later became an astute farmer and businessman, operating a distillery, a quarry, gristmills, sawmills, and a general store in the area.

Nelly Madison Hite died in 1803. Isaac remarried and had 10 more children, in addition to the two surviving children he had with Nelly. Interestingly, after the second Mrs. Hite died in 1850, none of the children wanted the house, so it was sold.

In the fall of 1864, Union general Philip Sheridan used the house as his field headquarters. One of the South's most promising young men, Major General Stephen Ramseur, was wounded at Cedar Creek and taken to Belle Grove, where he died in the library the day after the battle. Several Union officers who had been his classmates at West Point sat at his bedside, including—the tradition goes—Major General George A. Custer.

From 1900 until the 1930s, Belle Grove was operated as an inn. One of its frequent guests was a botanist from New York, Francis Welles Hunnewell, who later bought the house and began to painstakingly restore and furnish it. He died in 1964 and deeded the property to the National Trust for Historic Preservation.

Continue a short distance north on U.S. 11 from Belle Grove to Cedar Creek Battlefield Park. The park is owned by a private nonprofit foundation that purchased 158 acres in 1988—land that had been zoned as an industrial park. After almost losing this historic area to development, the foundation's members might have reflected on General Sheridan's comments after the Cedar Creek battle: "Disaster has been converted into a splendid victory." A visitor center was added in 1996.

The battle began as a surprise attack on 30,000 sleeping Union troops by 17,000 Confederates led by General Jubal Early before dawn on October 19, 1864. The Union had won important victories the previous month at Winchester and Fisher's Hill, and "The Burning" of the Valley—a devastating attempt to cut off food and supplies to Confederate troops in eastern Virginia—had begun that fall. Early's men drove the Federals past Belle Grove and through Middletown, where they stopped to regroup.

In the meantime, General Sheridan, who had been in Winchester when the attack at Cedar Creek began, rode his horse down the Valley Pike (inspiring the poem "Sheridan's Ride") and organized a successful counterattack. This battle marked the end of the Confederates' military power in the Valley and helped ensure President Lincoln's reelection just three weeks later. Interestingly, two future United States presidents fought in the battle for the Union side: Colonel Rutherford B. Hayes and Major William McKinley.

Continue a mile up the road to **Middletown**. This community was called Senseney Town, after its founder, when it was chartered in 1796. The current name grew out of the fact that the town is halfway between Stephens City and Strasburg.

Wayside Inn

You will pass the Wayside Theater, one of a dwindling number of small-town summer-stock theaters left on the East Coast. It occupies a 1940s building that was once the town's movie house.

Not historic but fun is the Route 11 Potato Chip Company, also located on the left. On weekends, the factory is open to let visitors watch chips being made. The company's product has been praised by *Gourmet* magazine. The owners claim they operate the smallest potato chip factory in the nation.

The stretch of U.S. 11 around Middletown was the scene of much Civil War action, as noted by the numerous state historical markers between here and Winchester. The marker in front of the Wayside Inn cites this as the place where, on May 24, 1862, General Stonewall Jackson's army attacked General Banks's forces, which were retreating from Strasburg. Banks was forced to divide his army.

The original portion of the Wayside Inn was built in 1797. It was first known as Wilkinson Tavern and later as Larrick's Hotel. In the 1800s, it served as a stagecoach relay station. In the early 1900s, it was enlarged by new owners and began catering to automobile traffic. In fact, it still advertises itself as the nation's first motor hotel.

Just north of Middletown is the campus of Lord Fairfax Community College. The historical marker in front of the school notes that during the Battle of Cedar Creek, Confederate general Early stopped his advance here on the morning of October 19, 1864, and was pushed back by General Sheridan later that day.

It is 1 mile farther on U.S. 11 to another historical marker. This one commemorates the end of Sheridan's ride and marks the place where the Union army stood when he rejoined it during the Battle of Cedar Creek, thereby halting the Union retreat.

Continue on U.S. 11 to **Stephens City**. As you approach the town, you'll pass a reminder of mid-20th-century history—one of the few remaining family-style drive-in theaters on the East Coast.

Just under a mile past the drive-in, you'll pass La Grange, a handsome old stone farmhouse on the left. Built by a local physician around 1828, it was once known as the McLeod House.

Frederick County's second-oldest town (after Winchester), Stephens City was founded by one of Jost Hite's original settlers, Lewis Stephens, and chartered as Stephensburg in 1758. Around the time of the California gold rush, the town became well known for its 13 wagon-making shops. The wagons, called Newtown wagons, were praised for their sturdiness. Stephens City narrowly escaped being burned during the Civil War. Today, it is an attractive and well-preserved town with many lovely old homes and churches.

Continue about 1 mile out of Stephens City to where U.S. 11 dips as it approaches Opequon Creek. After the sign for the creek, look for a house on the right behind a stand of trees. This old stone home is Springdale. As the historical marker in front notes, Springdale was built by one of Jost Hite's sons, John, in 1753 near the site of Jost Hite's original homestead of the 1730s. John Hite was a county justice, a militia colonel, and a close friend of George Washington, who once visited him here. This house is thought to have served for a time as the headquarters of one of Sheridan's generals, William Dwight.

About 1 mile from Springdale, U.S. 11 passes under I-81. **Kernstown** *is* *about 1.5 miles down the road.* One of the first religious congregations in the Shenandoah Valley was formed here by some of Jost Hite's settlers in 1736. Today, Opequon Presbyterian Church, west of U.S. 11 on Route 706, holds services in an 1897 building that stands on the site of two earlier churches.

Kernstown is best known for the two Civil War battles that took place here. The First Battle of Kernstown—considered to be Stonewall Jackson's only military defeat—was fought on March 23, 1862, as Jackson's men attacked Union general James Shields, hoping to regain the Valley. Unfortunately for the Confederates, Jackson relied on Colonel Turner Ashby's reports of Union troop strength, which were greatly underestimated. But the battle did achieve one of Jackson's goals: it kept 35,000 Union soldiers engaged in the Valley, away from Richmond.

About 2 miles past Kernstown, you'll reach the outskirts of **Winchester**. A historical marker just past the intersection with Shawnee Drive describes the Second Battle of Kernstown, fought on July 24, 1864. It was begun by Confederate general Jubal Early, who believed that some of the Union troops

The Three Battles of Winchester

Winchester was the site of three major Civil War battles, a result of its strategic location at the junction of railways and major roads. Its terrain was flat and not easily defended. When attacked by one side, the other side evacuated—this occurred an estimated 72 times in all. One historian called the town "basically indefensible."

The First Battle of Winchester occurred on May 25, 1862. Stonewall Jackson chased out Union general Banks's forces, already on the run after their defeat a few days earlier in Front Royal. The battle took place on Bowers Hill, behind what is now Handley High School, and on Camp Hill, on what is now South Kent Street.

The Second Battle of Winchester took place June 13 through June 15, 1863. Confederate general Richard Ewell, on his way to Gettysburg, found General Milroy's troops occupying Winchester. Ewell struck from two sides (the northwest and the northeast), forcing the Union troops into retreat. Action took place at Star Fort, West Fort, and Stephenson Depot, north of town.

The Third Battle of Winchester occurred on September 19, 1864, when Union general Philip Sheridan drove General Jubal Early's forces from what is now Route 7 down the Valley Pike to Fisher's Hill, south of Strasburg. He defeated the Confederates once more a few days later.

in Winchester had returned to Washington. When Union general George Crook heard that Early's men were marching toward Winchester from Strasburg, he ordered his 12,000 men to meet them at Kernstown. Early failed to contain the Union army, which managed to retreat to Bunker Hill, north of Winchester.

During the Civil War, what is now U.S. 11—then the Valley Pike—was one of the few macadamized roads in the region, and it was operated as a toll road. One of the Valley's most enduring tales describes how, in 1864, a young tollkeeper on a stretch of the turnpike south of Winchester lowered her barrier to collect tolls from General Sheridan and his Union troops. The general and his staff paid up, but they told her she'd have to collect from the United States government for everyone else. And after the war was over, she did.

Continue straight on U.S. 11 (now called Valley Avenue) through the traffic light at Weems Lane and the Ward Plaza shopping center. It's a good idea to stay in the left lane for the next mile. You'll begin to see beige-and-green signs directing the way to Old Town Winchester and bright blue signs for the visitor center; be aware that the present tour route diverges from these signs in a few places.

You'll soon enter a residential area of old homes. Shortly, you'll see the huge front lawn of Handley High School on the left. This grand high school looks more like the main building of an elite college. It was built in the early 1900s from funds left to the city by Pennsylvania judge and philanthropist John Handley (who is covered later in this tour). The First Battle of Winchester took place on Bowers Hill, behind the school, as well as on South Kent Street. Here, Stonewall Jackson's forces chased Union general Banks's army out of Winchester.

Handley High School

At the first intersection past Handley High School, turn right on to Gerrard Street (which becomes Millwood Avenue). At the next traffic light (at South Loudon Street), note Gault's Drug Store on the right. Famous country-and-western singer Patsy Cline worked the soda fountain here as a teenager. The drugstore's walls hold many pictures of her.

At the third traffic light, turn left on to Pleasant Valley Road. This busy intersection is the spot where one of General Jackson's regiments was ambushed during the First Battle of Winchester.

Patsy Cline

Gault's Drug Store, where Patsy Cline once worked

Patsy Cline was a well-known country-and-western singer who died tragically in a plane crash in 1963, just as her career was taking off. She was born in nearby Gore, Virginia, grew up in Winchester, and began singing at area clubs and dance halls in the 1950s. One of her biggest hits, "Crazy," was written for her by Willie Nelson.

The Kurtz Cultural Center—which houses Winchester's downtown visitor center—features a display on the singer.

She is buried at Shenandoah Memorial Park, about 4 miles south of town on Route 522 South. *If you want to see her grave, follow the signs to Route 50 East from downtown Winchester or from Exit 313 off I-81. Turn on to Route 522 South toward Front Royal. Enter the cemetery at the north gate and take the first right to the bench on the left.*

Abram's Delight

Drive 0.1 mile to the visitor center, on the right. The visitor center grounds are the site of the oldest house in Winchester, Abram's Delight. Around 1729, Abraham Hollingsworth built a log cabin here, close to a Shawnee Indian village of 100 or so people. The legend goes that he bought more than 500 acres of land around Shawnee Springs from the Indians in exchange for a cow, a calf, and a piece of red cloth.

The Indians remained in the area until 1754, when they headed west to the Ohio Valley to join other tribes in siding with the French in their conflict with the British over territorial claims. That same year, Hollingsworth's son, Isaac, built the first portion of the stone house that stands here today. His father's statement that the spot was "a delight to behold" was the inspiration for the home's name. According to the Virginia Landmarks Register, the stonemason of record for Abram's Delight was Simon Taylor, who also worked as a stonemason at Springdale, the Hite home mentioned earlier in this tour.

The Winchester–Frederick County Historical Society owns this and two other historic properties in Winchester. It offers tours of Abram's Delight and a nearby furnished log cabin daily from April through October. The visitor center, across the parking lot from Abram's Delight, is located next to a large city park and shares an old stone mill building with the local chamber of commerce. The center can provide information on historical sites, lodging, and restaurants; a second visitor center, located in the city's Old Town area (the next stop on the tour) offers art and history exhibits.

Winchester was the first town in the Shenandoah Valley and the first English-speaking settlement west of the Blue Ridge. It was settled largely by Germans and Scots-Irish who came to Virginia from Pennsylvania. The first homes in what is now the downtown historic district are thought to have been built before 1732.

Frederick County was formed from Orange County in 1738. Its name honors Frederick, prince of Wales. This community was first known as Frederick Town; the name was changed to Winchester to honor the English birthplace of the town's founder, James Wood, and to avoid confusion with Frederick, Maryland.

James Wood worked as a surveyor for Orange County, which in those days stretched into this part of the Shenandoah Valley. While surveying here, he decided he liked the area. He subsequently obtained a grant for 1,300 acres from Royal Governor Gooch of Virginia. He began laying out the town in 1744—but only after having to accede to Lord Fairfax's claim that the grant made to him by Governor Gooch was illegal.

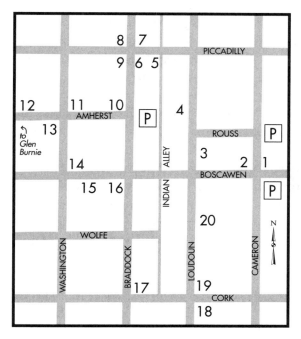

DOWNTOWN WINCHESTER

1 Kurtz Cultural Center/Old Town Visitor Center
2 Rouss City Hall
3 Frederick County Courthouse
4 Taylor Hotel
5 Philip Williams House
6 George Reed House
7 Old post office building
8 Handley Library
9 Logan House
10 McGuire House
11 Alexander Tidball House
12 Daniel Morgan House
13 Ambler Hill
14 Christ Episcopal Church/Lord Fairfax tomb
15 Josiah Massie Hatter Shop
16 Rouss Fire Hall
17 George Washington's Office Museum
18 Red Lion Tavern
19 First Presbyterian Church
20 Godfrey Miller House
P Parking

His Lordship held title to all the lands in the Northern Neck, which extended well into the Shenandoah Valley. Any settlers who had received land grants from the colonial government before Lord Fairfax's arrival were required to reapply for their land and pay annual "quit rents," which were similar to property taxes. This unexpected requirement meant that they had to buy the land twice and live in constant uncertainty as to whether they held clear title. Needless to say, Lord Fairfax was not a popular figure. Jost Hite resented Fairfax's demands and began a court battle that wasn't resolved for more than 40 years, until after both men were dead; the Hite family won in the end. (For more about Lord Fairfax, see The White Post to Millwood to Berryville Tour, pages 54–55.)

Winchester was chartered in 1752, with 80 lots. Wood named many of the streets after French and Indian War heroes; Lord Fairfax, who also owned land in town, named his streets after places in London. Wood later became a colonel in the militia, the first clerk of court in Frederick County, and the man who launched George Washington's political career. In 1760, he built a home a mile west of downtown on land that later served as the site of the family's mansion, Glen Burnie. Members of the Wood family lived at Glen Burnie continuously until 1992; the mansion was opened to the public in 1998. (More information about Glen Burnie is included later in this tour.)

During the Civil War, three major battles were fought in Winchester. For most of the war, the town was under Union control. Its proximity to Washington, D.C., its value as a supplier of food and materials to the Confederacy, its railroads, and its location on the Valley Pike, a macadamized road stretching south past Staunton, gave the area its strategic importance.

After recovering from the devastating effects of the war, Winchester began to grow at a rapid rate in the late 1800s, thanks largely to the health of its apple, wheat, and woolen industries. Today, apples are still important to the local economy, which is also supported by light manufacturing and a growing educational institution, Shenandoah University, formerly the Shenandoah Conservatory of Music, which moved here from Dayton, Virginia, in 1960. (See The Edinburg to Singers Glen to Mount Jackson Tour, pages 108–9, for the early history of the school.) The city is well known throughout the Mid-Atlantic region for its Shenandoah Apple Blossom Festival, an event held every May since 1924.

Traffic Congestion, 1700s-Style

By the late 1780s, Winchester had established itself as a major trade center. According to one estimate, some 132,000 barrels of flour were sent from Winchester to Alexandria each year. The traffic between the two cities became so heavy that merchants petitioned the Virginia assembly for new roads and for additional ferries across the Shenandoah River, especially where the Winchester-Alexandria Road (what is now Route 7) crossed. They claimed congestion was so bad that wagons often had to wait two or three days before they could get across the river.

To reach Old Town Winchester from Abram's Delight, turn right back on to Pleasant Valley Road, drive about 0.8 mile to Cork Street, and turn left. Beige-and-brown signs point the way. The large cemetery on the corner, Mount Hebron, actually contains four separate cemeteries. If you care to make a brief side trip to visit them, turn right on to Kent Street at the next intersection. Many early Valley settlers (including Revolutionary War hero Daniel Morgan) are buried here, as well as thousands of Union and Confederate soldiers. Some 3,000 known and 829 unknown Confederates are buried in Stonewall Cemetery. About 5,500 veterans of all United States wars, including Union soldiers from the Civil War, are buried in Winchester National Cemetery, north of Stonewall Cemetery.

Continue down Cork Street to Cameron Street and turn right. Drive one block to the Downtown Welcome Center—also known as the Kurtz Cultural Center— at the corner of Cameron and Boscawen Streets. Park at the garage across Boscawen Street, in the Judicial Center lot, or at one of the meters on the street to take a brief walking tour of downtown Winchester. A bronze statue in front of the Judicial Center honors Admiral Richard E. Byrd, a pioneer navy aviator and polar explorer who was born in Winchester at 326 West Amherst Street; the house no longer stands.

The Kurtz Cultural Center, housed in an 1836 building, provides tourist information, art exhibits, and an exhibit called "Shenandoah: Crossroads of the Civil War." Open daily year-round, it offers special programs and guided 90-minute walking tours on weekends from mid-May to mid-October. If you are interested in a self-guided walking tour of the historic district, ask at the counter for a printed guide. Two are available; one covers sites of importance during the Civil War, and the other emphasizes history and architecture.

Rouss City Hall

The impressive building directly across Cameron Street is Rouss City Hall, built in 1900 and named for local merchant C. B. Rouss, who funded this and other city projects. After the Civil War, Rouss moved to New York, opened a general merchandise store on Broadway, and eventually became a millionaire. He remembered his hometown of Winchester with several generous financial gifts.

To reach the downtown mall area, walk across Cameron Street, turn right to walk past city hall, and turn left on Rouss Avenue. A few steps away on the left is the Frederick County Courthouse. Built in 1840 in the Greek

Revival style, it is considered by some to be one of the prettiest court-houses in the state. Plans are under way to open a Civil War museum in the courthouse.

From the front of the courthouse, turn right on the downtown mall (which runs along Loudon Street) and walk to the three-story blue-painted building with large white columns at 125 North Loudon. For most of the 20th century, this building housed a variety store. But in the 1800s, it had porches on all three levels and was known as the Taylor Hotel. Its guests included Henry Clay, Daniel Webster, and Stonewall Jackson. Built in 1836, it served as both Union and Confederate headquarters, depending on which side controlled Winchester at the time. One story goes that the hotel changed hands four times in one day. It was here that Stonewall Jackson promoted Turner Ashby to the rank of general, a title he held for only 10 days until his death near Harrisonburg in June 1862.

Continue down Loudon Street and turn left on to Piccadilly Street. Just across Indian Alley, at 25 West Piccadilly, a gift store occupies a beautiful old white-painted brick house with extensive ironwork. The home was built in 1845 by a local attorney, Philip William. Local legend says that the ironwork was taken down and buried during the Civil War so it wouldn't be confiscated and melted down for ammunition. George S. Patton, the grandfather of the famous World War II general of the same name, was wounded during the Third Battle of Winchester and was brought to this house, which belonged to his cousin. He died here.

The stone house at 35 West Piccadilly (now occupied by a bank) was built in 1797 by George Reed, a coppersmith whose shop was next door. It is typical of stone structures in early Winchester, featuring two stories with two rooms on each level. As in most houses like this one, the dormers were added later.

Directly across the street is the Old Post Office Building, an Italian Renaissance Revival structure that now houses a bank.

Continue to Braddock Street. You can't miss the large red apple sitting on the front lawn of the white Greek Revival house across Braddock. Now a gift and furniture store, it was built in 1850 by tobacco merchant Lloyd Logan. The house was once the headquarters of Union generals Milroy and Sheridan; the town was outraged when Milroy moved in and literally threw

Winchester's downtown mall

the Logan family out on the street. From 1874 to 1909, the structure housed the Episcopal Female Institute. The large porch is a 20th-century addition.

Logan House

The impressive building on the corner across the street is the Handley Library. This Beaux-Arts building was built between 1908 and 1913 from funds left to the city by a man who never lived here. He was Judge John Handley of Scranton, Pennsylvania, who first visited friends in Winchester in 1869 and became quite fond of the city. Handley made a fortune in coal investments. When he died in 1895, he left the city a bequest (which grew to nearly $2 million) for the purpose of building and maintaining a public library and a high school. Judge Handley was buried in Mount Hebron Cemetery.

The Handley Library was designed by two New Yorkers, Stewart Barney and Henry Otis Chapman. It has a large copper dome (with a stained-glass dome inside) and coupled columns on either side of the entrance porch. The design was intended to represent a book, the rotunda serving as the spine and the two side wings as the opened pages. As the library grew, the problem arose of how to expand the building. Hard as it is to believe, one consultant advised tearing down the structure and starting anew. Instead, a wing was added in 1979, and it fit in so well with the original design that the library won an award from the American Institute of Architects.

Walk up North Braddock Street. Just past the rear of the library, look for a small historical marker across the street at the corner of Fairfax Lane. It states that George Washington once owned this lot (designated as lot 77). He bought it in 1753 while living in Winchester as a young man. The black-smith shop that originally stood on the site made iron for nearby Fort Loudon, one of the many forts Washington was charged with building in the 1750s to protect Valley settlers from Indian attacks. Washington purchased about 1,000 acres in the Winchester area. Lot 77 and lot 16 in the downtown area were mentioned in his will, the only Winchester properties he still owned at the time of his death in 1799.

Handley Library

Continue walking two and a half blocks up North Braddock Street. The house set back from the street on the left at 415 North Braddock served as Stonewall Jackson's headquarters between November 1861 and March 1862.

A charming Gothic Revival structure with diamond-pane windows, the house was built in 1854 and sold two years later to Lewis T. Moore. A

George Washington's Early Years in the Shenandoah Valley

George Washington first came to the wilderness that was the Shenandoah Valley in 1748 as a boy of 16, when he accompanied a surveying party. A year later, he began working for Lord Fairfax as a paid surveyor on His Lordship's huge landholdings west of the Blue Ridge.

Washington learned much about survival while living in this wilderness area. It was that experience that led Lieutenant Governor Robert Dinwiddie of Virginia to select him in 1753 to deliver a letter of protest from King George II to the French in the Ohio Valley. At the time, the Ohio Valley was claimed by both the French and the British. During his journey, Washington experienced several months of harrowing adventures and close calls. A member of the Virginia Regiment, he hoped for a promotion to colonel in the regular British army, but when it didn't come ("provincials" like Washington could receive no commission higher than captain), he quit and returned to Mount Vernon to become a planter.

By 1755, he was back in the British army, this time as an unofficial aide to General Braddock during the disastrous defeat at Fort Duquesne. After that, the British abandoned their interest in the area west of Virginia. As a result, the Virginia assembly decided to create its own army to defend its western lands. It named the 22-year-old Washington "the Colonel of the Virginia Regiment and Commander in Chief of all Virginia forces." He was put in charge of building small forts along Virginia's long Allegheny border in an attempt to protect settlers from French and Indian attack. He used Winchester as his base of operations for several years.

The task was impossible from the start, but Washington gained valuable experience in dealing with day-to-day problems of managing shortages of funds and troops and reporting to incompetent British authorities. Many historians believe that the hard times he experienced during his early years in Winchester prepared him for his leadership role in the American Revolution. And it was in Winchester in 1758 that Washington, age 26, was elected to his first political office—Frederick County representative to the Virginia House of Burgesses in Williamsburg.

colonel with the Fourth Virginia Volunteers, Moore was injured at First Manassas. While he was hospitalized, he learned that Jackson needed a headquarters in Winchester and offered the general the use of his home. Jackson used the home's parlor as his office; it is furnished today much like it was when he was here. In a letter to his wife, Jackson commented on the beautiful gilded wallpaper in the parlor. More than 100 years later, the wallpaper was faithfully reproduced and rehung, a gift from actress Mary Tyler Moore, a great-granddaughter of Colonel Moore. The house is now operated as a museum by the Winchester–Frederick County Historical Society. Open daily from April through October, it features many Jackson mementos and artifacts, including his prayer book and the chair and desk he used while staying here.

Stonewall Jackson's headquarters

Turn around and walk back down North Braddock Street, passing the library and the big red apple. Turn right on to Amherst Street. The house across Amherst on the corner at 103 North Braddock is known as the McGuire House. It dates to around 1790. This was the boyhood home of Stonewall Jackson's personal physician during the Civil War, Dr. Hunter Holmes McGuire. Dr. McGuire also served as the medical director of the Army of Northern Virginia.

At 123 North Amherst is the Beall House, built by schoolteacher Eli Beall in 1820.

At 138 North Amherst is the Alexander Tidball House, built around 1835. Tidball was a prominent attorney in Winchester.

As you walk the streets in this neighborhood, look at the chimneys on the homes and buildings. Many lean markedly northward. This happened when the mortar on the south side of the chimneys dried and expanded faster than that on the north side.

Cross North Washington Street into the next block. At 223 North Amherst is Ambler Hill, a yellow clapboard house of frame peg construction built by local merchant John Norton in 1786. The house took its name from the man Norton's widow married after his death in 1797.

At 226 North Amherst is the Daniel Morgan House, the southeastern portion of which was built by George Flowerdew Norton around 1786. The home was purchased and enlarged by Daniel Morgan for his daughter in 1800. Morgan died here in 1802. (For more about this fascinating Revolutionary War hero and United States congressman, see The White Post to Millwood to Berryville Tour, pages 59–60.) In the late 1800s and early 1900s, this house was owned by two sisters who ran a school on the grounds. Two of their more famous students were Harry F. Byrd, a future Virginia governor and United States senator, and his brother, the explorer Richard E. Byrd, mentioned earlier.

Return to the corner of Amherst and Washington Streets and turn right on Washington. Walk one block and turn left on West Boscawen Street. The large church on the corner is Christ Episcopal, built in 1829; a church first occupied this site in 1752. The tomb of Lord Fairfax is in the courtyard on the right side of the church.

The large house diagonally across the intersection at 5 South Washington Street is called The Gables; it was built in 1899 for the Baker family, of baking chocolate fame. The Baechters came to Winchester from Germany

The Gables

143 Boscawen Street

Weathervane of the Rouss Fire Hall

around 1755, and several family members became merchants. William H. Baker (the Anglicized version of Baechter) founded Baker Chocolate in New York; he also served as president of the Shenandoah Valley Bank and as vice president of the Virginia Woolen Company, once an important Winchester industry.

Farther down the block on West Boscawen Street are several buildings that look much as they did in the 1800s. The stone building at 143 West Boscawen was built by a tanner. The house at 125 West Boscawen is an early log home that was later covered with clapboards; built between 1806 and 1815, it was once a hatter's shop and is now home to a law firm. On the corner is the Rouss Fire Hall, built in 1896 with funds from former citizen and successful New York businessman Charles B. Rouss.

From the fire hall, turn right on to North Braddock Street and walk two blocks to Cork Street. The dark brown log-and-stone cabin at the corner of Braddock and Cork is George Washington's Office Museum. The stone portion of this structure is said to have been used as an office by Colonel Washington in 1755 and 1756, when he was in charge of building a series of forts along a 300-mile stretch of frontier to protect settlers from attacks by the French and the Indians. (According to the Virginia Landmarks Register, no documentation exists to prove that Washington worked here, although local tradition to the contrary is strong.) The museum is open daily from April through October.

To complete the downtown walking tour, follow Cork Street across Indian Alley to South Loudon Street. The stone structure on the corner diagonally across the street was once the Red Lion Tavern, built around 1783 by one of Daniel Morgan's Revolutionary War Riflemen, Peter Lauck.

Turn left on South Loudon, which will put you at the other end of the downtown mall. The lovely old stone house at 28 South Loudon dates to 1785 and was bought in 1850 by merchant Godfrey Miller.

One other important old home of interest is Glen Burnie, mentioned earlier in the tour as the home of the James Wood family and its descendants from the 1790s to 1992. Now open to the public for tours, it is elegantly furnished with historically valuable paintings (including an 1850 portrait of George Washington by Rembrandt Peale) and fine antiques. Most were collected by the last descendant to live in the house, Julian Wood

Glass, Jr., who died in 1992. He left the property to a foundation and stipulated that it was to be run as a house museum; it opened to the public in April 1998 and may be visited daily except Mondays from April through October.

Glen Burnie is at 530 Amherst Street. To get there from the Kurtz Cultural Center, drive north on Cameron Street (the one-way street in front of the center) to the first intersection, which is Piccadilly Street. Turn left, drive three blocks (past the library and the big red apple) to Washington Street, and turn left again. Turn right on to Amherst Street at the next corner. After you pass a group of dental offices on the right, look to the left for signs pointing to the left-hand turn into Glen Burnie.

Winchester's founder, James Wood, built a log-and-stone house on this site in 1737. One of his sons, Robert, built this brick house between 1794 and 1798. The property features 25 acres of formal English-style gardens, including the Pink Pavilion, a garden structure furnished with antiques.

Robert's brother, James Wood, Jr., was born in 1741 in an earlier structure on the grounds of Glen Burnie. James was only 19 years old when he became his father's deputy clerk of court for Frederick County. Between 1766 and 1775, he represented Frederick County in the Virginia House of Burgesses. He was also an Indian fighter and a Revolutionary War general. In 1796, he was elected governor of Virginia. He went on to serve three terms.

The tour ends here. To return to the interstate, go back to the downtown area and follow the I-81 signs on Cameron Street. Cameron Street is also U.S. 11. As it continues north, it passes several Civil War historical markers before eventually connecting with I-81 a few miles north of the city (where The Clearbrook to Martinsburg Tour begins).

George Washington's Office Museum

Willa Cather's Birthplace

Novelist Willa Cather was born near Gore, 13 miles west of Winchester on U.S. 50, in 1873. She spent her early childhood in the home of her maternal grandmother. Known as Willow Shade, the house still stands on Route 50, its location noted by a historical marker. Cather moved with her parents to Nebraska when she was nine years old.

In 1923, she won the Pulitzer Prize for her novel *One of Ours*. Only her last book—*Sapphira and the Slave Girl*—dealt with the Gore area. That novel drew on the many tales her grandmother once told her.

The White Post to Millwood to Berryville Tour

The White Post to Millwood to Berryville Tour

The tour begins in the historic hamlet of **White Post**. *There are two ways to reach White Post, depending on the direction you're coming from.* **From the Baltimore–Washington, D.C., area**, *take Exit 6 off I-66 and follow the sign toward Winchester, which will put you on U.S. 340 North. In about 10 miles, you'll pass a state historical marker on the right at the boundary of Clarke County. About 0.8 mile after the marker, turn left at the traffic light at Double Tollgate to stay on U.S. 340 North to White Post and Boyce.* **From I-81**, *take Exit 307 (marked "Stephens City to Route 340"), then turn at the sign that says, "To U.S. 340." You are now on Route 277 (Fairfax Pike). In 4.6 miles, you'll come to a traffic light at the U.S. 340 intersection at Double Tollgate. Continue straight through the light toward White Post as the road becomes U.S. 340 North.*

In 1.8 miles, turn right on to Route 628 (White Post Road) just before a barbecue restaurant.

Clarke County was formed from Frederick County in 1836. It was named to honor George Rogers Clark, the Revolutionary War hero who (at his own expense) led his 175 soldiers to help secure the Old Northwest Territories—what are now Kentucky, Ohio, Indiana, Illinois, and Missouri—for America. For reasons unknown, an *e* was added to the county name.

This area was settled mostly by well-to-do English and Americans of English descent. Families like the Carters, the Burwells, the Randolphs, the Washingtons, and the Byrds began coming here in the 1780s and early 1800s from the Tidewater area of eastern Virginia. For them, the main attractions were a better climate and plenty of fertile farmland on which to grow wheat, by that time a more profitable crop than tobacco.

This tour covers Clarke County, on the northeastern edge of the Shenandoah Valley. This area was settled by immigrants and landed gentry alike, the most famous of the latter being the largest Valley landowner of the time, Lord Fairfax. The other famous families who built homes and estates here—including the Washingtons, the Carters, the Byrds, and the Burwells—were attracted by the area's pleasant climate and fertile soil.

The tour starts in the village of White Post, where the young George Washington worked for Lord Fairfax as a surveyor. It continues down a Virginia Byway to the old railroad town of Boyce and the 1700s settlement of Millwood. Along the way, it pauses for a visit to the little-known State Arboretum of Virginia. It ends at the county seat of Berryville—originally called Battletown, not because of any involvement in military events but because of its rough-and-tumble reputation as a pioneer town.

Total mileage:
Approximately 55 miles

The county's most famous resident was probably Thomas, the sixth Lord Fairfax. He had inherited from his mother (the daughter of Lord Culpeper) the lands known as the Northern Neck Proprietary—some 5 million acres that stretched from the Rapidan River in southeastern Virginia to most of northern Virginia, including parts of the Shenandoah Valley. For a small fee—10 shillings per 100 acres, plus office costs—and an annual rent, he granted settlers parcels of land for the asking.

Lord Fairfax first came to America to check out his landholdings in 1736, when he was 53 years old. After a year here, he returned to England for 10 years, leaving his cousin, William Fairfax, in charge of assigning land grants and collecting rents. Lord Fairfax came back to Virginia for good in 1747. For a while, he lived with William Fairfax in the family mansion, Belvoir, on the Potomac River near Mount Vernon. (William's daughter, Anne, married Lawrence Washington, George's elder half-brother and the builder of Mount Vernon.)

By the late 1740s, most of the remaining Fairfax lands were located west of the Blue Ridge, so Lord Fairfax decided to move his land-office operations from Belvoir to a spot near what came to be called White Post. Here, he built a complex of buildings, including a relatively modest house (no longer standing) and several other structures. He called his new land office Greenway Court, after his mother's estate in Kent, England. The land office, a National Historic Landmark, survives today, but it is located well beyond the road on private property. The only original Greenway Court building that can be viewed from the road stands practically on it about a mile from White Post. That structure is visited later on this tour.

Lord Fairfax believed that any land grants made by the colony of Virginia for his lands before he arrived in America were illegal, and he didn't hesitate to demand payment from those he considered to be squatters. Some people paid up just to be able to stay on their land without fear of reprisal. Others rebelled. Lord Fairfax thus became involved in lengthy legal squabbles with the Virginia colonial authorities—and in particular with Jost Hite, one of the Valley's original settlers.

Some historians say that Lord Fairfax's intention was not to take away settlers' lands but rather to clarify ownership and boundaries—and also to be able to collect annual rents. Others say that he was determined to exert control and didn't want to miss out on any potential source of income; even in those days, many English lords were short of cash. The lawsuit involving the Hite family went on for years and was finally resolved after both Jost Hite and Lord Fairfax were dead. After the Revolution, the Virginia assembly abolished the system of "quit rents" entirely.

The story goes that Lord Fairfax never married because his fiancée jilted him for a wealthier suitor just before the wedding. He apparently never overcame his distrust of women after that painful episode.

Although Lord Fairfax entertained frequently, he did not live ostentatiously. He became involved in local political affairs but tried to remain neutral throughout the Revolution. He lived to be 90 years old and was buried in Winchester, where his tomb can be visited today (see The Middletown to Winchester Tour, page 49).

It was in 1749 that Lord Fairfax hired his cousin's Mount Vernon neighbor, the young George Washington, to help survey the western boundary of his holdings. Unable to attend college because of the death of his father a few years earlier, Washington needed a paying job. He could not have realized at the time that this assignment would give him a knowledge of the Allegheny wilderness that would qualify him for his first military appointment just a few years later.

The white post

For several years, Washington worked out of Greenway Court, where he is said to have used Lord Fairfax's library to further his education. Legend has it that in 1750, Lord Fairfax directed Washington to erect the now-famous white post near the Ashby Gap–Winchester Road (also called the Old Dutch Trail, today's U.S. 340) to mark the way to Greenway Court. Unless it has been knocked down again by a motorist surprised by its placement in the middle of the intersection, you can't miss seeing this post; it stands where Routes 628 and 658 meet.

The village of White Post is a Virginia Landmarks Register Historic District. Its two churches and more than 20 old homes from various eras are set on lush green lawns and shaded by huge old trees. A short distance north on Route 658 is Bishop Meade Memorial Episcopal Church, built in 1875 and named for the third Episcopal bishop of Virginia, a local resident. After the War of 1812, Meade led a revival of the Episcopal Church in Virginia.

Meade Memorial Episcopal Church

Meadea

Mesilla

Continue straight past the white post on Route 628. The second house on the right is a one-and-a-half-story clapboard (over log) home with two stone chimneys. This is Meadea, built in the 1780s. One of the oldest homes in Clarke County, it is typical of early homesteads in the area.

Head back toward the white post and turn left to go south on Route 658. On the right after 0.6 mile, you'll see a mid-1800s Greek Revival brick house called Mesilla. On the right after another 0.5 mile is Porter's Lodge of Greenway Court, an old stone building with clapboard additions at the back. Built around 1760, it is one of only four original Greenway Court buildings still standing—and the only one visible from the road. Lord Fairfax's manor house here was torn down in the 1830s.

Route 658 veers sharply to the left after Porter's Lodge. Continue for 2.3 miles, then turn left on to Route 622, which is a designated Virginia Byway. After 0.3 mile, look to the left for the first set of entry gates for Federal Hill. Built by Samuel Baker in the early 1800s, this structure was home to three generations of his family. Federal Hill is best seen from the second set of stone gate posts, located 0.2 mile down the road from the first set. The house sits high on a hill well back from the road, facing the Blue Ridge Mountains. It remains a working farm today.

Porter's Lodge, Greenway Court

The Bakers and their neighbors at nearby Guilford (located on Route 644 just beyond the turnoff to Route 622) were related by marriage. Guilford was built between 1812 and 1820 by the family of James Madison Hite, who was a son of Isaac Hite and a nephew of President Madison. Guilford was later the home of the Ashby family.

Long Branch

Continue on Route 622 past where it intersects Route 627. When you come to the intersection with Route 626 in 0.6 mile, turn left to stay on the Virginia Byway. In another 0.7 mile, stay straight through the Route 628 intersection—don't turn left. Route 626 is renumbered Route 628 after a short distance. There are several interesting old homes along this road.

In 0.8 mile, you'll see a driveway on the right and a sign pointing to Long Branch. A state historical marker describing Long Branch is located nearby.

If you are here on a weekend afternoon between April 1 and October 31, you may want to consider touring Long Branch. It's one of the few great old homes in the area open to the public for tours. Even if you decide not to take the tour, go up the long drive to see the house and its extensive grounds and horse farm. The estate occupies a magnificent setting, with wonderful views of the Blue Ridge Mountains in the distance.

Long Branch was built around 1811 by Robert Carter Burwell, originally of Carter's Grove on the James River in the Tidewater area. Burwell inherited the land from his grandfather, Robert Burwell, who inherited it from Robert "King" Carter, the wealthy agent for Lord Culpeper and later for Lord Fairfax. Robert Carter Burwell obtained design help—including suggestions for the home's dramatic curved hanging staircase and its piazza—from America's first professional architect, Benjamin Henry Latrobe. Burwell died in the War of 1812.

Long Branch was bought in 1842 by a Burwell descendant, Hugh Mortimer Nelson, who remodeled it in the Greek Revival style. Nelson also died in war—the Civil War—but the estate remained in his family well into the 20th century.

View of the Blue Ridge from Long Branch

By 1986, the house had begun to deteriorate. It was purchased by Baltimore textile executive Harry Z. Isaacs, who restored the property in less than three years. During that time, Isaacs traveled all over the world to find antique furnishings, fabrics, and wallpaper that were right for the house. The results of his labors are impressive. He also made the surrounding 400 acres into a working horse farm. Before he died in 1990, he established a

Orland E. White Arboretum

An Amazing Collection of Plants

More than 5,000 species of plants are collected at the State Arboretum of Virginia, including the largest selection of boxwood cultivars in North America (the arboretum is headquarters of the American Boxwood Society). The arboretum also has representatives of more than half the world's pine species. Its ginkgo planting area contains more than 500 trees, one of the largest groves outside China. Other planting areas include those for maples, oaks, chestnuts, dogwoods, hollies, magnolias, roses, azaleas, irises, daylilies, herbs, and perennials. The arboretum's buildings date to around 1825 and were once slave quarters for the nearby Tuleyries estate. The grounds are open free to the public year-round from dawn to dusk. Picnickers are welcome. Rest rooms and a gift shop are in the Quarters Building.

private nonprofit foundation to maintain the estate and open it for public tours, which are led by local volunteers.

Leaving Long Branch, turn right at the end of the driveway to continue in your original direction on Route 628. Go to the stop sign at Route 624 and turn left. In about 0.5 mile, you'll come to Route 17/Route 50, a four-lane divided highway. Turn left. In about 1 mile, you'll see a brown highway sign announcing the turnoff for the Orland E. White Arboretum, also known as the State Arboretum of Virginia at Blandy Experimental Farm. Turn left into the arboretum.

The beautiful grounds of the arboretum make it a perfect place to stop for a picnic lunch. It's also a great place for walking along marked trails and learning about an enormous variety of trees and other plants. If time is short, you can take a 3-mile loop driving tour around the property and catch a glimpse of a historic old home, Tuleyries, still a private residence. Maps showing self-guided trails and the loop driving tour are available at the information kiosk next to the arboretum parking lot.

Tuleyries was built around 1833 by Colonel Joseph Tuley, Jr., who was originally from New Jersey. Tuley and his father had made a fortune as tanners in Millwood. The locals thought the name for the house—which was derived from Tuley's own name but alluded to the French royal palace called Tuileries—was a bit much. Wryly, they suggested a better name might be "Hide Park."

Tuleyries was owned later by Upton L. Boyce before being bought by Graham F. Blandy, a New Yorker, in 1903. Upon his death in 1926, Blandy deeded the land to the University of Virginia, which uses the farm as an educational center.

From the arboretum entrance, turn left back on to Route 17/Route 50, drive 1.5 miles to the traffic light, and turn right on U.S. 340 North at **Waterloo**. *After 1.5 miles, turn right at the yellow flashing light on to Route 723. This will take you into the old part of* **Boyce**, where you'll see a mix of restored and original buildings and Victorian homes. Once a thriving railroad town, the community was named for Colonel Upton L. Boyce, who purchased Tuleyries after Tuley's death. An attorney for the Norfolk and Western Railroad, Boyce is said to have helped bring the Shenandoah Valley Railroad through Clarke County in 1879. The Winchester chapter of the National Railway Historical Society plans to restore the 1913 train station and turn it into its headquarters and a museum.

Continue over the railroad tracks on Route 723. The 1780 estate known as Saratoga—a National Historic Landmark—is just ahead on the right. Unfortunately, it is privately owned and is not visible from the road. It was built by Revolutionary War hero Daniel Morgan and named after the victory he helped secure at the Battle of Saratoga in New York.

Boyce Train Station

An original American success story, Morgan was the son of Welsh immigrants to New Jersey. He made his way to Virginia in 1753, when he was just 17 years old. Having no prospects and no money, he took whatever work he could find—as a farm laborer, as manager of a sawmill, and as a wagon driver hired by Robert Burwell, one of the local gentry. Morgan was soon able to buy his own wagon, after which he found work hauling supplies for General Braddock during the French and Indian War.

Years later, as a captain of the local militia in 1775, Morgan wasted no time in responding to General George Washington's call for troops. He recruited his 93 Riflemen and took just 26 days to march them 600 miles to join Washington's forces at Cambridge, Massachusetts. By December 1775, Morgan was fighting under General Benedict Arnold's command during the assault on Quebec, where he was forced to surrender. He remained a prisoner of war there for five months. In 1777, he joined General Horatio Gates in the Battle of Saratoga.

Ill health forced Morgan to resign from the army in 1779, after which he began building his estate in Boyce. At that time, hundreds of Hessian prisoners of war were being held in the Winchester area. Local lore says that these German mercenaries for the British army were put to work as stonemasons and woodworkers for the many fine homes being built in the area. Some historians dispute that story, saying that the prisoners were not held in the area for the several years needed to construct such large homes. Nevertheless, more than 40 percent of those prisoners chose to remain in America once freed. They may well have offered their skills to area residents as paid workers.

Morgan was recalled to service in 1780 after the Americans were badly defeated at the Battle of Camden in South Carolina. He won a surprise victory against a larger British force at Cowpens, also in South Carolina, and was made a brigadier general.

After the war, he served a term in the United States Congress. He saw military action once more, in 1794, when he was sent to command troops to put down the Whiskey Rebellion in western Pennsylvania. He died in Winchester in 1802 at the home he bought for his daughter (see The Middletown to Winchester Tour, page 49).

After Morgan's death, his daughter inherited Saratoga. Her descendants later sold it to Nathaniel Burwell, son of Colonel Nathaniel Burwell of Carter Hall (visited later on this tour). General Robert E. Lee camped on its grounds during the Civil War.

Saratoga remains a working farm today.

Almost directly across the road from Saratoga, you'll see an impressive-looking set of gates marked "Kentmere." Kentmere is part of an estate called Scaleby just up the road. The mansion—all 30,000 elegant square feet of it—was built between 1910 and 1912 by Mr. and Mrs. Henry Gilpin, part of a famous New York railroad family, and named for the family's ancestral seat, Scaleby Castle in Cumberland County, England.

Continue on Route 723 toward **Millwood**, *located about 1 mile ahead.* This portion of the road is lined on both sides with beautiful limestone walls. Several old frame houses front the narrow road as it enters town. Clark House, located on the right, was built in 1842 and originally served as a tavern. During the Civil War, it was the location of a meeting to negotiate the surrender of Confederate colonel John Mosby.

The community of Millwood formed around a large mill completed in 1785 by Colonel Nathaniel Burwell (who also built Carter Hall) and Daniel Morgan. The mill is just ahead on the right.

Burwell (pronounced "Burl" by the locals) predicted, correctly, that wheat would be a profitable crop for the area in the years following the Revolutionary War, and that building a large mill to turn the grain into flour would be an even more profitable endeavor. Probably with the help of Hessian craftsmen, Morgan oversaw the construction of the limestone mill, which was worked around the clock during its heyday.

The Burwell-Morgan Mill is open to visitors daily except Tuesdays from May through October. It has recently undergone a major renovation, its second since it ceased operating as a commercial mill in 1953. Now owned by the Clarke County Historical Association and first restored in the 1960s, it is well worth a stop. A video describing the mill and local history is shown, and local volunteers give tours and explain the operations. In

Burwell-Morgan Mill

days gone by, barrels of flour and cornmeal from this mill were taken to the Shenandoah River and floated on barges to Harpers Ferry, where they were loaded on canal boats for shipment to the ports of Georgetown and Alexandria.

Burwell was living at Carter's Grove in the Tidewater area at the time of the mill's construction and during its early days of operation. He built Brookside, the frame house across from the mill, in 1786 as a summer home and a place to live while he constructed his mansion, Carter Hall, nearby. The other frame house on the property was the miller's house. Located behind the mill, it dates to 1820.

Brookside

Millwood has a real old-time feel about it and has several great shops to explore. Jackie Onassis is said to have shopped here in the early 1990s. In addition to the many antique stores in town, don't miss Locke's General Store, across the street from the mill. Located on the site of the first store in Millwood, this is an authentic early-1900s general store complete with pressed-metal ceilings.

From the mill's parking lot, turn left, go past Locke's General Store, and make an immediate right on to Route 255 North. This road will take you past more old homes and antique shops.

After 0.2 mile, you'll see entrance gates on the right for Project Hope. This is actually the entrance to Carter Hall, the beautiful stone mansion Colonel Nathaniel Burwell built in the 1790s. Today, it is the headquarters for Project Hope, an international health science educational foundation; it is not open to the public.

Burwell's grandfather was Robert "King" Carter, who built Carter's Grove (now owned by Colonial Williamsburg); Nathaniel Burwell inherited Carter's Grove when he was only five years old, after the death of his father. King Carter's 50,000 acres of land included what was called the Shenandoah Tract, here in Clarke County. After graduating from William and Mary, Nathaniel came here in the 1770s to manage the estate.

Millwood Antique Shop

In 1862, General Stonewall Jackson set up temporary headquarters on the grounds of Carter Hall, refusing offers to use the house itself.

On the left just across the street from the state historical marker for Carter Hall is Christ Episcopal Church of Cunningham Parish, a Gothic stone structure dating to 1832. It was built under the direction of its rector,

William Meade, who was then bishop of the Episcopal diocese of Virginia. The small white building with the red door to the right of the church is Cunningham Chapel.

Continue down Route 255 for another 2.8 miles, past farms and old homes. Just as the road passes under a railroad bridge and veers left toward its intersection with busy U.S. 340, look to your left. The small stone building (which has an unpaved driveway you can turn into) is known as Old Chapel. This is one of the earliest Episcopal churches west of the Blue Ridge. It was built in 1793 to replace a 1740s log church that was located nearby, thanks to a donation of land from Nathaniel Burwell.

Cunningham Chapel

Though the congregation later moved to the larger Christ Episcopal Church in Millwood, the parish still holds a special annual service at Old Chapel. Many of the area's original citizens are buried in the chapel's graveyard, including Nathaniel Burwell and Edmund Jennings Randolph. Randolph was a governor of Virginia, the first United States attorney general, and a United States secretary of state. He died at Carter Hall while visiting there in 1813.

From Old Chapel, continue a short distance on Route 255 to the intersection with U.S. 340 and turn right on to U.S. 340 North. On the left soon after the turn is a stone home called Chapel Hill. The oldest section of Chapel Hill was built around 1826 by Dr. Charles Byrd, who sold the house that year to Phillip Burwell. In the 20th century, it was the home of William "Wild Bill" Donovan, head of the OSS (today's CIA) during World War II.

Continue for 0.6 mile, then turn left on Route 633 (Annfield Road). Drive about 1.5 miles to Annfield, on the right. Annfield has been called one of the most beautiful mansions in Virginia. A prime example of Federal-style architecture, it is typical of the homes built by families who came here from the Tidewater area. Annfield was constructed in the 1790s by Matthew Page, who named it for his wife, Ann Randolph Meade Page. She was a sister of Bishop William Meade and an early abolitionist well known in her own right.

Annfield was the birthplace of Mary Custis, Robert E. Lee's wife, who was born in the house while her mother was a guest here in 1808. The home is built of limestone blocks and has a two-story pedimented portico, with each level supported by four white columns; a Chippendale railing encloses the upper porch.

TOURING THE SHENANDOAH VALLEY BACKROADS

The roads on this part of the tour are idyllic—if slightly upscale—country byways with huge stands of old trees, miles of stone walls, brown-fenced horse farms, and rolling green fields. Every so often, an apple orchard comes into view.

Continue 0.8 mile to Route 652, a gravel road. Turn right. Go 1.5 miles to the stop sign at Route 657, turn right again, and go 2 miles to Avenel, on the left. Surrounded by a grove of large white oaks, Avenel was built by the Gold family in 1814. Mosby's Rangers skirmished with the Sixth New York Cavalry nearby in September 1864; at that time, the estate was known as Gold's Farm. The beautiful barn on the property was one of the few to escape Sheridan's burning of the Shenandoah Valley in 1864. In the 1930s, United States senator Harry Flood Byrd, Sr., bought the property. He later gave it to his son, Richard E. Byrd.

Continue on Route 657 for 1 mile until you reach U.S. 340. Turn left on to U.S. 340, which will take you into Berryville. Turn right at the traffic light on to West Main Street (Route 7 Business) to enter the downtown area.

Berryville began in the mid-1700s as a frontier settlement known as Battletown, so named because some of its early residents spent their evenings drinking and fighting at local taverns. According to records, one of the regular participants in these activities was the young Daniel Morgan. The hamlet formed at the intersection of the Winchester-Alexandria Road

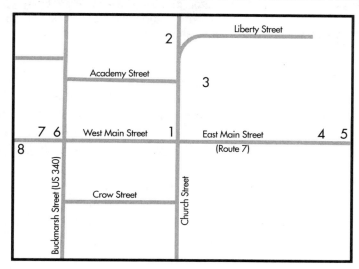

DOWNTOWN BERRYVILLE

1 Site of Daniel Morgan's favorite tavern (flower shop)
2 Grace Episcopal Church
3 Clarke County Courthouse
4 Former Coiner's Department
5 The Nook
6 Hawthorne Building
7 Battletown Inn
8 Berryville Presbyterian Church

Historic Sites Just North of Berryville

Quite a bit of history surrounds the area above Berryville north of the intersection of U.S. 340 and Route 7.

Drive north on U.S. 340 from the Route 7 interchange. The fields immediately to the right are where Confederate generals Lee and Longstreet camped on their way to Gettysburg in June 1863. And in August 1864, Mosby's Rangers attacked Union general Sheridan's 7-mile-long wagon train here, capturing 600 horses and mules and 200 prisoners.

About 1 mile farther up U.S. 340 is one of Virginia's most intriguing state historical markers. Titled "Buck Marsh," it notes that pioneer Joseph Hampton and his two sons lived near here in a hollow sycamore tree for several months in 1744.

Another 2.1 miles north on U.S. 340 is the site of a beautiful old limestone house called Fairfield. It was built by Warner Washington, a cousin of George Washington, sometime before 1770. A sign at the entrance marks the spot, but the home is a private residence and is difficult to see from the highway.

Fairfield is said to be one of the finest Washington homes still standing. Its interior is similar to that of Kenmore in Fredericksburg, Virginia, the home of George Washington's sister. Some think that architect John Ariss designed both houses. Fairfield's wings and dormers were added in the 1900s.

Warner Washington's second wife was Hannah Fairfax, the daughter of William Fairfax of Belvoir and the sister of George William Fairfax, who sold Warner Washington 1,600 acres here soon after his marriage to Hannah in 1764. George and Martha Washington and Martha's daughter Patsy visited Fairfield in 1769 on their way to the resort now known as Berkeley Springs. The house remained in the Washington family until 1815.

(today's Route 7 Business) and the road to Lord Fairfax's land office at Greenway Court (today's U.S. 340). It was renamed Berryville in 1798 for Benjamin Berry, who donated the land and helped develop the town site. When Clarke County was formed from Frederick County in 1836, Berryville became the county seat. More recently, it was home to former United States senator Harry F. Byrd, Jr.

The best way to see the town—a mix of old and new—is to park and walk. Turn left off West Main Street on to Church Street and leave your car near the Clarke County Courthouse complex. The complex includes the old red-brick courthouse, built in the Roman Revival style in 1838, and a more modern structure built in 1978.

Clarke County Courthouse

TOURING THE SHENANDOAH VALLEY BACKROADS

On the ground floor just off the covered walkway on the left of the old courthouse is the Clarke County Historical Association Museum, which is open Thursday through Saturday.

At the top of the street above the courthouse complex is Grace Episcopal Church, built in 1852. General Robert E. Lee is said to have attended a service here on his way to Gettysburg.

Walk back to Main Street to see several other buildings of historic interest. Turn left on Main.

At 24 East Main is a gift shop that until recently was Coiner's Department Store, which occupied this location from 1896 to 1996. During that entire time, clerks used a pulley-operated cash carrier to transfer money back and forth to the cashier.

At 106 East Main is The Nook, thought to be the oldest home in Berryville. The central portion, of painted clapboard construction, was built in 1765 by Major Charles Smith, who came to the area from Prince William County after serving in the French and Indian War; he later served in the Revolutionary War and as high sheriff of Frederick County. He bought 20 acres of land here from his father-in-law, John Hite. Smith positioned

The Nook

Battletown Inn

the house so that its corners matched the four points of the compass. His son later sold the property to Benjamin Berry. In the years following the Civil War, a woman named Harriot Hammond ran a girls' school in the house.

Turn around and walk west on Main Street.

On the corner at 2 West Main, a flower shop stands on the site of one of the old 1700s taverns whose regulars gave the town its early name of Battletown. The tavern at this location was supposedly a favorite of Daniel Morgan.

At 100 West Main Street, across U.S. 340, is the Hawthorne Building, which has stood here since around 1820. Portions of the structure reportedly date to 1795.

The Hawthorne Building

Next door at 102 West Main is the Battlefield Inn, built around 1809 and once known as the Sarah Stribling House.

Berryville Presbyterian Church, at 123 West Main, was built around 1854 and is the oldest church still standing in town. It was used to house troops during the Civil War.

Return to your car; the tour ends here in Berryville. **To reach the Washing-**

TOURING THE SHENANDOAH VALLEY BACKROADS

ton, D.C., area, follow Route 7 Business (Main Street) to Route 7 and turn right (east). This will take you past Leesburg, into the Tysons Corner area of northern Virginia, and to I-495, the Washington Beltway. **To return to I-66, take U.S. 340 South to Front Royal. To return to I-81,** take Route 7 Business West, which intersects Route 7 West; turn left to go toward Winchester.

If you take Route 7 East toward Washington, you'll pass Audley Farm, one of several homes in this area once owned by the Washington family. The farm is visible at the intersection of Route 7 Business and Route 7; look directly across the highway before you turn right.

Audley was built by Warner Washington's son, Warner Washington II, around 1795. Nelly Parke Custis Lewis, George and Martha Washington's granddaughter, and her husband, Major Lawrence Lewis, bought the house in 1825. But the couple never lived here, residing instead at Woodlawn, the house George Washington built for them near Mount Vernon in Alexandria. The Lewises' son, Lorenzo, inherited Audley from his father in 1839. Lorenzo and his wife lived here until he died in 1847. Nelly moved to Audley to be with her son shortly after her husband's death; she lived here until she died in 1852.

The house, privately owned, has been remodeled several times since the early 1800s. Today, Audley Farm is well known as a racehorse breeding farm.

Side Trip to Holy Cross Abbey

Holy Cross Abbey—known in the Washington, D.C., area for its Christmas fruitcakes and other baked goods—is about 5 miles east of Berryville, past Audley Farm. Take Route 7 East and turn left on Route 603 just before the Shenandoah River bridge. The entrance to the abbey is 1 mile down the road.

The abbey is a monastery of the Cistercian Order of the Strict Observance (Trappists). The main part of the abbey is housed in a 1784 home once known as Cool Spring. In 1864, the grounds were the site of a Civil War battle between Confederate general Jubal Early's troops and units of the West Virginia army; the Confederates won.

Holy Cross Abbey is supported largely by its bakery. Visitors are welcome at the abbey's chapel, gift shop, and information center seven days a week.

The Strasburg to Fort Valley to Front Royal Tour

The Strasburg to Fort Valley to Front Royal Tour

The tour begins in **Strasburg**. *Take Exit 298 off I-81 and follow U.S. 11 South toward town for about 1 mile to the brown road sign pointing to the Stonewall Jackson Museum at Hupp's Hill, located on the right.*

This modern, privately run museum sits high above the town. The museum grounds contain the ruins of trenches and earthworks built by Union general Nathaniel Banks as protection for his men against enemy fire. Banks's 8,000 soldiers camped at this spot in May 1862 to control access to the Valley Pike and the railroad through Manassas Gap.

Caught by surprise when Confederate general Stonewall Jackson attacked 1,000 of his men at nearby Front Royal on May 23, Banks quickly left Strasburg and headed up the Valley Pike toward Winchester. The next day, Jackson's troops engaged some of Banks's men at Cedar Creek, resulting in a Union defeat. On May 25, Banks and Jackson had another encounter—now known as the First Battle of Winchester—which the Confederates also won.

The museum explains Jackson's famous Valley Campaign of 1862 and features a 100-foot mural of the history of war and a special hands-on children's section. A few shaded picnic tables are available on the grounds.

Also at Hupp's Hill are the Crystal Caverns, recently reopened after being closed to tours for 27 years. Paleontologists believe the cave site was occupied by humans at least 3,000 years ago, and perhaps thousands of years

This tour begins in Strasburg, settled by the Alsatian pioneer Jost Hite around 1730 and best known today for its many antique shops and nearby Civil War sites. The tour then heads south down the old Valley Pike (U.S. 11) to the northern edge of Woodstock, where it turns to climb Massanutten Mountain to the Woodstock Tower, which offers a bird's-eye view of the "Seven Bends" of the Shenandoah River and panoramic views to the east and west. The tour then descends into Fort Valley, a sparsely populated and picturesque "valley within a valley" that has a timeless feel about it. It ends in Front Royal, known as Helltown during its wilder days in the 1700s. Front Royal saw much Civil War action and was the setting for the exploits of legendary Confederate spy Belle Boyd.

Several museums covering various aspects of local history and the Civil War are included in this tour.

Total mileage:
Approximately 50 miles

Stonewall Jackson Museum at Hupp's Hill

Old distillery at Hupp Homestead

before that. It is said that in the 1800s, the caverns sheltered runaway slaves and Civil War soldiers.

Just past the museum, also on the right, is the Hupp Homestead, built around 1755. George Hupp, who once lived here, was a paymaster during the War of 1812. He was a prominent citizen who owned or had an interest in several of the county's iron furnaces. His wife's ancestors, the Spenglers, are thought to have built this house and a second stone structure, located to the left.

Like so many of the 18th-century limestone structures in the Valley, the Hupp Homestead served as a fort to protect its inhabitants and their neighbors from Indian attacks during the French and Indian War. A spring ran into the cellar of the house, which meant that residents didn't have to venture outside for water during dangerous times. In later years, the spring also provided a steady supply of water for a distillery that occupied the stone building to the left of the homestead. Today, both buildings are private homes, but signs invite visitors to look around. The lush grounds behind the homestead include a creek and a pond.

Later generations of Hupps lived in the brick mansion across the street. During the Civil War, Union generals Banks and Shields used it as their headquarters.

Continue into town on U.S. 11, now called Massanutten Street. After passing under a railroad bridge, you'll begin to see a few of the town's many antique shops—Strasburg calls itself the "Antique Capital of Virginia." The largest, the Strasburg Antique Emporium, is on the left as you approach the traffic light at the intersection with King Street, the town's main street.

Next door to the Strasburg Antique Emporium is the Museum of American Presidents, which features a 60-year private collection of presidential portraits, autographs, and artifacts.

On the left at the end of the block is a log structure once known as Dosh House, which has been expanded over the years and now houses an antique shop. Built sometime after 1778, it is probably the oldest structure in Strasburg. It is thought that the rear portion once housed a tannery. The Dosh family bought the house in 1846, and they and their descendants lived here for almost 100 years.

The Colonial Inn, the three-story green-painted brick building on King

Street at the intersection, is thought to have been built in the early 1800s by a descendant of Anthony Spengler, a prominent early citizen. It most likely served originally as an inn and stagecoach stop. John Wayland, the prominent Valley historian, noted that much of the area's history passed in front of this inn: "Here the Blue and Gray passed and repassed from 1861 to 1865." Two highways cross at this spot as well—today's Routes 11 and 55.

The Colonial Inn

Turn left at the intersection and go 0.2 mile to the Strasburg Museum, housed in the old train station on the right. Strasburg was once a key railroad center. Its depot served both the B & O Railroad and the Southern Railroad. During the Civil War, Confederate general Stonewall Jackson called Strasburg the "fountainhead of rail traffic for the South." From here, he sent captured enemy locomotives and railroad cars to points south to aid the war effort. Those engines and cars—their wheels fitted with broad tires—had been taken in Martinsburg and dragged by teams of horses down the Valley Pike to Strasburg.

Strasburg, one of the oldest towns in the Valley, has an interesting history dating back to the 1730s. The area was settled by Jost Hite (1685–1761), one

---

of the Valley's earliest pioneers. Historians believe that he and some of the settlers he brought with him were from Strasbourg in the Alsace region of France—located near the German border and once part of Germany—and that they named the town after their old home. This mostly German settlement began to take shape after 1749, when Peter Stauffer (Anglicized as Stover) laid out a plan for what was called Staufferstadt, or Stover Town. But by 1761, when the settlement was officially chartered as a town, it had been renamed Strasburg (pronounced "Strawsburg" by the locals).

Strasburg was well known by the 1830s and 1840s for its many pottery shops, which originally produced salt-glazed crocks of blue and gray for everyday use and later specialized in fancy ware in multicolored glazes of green, cream, and brown. From 1809 until the end of the 19th century, at least 10 potters had shops in town. The most noted were the Bell brothers—Samuel and Solomon—and their descendants, who produced high-quality stoneware from 1834 to 1908. All old Strasburg pottery is highly valuable, but pieces marked with the Bell name are particularly treasured today. Though the community gained the nickname of "Pot Town" after the Civil War, the demand for pottery declined once cheaper glass jars became plentiful, and most of the shops had disappeared by the early 1900s. The craft has not been forgotten, however. The Shenandoah Pottery Guild carries on the town's tradition today.

The Strasburg Museum has several examples of this folk pottery. Housed in a grand old 1891 building that originally served as a pottery factory and later as a train depot, it is well worth a visit. It contains extensive exhibits of everyday life in the area from the 1700s into the 1930s and 1940s, including an old telephone switchboard, a scary-looking 1930s permanent wave machine from a local beauty shop, railroad memorabilia, an old still, Indian relics, Civil War swords and rifles, a re-created country store, and many other interesting displays. Don't miss the perpetual motion machine patented in 1910 by a local inventor; it is kept in a case near the middle of the ground-floor exhibits. Many loose pieces surround the contraption; a small sign on the case explains that the current owner could not figure out how to reassemble it. The museum, staffed by local volunteers, is open daily from May through October.

From the museum, head back down King Street into the downtown area. Once upon a time, King Street was lined on both sides with huge old trees; the trees had to be cut down when U.S. 11 was widened in the 1930s. But stately trees still line Strasburg's neighborhood streets; the streets east of King in particular are reminiscent of small-town America from decades past.

During its long history, Strasburg has experienced the terror of war more than once.

Several early residents were the unfortunate victims of random Indian attacks (then called "outrages") before and during the French and Indian War. One of the oldest structures from that era is Frye Fort, built in 1747 with 32-inch-thick stone walls as a defense against Indian attacks. The fort still stands as a restored private home on Cedar Creek, several miles northwest of Strasburg. Amazingly, the house was occupied by the original owner's descendants or relatives by marriage for more than 220 years, until the 1970s.

In 1764—a year after the French and Indian War officially ended—George Miller, his wife, and two children were working in the field near their home north of Strasburg when they were killed by a group of eight Indians and one white man. The Indians entered the Miller house, placed a burning coal on the family's opened German Bible, and closed the book. The fire burned through several pages but soon died out, leaving the volume intact. That Bible can be seen at the Strasburg Museum. On that same horrible day in 1764, another local citizen, John Dellinger, was also killed by an Indian party. His wife, Rachel, and their infant child were captured at their home south of town. The child was killed, but neighbors were able to rescue Mrs. Dellinger.

Almost a hundred years later, the town found itself in the middle of the Civil War. Strasburg's status as a crossroads and a railhead made it strategically valuable to both sides, and its proximity to Massanutten Mountain—which begins its 50-mile stretch to the south near here—provided General Jackson with places to confuse and spy on Union troops after the Battle of Kernstown in March 1862.

Throughout the Civil War, the summit of Three Top Mountain—also known as Signal Knob, the prominent northern end of Massanutten Mountain above Strasburg—served as a critical communications and observation post for both the North and the South. Using flags during the day and torches at night, the Confederates sent signals up and down the Blue Ridge

Signal Knob

Spengler's Mill

Fisher's Hill post office and general store

from Signal Knob. (Hikers can follow a 7-mile trail to the top of Signal Knob that begins about 0.5 mile east of the Elizabeth Furnace Recreation Area—see details in the Fort Valley section of this tour—and ends at Route 55 about 2 miles east of Strasburg.)

In the spring of 1862, General Jackson marched his 16,000 men through Strasburg several times. That November, he brought 40,000 troops through the town.

Two significant Civil War battles were fought nearby in 1864—the Battle of Cedar Creek (see The Middletown to Winchester Tour, pages 37–38) and the Battle of Fisher's Hill, which is the next stop on this tour.

From downtown Strasburg, continue down King Street (U.S. 11 South) toward Woodstock. Shortly after the road curves to the left out of the main business district, you'll see an old mill—now a restaurant—on the left. This stone structure, once known as Spengler's Mill, was probably built in the late 1700s by Anthony Spengler, a local farmer who sent weekly shipments of produce and flour by wagon to Alexandria.

Drive south on U.S. 11 for 1 mile until you see a brown road sign marking the turnoff for Fisher's Hill Battlefield. Turn right on Route 601 (Battlefield Road) and follow the signs as the road twists and turns for almost 2 miles to the battle-field. As the road traverses a low concrete bridge and enters the hamlet of Fisher's Hill, note the restored old mill upstream on the left. Once known as Keller's Mill, it dates to the 1700s. A combination post office and general store—a dying breed—occupies a low white building on the right a little farther up the road.

Fisher's Hill, often called "the Gibraltar of the Confederacy," was the scene of five different Civil War engagements. The best known took place in September 1864. General Jubal Early had retreated to Fisher's Hill after the Confederate defeat at Winchester. Union general Sheridan's surprise attack with 20,000 men here proved too much for General Early's 12,000 troops. It was after the Battle of Fisher's Hill that Sheridan ordered the destruction of the Valley's barns, mills, crops, and livestock—a campaign known as "The Burning"—in an effort to cut off food and supplies destined for Confederate troops in other parts of the state.

In the years following the war, families from as far away as Washington, D.C., came to Fisher's Hill each August to honor war veterans with a grand picnic complete with bands, a merry-go-round, speeches, and dancing. Today, the battlefield is maintained by the Association for the Preservation of Civil War Sites.

From the battlefield, retrace your route to U.S. 11. Turn right and proceed 3.4 miles to the village of **Toms Brook.** Not much is known about the early history of the town, or even how it got its name—which it has had since surveyors first noted it in 1744. Local citizens claim it's the only town with that name in the United States. Toms Brook is a quiet place these days. If you care to make a quick side trip to visit North Mountain Winery, located a short distance north of town, turn right off U.S. 11 on to Route 653 (Brook Creek Road).

The Battle of Toms Brook was fought northwest of town on October 9, 1864, during the period when Sheridan was destroying the Valley. Confederate soldiers found themselves helpless to stop the devastation but continued to attack Federal forces whenever they had a chance. Their actions finally irritated Sheridan to the point that he ordered his men to confront the Confederates at Toms Brook. Far outnumbered, the Southerners quickly retreated down the Valley Pike toward Woodstock. The Union soldiers are said to have referred jokingly to this retreat as "the Woodstock Races."

Continue along the Valley Pike about 1 mile to the next village, **Maurertown.** Pronounced "Morrytown," it also dates to the mid-1700s. It was probably named for Charles Maurer, who owned much of the land in the area. That surname was common in the area and was spelled many ways, including Mowrey, which sheds some light on the pronunciation of the town's name. Much larger in days gone by, Maurertown once boasted a train station, a chair factory, three mills, and even an undertaker.

The Shenandoah River meanders along the foothills of Massanutten Mountain just east of Maurertown. This is the area of the river's famous "Seven Bends," which you will be able to see from the Woodstock Tower, the next stop on this tour. In this part of the Valley in 1964, an archaeological team sponsored by the Virginia State Library excavated about 15 percent of the remains of an Indian village that they dated to between the years 900 and 1600. The village was about 250 feet in diameter and contained circular structures, food storage pits, and graves.

From Maurertown, continue south on U.S. 11 for 3.5 miles. Less than 0.5

Fort Valley farm

mile after you pass the Woodstock city limits sign, you'll see a large brick building on the left, once the local middle school and now the county administration center; turn left on to Mill Road (Route 665) and go 1.5 miles to a stop sign at Cemetery Road. Turn left; you are now on Woodstock Tower Road (Route 758). As you approach Massanutten Mountain straight ahead, the road curves left and crosses the North Fork of the Shenandoah River in about 0.5 mile. After you cross the bridge, stay to the right to remain on Woodstock Tower Road. It is mostly gravel but wide and well maintained for the rest of the hairpin-curve drive up the mountain. This area is part of George Washington National Forest.

When you approach the top of the mountain, park in one of the gravel areas along the road. Look to the right for a sign that points the way to the 0.25-mile trail to the 40-foot Woodstock Tower, located high above the town on a ridge of Massanutten Mountain. The short and relatively easy climb to the top offers a magnificent view in two directions. Facing west, you'll see the town of Woodstock directly below, with Great North Mountain and layers of Allegheny ridges in the distance. In particular, you'll get a great view of the often-photographed "Seven Bends" of the Shenandoah River, some 1,200 feet below. In fact, the meandering Shenandoah twists and turns to form 16 bends between Woodstock and Strasburg, traveling a distance of 35 miles over just 12 miles of land. Turning around to face east, you'll see Fort Valley (the next stop on the tour) and the Blue Ridge Mountains.

The tower was built by the Civilian Conservation Corps as a joint venture with the people of Woodstock in the 1930s.

Leaving the tower, continue driving east down the mountain. After 0.7 mile, you'll reach a crossroad; turn right. This road descends into Fort Valley past neat farmhouses, stocked trout streams, and Little Fort Recreation Area. In 3.3 miles, you'll come to a stop sign at Fort Valley Road (Route 678) at **Detrick**. *Turn left.* The Fort Valley Country Store is located to the right near this intersection, in case you need picnic supplies to take to the park a few miles down the road.

Fort Valley is a "valley within a valley," carved out by Passage Creek and enclosed by two parallel ranges of Massanutten Mountain. Until you look at a map of the area, you may not even realize this little valley exists.

Its peaceful farms and rolling hills take you back to a remote time and place far removed from the stresses of daily life. There are no shopping centers, no fast-food restaurants, no billboards, no signs of commercialism anywhere.

Fort Valley measures about 5 miles at its widest point and extends 23 miles from the town of Waterlick in the north to near New Market Gap in the south. (This tour covers the northern part of Fort Valley; see The Massanutten Mountain–Page Valley Tour, page 145, for more about the southern end.) Fort Valley was part of the area George Washington surveyed for Lord Fairfax in 1748 and 1749. The story goes that Washington remembered this little valley during the Revolutionary War, thinking it could provide him with a military advantage if the British drove him west.

Many arrowheads and stone tomahawk heads have been found on farms in Fort Valley, confirming that this secluded area was long used as a hunting ground by various Indian tribes, some of which apparently set up temporary villages. An Indian burial ground has been discovered near one of the farms here. According to the reports of one early settler, the Indians called the valley *Massanutton*, an Indian word for basket, supposedly because its shape was similar to that of baskets they made. Later, the entire mountain range was given that name.

Fort Valley's first non-Indian resident is thought to have been a man named Powell, a hermit-type character who claimed to have found gold and silver in the surrounding hills. He is said to have made high-quality counterfeit coins from his finds, but the authorities were never able to catch up with him in the wilds of the mountains. Powell's operation was so secure, in fact, that the locals took to calling the place Powell's Fort. The German settlers who came here in the 1730s began to call the area Powell's Fort Valley.

By the 1800s, Fort Valley's mineral deposits were attracting industrial activity. Manganese mines were developed, as were two iron-ore mines, which supplied the Fort Valley iron furnaces owned by a man named Blackford. He named those furnaces after two of his daughters, Elizabeth and Caroline. (Another Blackford-owned furnace, near Luray, was named for a third daughter, Isabella.) The furnaces were burned by Union forces during the Civil War and were never rebuilt.

About 1 mile down Fort Valley Road from the turn, you'll pass a sign for the small settlement of **Seven Fountains**. A resort of the same name once stood here; it was one of Virginia's many popular mineral springs resorts. From 1850 until the Civil War, as many as 600 people at a time filled the large hotel and private cottages to escape the city heat and take the waters. Most visitors came from the Washington, D.C., area, riding the train into Strasburg and then taking a horse-drawn carriage into Fort Valley. In 1853, Seven Fountains became the location of the first post office in Fort Valley; before then, residents had to travel over the mountains to Woodstock to get their mail. The resort never reopened after the Civil War.

Continue on Fort Valley Road for about 0.5 mile to the Fort Valley Museum, the small red-brick building on the left at the intersection with Route 770. This structure originally housed the Old Brick Church at Dry Run, built in 1841. It was a "free" church, used by several denominations until the congregations could build their own churches. Today, the museum features textiles, local fossils, tools, and an exhibit of a one-room school. It is staffed by volunteers and is open on weekend afternoons from Memorial Day weekend through Labor Day.

Fort Valley Museum

Past the museum, Fort Valley Road begins to curve alongside Passage Creek, passing several marked hiking trails along the way. In some places, trail information is posted at parking places; for additional information, contact the United States Forest Service (see the listing in the appendix).

Drive about 6.5 miles to Elizabeth Furnace Recreation Area. This recreation area includes a campground and a day-use park at the site of the ruins of the old Elizabeth Furnace. The park offers toilets, picnic tables, shelters, trails, and fishing along Passage Creek.

Past the recreation area, continue a short distance to the northern entrance to Fort Valley and the settlement of **Fortsmouth**. Across from the Fortsmouth Fire and Rescue building is a 1785 home built by Samuel M. C. Richardson, who was a Revolutionary War soldier, a Shenandoah County magistrate, and the planner of the town of Front Royal. The red-painted brick house, still used as a residence, is partially hidden from view by a stand of trees.

In less than 1 mile, Fort Valley Road ends at a stop sign at Strasburg Road (Route 55); turn right. This is **Waterlick**. *In about 4 miles, you'll reach the* **Front Royal** *city limits. In another mile, the road meets U.S. 340; turn right and cross the Shenandoah River bridge into town. In less than 1 mile, you'll start to see brown road signs pointing to the historic downtown area and the visitor* center. *Following these signs, turn left at the first traffic light to stay on Route 340 South/Route 522 South/Route 55 East. Continue through two traffic lights. Turn left on to Main Street at the third light to reach the historic district and the visitor center.* (If you wish to bypass the town and go directly to the entrance to Skyline Drive and Shenandoah National Park, continue straight through the light.)

As you turn on to Main Street, you'll pass in front of the Warren County Courthouse, a handsome stone structure completed in 1936 by the Works Progress Administration (one of President Franklin Roosevelt's Depression-era work programs). It replaced the town's first courthouse, which was built in 1836, when Warren County was formed.

Drive two blocks to the Front Royal Visitor Center, on the left. The visitor center occupies the 1880s railroad station near the center of downtown; it

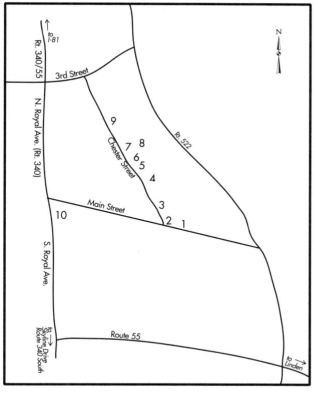

DOWNTOWN FRONT ROYAL

1 Visitor Center
2 Village Commons
3 Garrison House
4 Chester House
5 Balthis House
6 Warren Rifles Confederate Museum
7 Ivy Lodge/Warren Heritage Society
8 Belle Boyd House
9 Petty-Sumption House
10 Warren County Courthouse

John Lederer, Early Valley Visitor

One of the first European explorers in this area was German physician and scholar John Lederer. Although other explorers may have seen the Shenandoah Valley earlier, Lederer was the first European to record (in Latin) his journeys here. He made three trips to the Blue Ridge in 1669 and 1670. On the first, it appears that he reached the top of the Blue Ridge at or near Swift Run Gap in what is now Shenandoah National Park above Elkton. From that vantage point, he saw many more mountain ranges to the west—a discouraging finding for colonists wishing to expand settlement westward. On his third trip, in August 1670, he reached the top of the Blue Ridge near Manassas Gap or Chester Gap (his descriptions do not make the spot clear), southeast of Front Royal.

A small roadside monument recognizing Lederer is along Route 55 in Linden, east of Front Royal, in the area of Manassas Gap.

Skyline Drive and Shenandoah National Park

The north entrance to Skyline Drive is off U.S. 340 to the south of Front Royal. Skyline Drive winds for 105 miles atop the Blue Ridge Mountains through Shenandoah National Park and ends at the Blue Ridge Parkway near Waynesboro.

In the 1930s, the area hardly looked as lush as it does today. There were few trees, the result of decades of farming and logging activities. The area also suffered greatly from the chestnut blight of the early 1900s—it is estimated that every fourth tree in the Appalachian forests was a chestnut tree.

Although especially lovely in the fall, Skyline Drive—the only road through the park—tends to get crowded in October, so be forewarned. The park's 2 million visitors a year also come for the 500 miles of hiking trails (the Appalachian Trail passes through the length of the park), the numerous picnic spots, the five campgrounds, the four camp stores, the lodges and cabins, the restaurants, the visitor centers, the fishing, and other activities.

The gazebo at Village Commons

shares a parking lot with the Village Commons, which has a distinctive domed gazebo. The friendly, well-staffed visitor center offers plenty of information about local history and Civil War events in the area. You can also pick up a brochure for a 1-mile walking tour of the historic district.

Front Royal began as a crossroads where the trails through Manassas Gap and Chester Gap—the two lowest gaps across the Blue Ridge from the eastern part of the state—met. Front Royal's early name was Helltown, presumably a reflection on the rough-and-tumble lifestyle of the early residents. Some of the village's more conservative citizens later renamed it Lehewtown, after a French Huguenot settler who owned 200 acres and a tavern here in the mid-1700s.

For many years, reports of Indian attacks slowed the pace of settlement in the area. But after the Revolutionary War, land speculators came to the area and obtained a charter for a town they called Front Royal. No one is quite sure how the name originated. The most popular theory is that the drill sergeant of the local militia, frustrated when his less-than-professional volunteers failed to understand marching instructions, finally took to telling them to "front the royal oak," a huge tree on the town square. He figured it was the only way he could make all the men face the same direction. Amused onlookers repeated the story, and it is thought the name evolved from there.

The town's strategic location made it valuable to both sides during the Civil War. The North and South Forks of the Shenandoah River meet here, and roads, railroads, and bridges offered transport in all directions. The town suffered heavily during the war. After the fighting was over, not a single business was left in Front Royal. Its bridges were burned, its rail lines were gone, and most of its buildings were either damaged or destroyed. But the town was eventually rebuilt. By the mid-1930s, the opening of Skyline Drive and Shenandoah National Park and the development of Skyline Caverns (near the park entrance) brought tourism to the area virtually overnight.

Park at the Front Royal Visitor Center to take a short walk down Chester Street (the street across the Village Commons from the visitor center). This is Front Royal's oldest street, and you'll notice that the usual numbering scheme does not hold true. Here, you'll find ascending and descending numbers and odd and even numbers—all on the same side of the street.

At 46 Chester Street is Garrison House. Dr. Manley Littleton Garrison built this dwelling in 1883 after tearing down a small frame house that once stood here. He was a field and hospital physician during the Civil War and later practiced medicine for 50 years in a small building next to this house.

Chester House, at 43 Chester Street, is now a bed-and-breakfast but was once the home of the Samuels family.

Balthis House, the white frame house at 55 Chester Street, is the oldest home in Front Royal. Built around 1787, it was owned by the William Balthis family from 1838 to 1908. The brick wing in back was added around 1845. The first Mr. Balthis was a blacksmith who had a shop next door, on the lot where the Warren Rifles Confederate Museum stands today.

Next door at 95 Chester Street is the Warren Rifles Confederate Museum, which displays many local relics of the Civil War (including Stonewall Jackson's signal gun) and serves as a memorial to Confederate soldiers from throughout the South. The museum was conceived by the Warren Rifles chapter of the United Daughters of the Confederacy in 1937. This group spent more than 20 years raising funds and taking donations of materials and services to build the structure. The museum was dedicated in 1959; Senator Strom Thurmond of South Carolina cut the ribbon on opening day.

Next door at 101 Chester Street is Ivy Lodge, home of the Warren Heritage Society. One local history states that "this venerable house has been

The Oldest Street in Front Royal

Chester Street is Front Royal's oldest. It was first known as Chester's Road, an early trail across the Blue Ridge that connected Winchester with markets in eastern Virginia and Maryland. The name no doubt came from Thomas Chester, a settler from Pennsylvania who in 1736 became the first licensed ferryboat operator west of the Blue Ridge. Chester also served as sheriff. He once found himself in the unenviable position of having to charge his wife, Sarah, with selling "strong drinks commonly called Rye Brandy or Whiskey and Cyder without License." Fortunately for him, the case was dismissed for reasons never recorded.

Ivy Lodge

Belle Boyd Cottage

the home of more leading citizens, the center of more political, social, religious, patriotic, and cultural events that any other place left standing in Front Royal." No one is sure when it was built, but the fact that the window frames and floors are held together by wooden pegs, not nails, seems to date the structure to before 1825. It has served as a private school more than once in its history. Today, it contains a gift shop, exhibits about daily life in the area, and historical archives.

In the yard behind Ivy Lodge is the Belle Boyd Cottage, made famous by its association with a young woman of the Civil War. Belle Boyd became well-known throughout the United States and England for her exploits—never fully proved, however—as a self-appointed spy for the Confederacy.

It all started when, as a girl of 17, Belle shot and killed a Union soldier in her parents' home in Martinsburg on July 4, 1861. The soldier had told Belle's mother that he planned to raise the Union flag over the house. When Mrs. Boyd, whose husband was serving with the Confederates, declared that she and her children would rather die first, the soldier responded with an insulting comment that prompted Belle to pull out a pistol and shoot him. After a brief investigation, the soldier's commanding officer let Belle off the hook, even placing soldiers around the house to protect the Boyds from further harassment. Belle soon charmed these men, stealing their weapons and passing along information about Union plans to the Confederates.

Presumably to keep her out of trouble, she was sent to Front Royal to live with her aunt and uncle, who were the proprietors of the Fishback Hotel at 317 East Main Street. But she was soon back in the midst of Civil War intrigue.

In the spring of 1862, at the time General Stonewall Jackson was beginning his famous Valley Campaign, Union general Shields made the Fishback Hotel his headquarters. Belle, who lived with her relatives in the cottage behind the hotel, found herself in the perfect position to resume her covert activities. (Note that the cottage was moved to its Chester Street location in 1982.)

In her recollection of the times, Belle stated that General Shields "introduced me to the officers of his staff, to one of whom, Captain K., I am indebted for some very remarkable infusions, some withered flowers, and a great deal of very important information, which was carefully transmitted to my countrymen."

One night, she hid in a closet above the hotel parlor, where she could overhear, through a hole in the floor, Union war plans being made below. At one o'clock in the morning, after the meeting ended, she quietly saddled her horse and rode 15 miles to tell Colonel Turner Ashby what she had heard. Stonewall Jackson reportedly used her information to prepare for his surprise attack on Front Royal on May 23, 1862.

On that day, while Union troops in the town were in an uproar upon discovering they were under attack, Belle took revenge on a Union-friendly reporter who was staying at the hotel. Unwisely, the man had left his room key hanging on the outside of his door as he was packing to leave. "The temptation of making a Yankee prisoner was too strong to be resisted," Belle wrote. "Yielding to the impulse, I quietly locked in the 'Special Correspondent' of the *New York Herald*." Later, she watched from the hotel steps as he was taken prisoner; he reportedly yelled to her, "I'll make you rue this!"

Belle claimed that on the same day, in the midst of an ongoing attack, she once again carried military information to the Confederates, bullets piercing her skirts as she ran through the battle lines. According to Belle's journal, her efforts won her a personal note of praise and appreciation from General Jackson.

The Union officers were not as pleased with her, though. She was arrested six times and imprisoned twice in the Old Capitol Prison in Washington, D.C., where it is said she helped Confederate prisoners escape and even talked the warden into shopping for her wedding trousseau.

After the war, she continued to lead an interesting life, marrying a Federal navy ensign who had been assigned to guard her. The docents at the Belle Boyd Cottage can relate many more details about the life of this remarkable woman.

These are just a few of the many historic homes in Front Royal; pick up a copy of the walking-tour booklet at the visitor center for more information.

Return to your car to complete the tour. Drive north on Chester Street until it ends at Royal Avenue (Route 340/Route 522). Turn right and leave town the way you came in. Follow the signs to I-66. To reach I-81, take I-66 West, which merges with I-81 a short distance west of Front Royal.

Ice Cream Treats, circa 1940

At the north end of historic Chester Street is a business that captures a slice of the recent past: the Royal Dairy, a 1940s-style soda shop complete with tile floors and swivel stools at a long counter. The dairy makes old-fashioned milk shakes, crushed-fruit sodas, and ice cream sundaes to order. The address is 241 Chester Street.

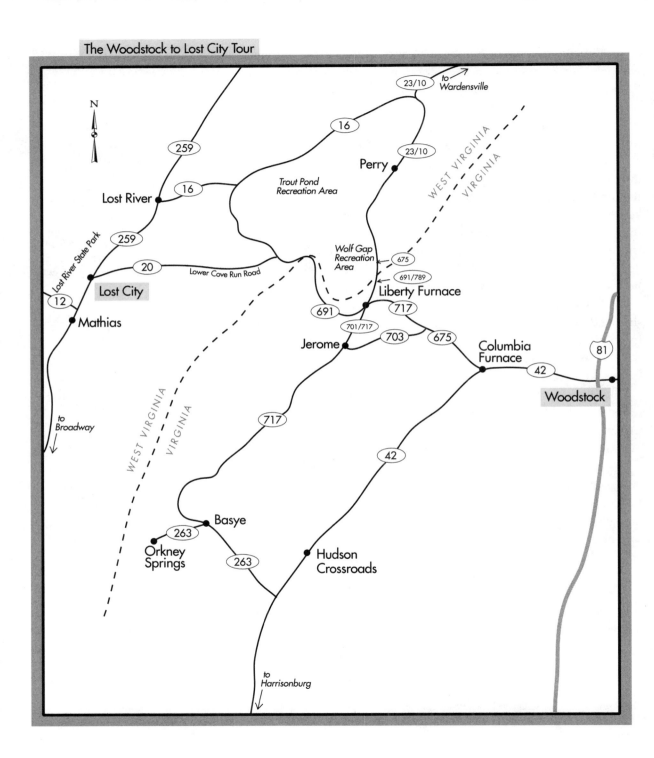

The Woodstock to Lost City Tour

N

to Wardensville
23/10

16

259

23/10
Perry

Trout Pond
Recreation Area

Lost River
16

WEST VIRGINIA
VIRGINIA

259

Wolf Gap
Recreation
Area
675

20
Lower Cove Run Road
691/789

Lost City
Liberty Furnace

12
691
717

701/717

Mathias
703
675

Jerome
Columbia
Furnace
81

42

Woodstock

717

WEST VIRGINIA
VIRGINIA

42

to
Broadway

Basye

263

Orkney
Springs
263
Hudson
Crossroads

to
Harrisonburg

The Woodstock to Lost City Tour

*The tour begins in **Woodstock**. Take Exit 283 off I-81, then follow Route 42 North to U.S. 11. Turn left on to U.S. 11, which is Main Street in Woodstock. On your way to the downtown area, you'll pass the campus of Massanutten Military Academy, which held its first classes in 1899. The first stop is the historic Shenandoah County Courthouse, on the left at the third traffic light.*

Woodstock was founded in 1761 and became the county seat when Dunmore County (named for Virginia's Royal governor at the time) was created in 1772. The governor's popularity didn't last long, though. During the American Revolution, Lord Dunmore burned Norfolk, among other dastardly deeds, prompting county residents to rename their county Shenandoah (then spelled *Shanando*) in 1778.

A German settler named Jacob Mueller laid out the town, which he called Muellerstadt, on a portion of a 2,000-acre grant he had obtained from Lord Fairfax in 1752. Like many other immigrants, he had first settled in Pennsylvania but later headed south to Virginia, where land was cheaper and more plentiful.

Woodstock has had several well-known residents. John Sevier, who was to become the first governor of Tennessee, moved here from New Market in 1770 but left three years later. Jonathan Clark, elder brother of Revolutionary War hero George Rogers Clark, was another early resident. Thomas Marshall, father of United States Supreme Court chief justice John Marshall, lived here sometime before the Revolutionary War in a large brick-and-limestone home that still stands at the corner of Court and Muhlenberg

This tour begins in Woodstock, one of the Shenandoah Valley's oldest towns, and winds toward Great North Mountain past the early settlements of Conicville and Hudson Crossroads, settled in the 1700s. It then begins a descent into a picturesque hidden valley and the longtime resort villages of Basye and Orkney Springs. From there, the tour skirts the foothills of Great North Mountain to Liberty Furnace, then begins the climb over this first ridge of the Alleghenies into West Virginia. After passing Wolf Gap Recreation Area at the top, it continues to Trout Pond Recreation Area and Lost City, West Virginia. A side trip to Lost River State Park is included. The tour returns toward Woodstock by way of a gravel mountain road that offers spectacular views of the Valley below and Massanutten Mountain to the east.

The tour includes honest-to-goodness backroads up and over Great North Mountain. Although it is easily done in a day, there are enough outdoor recreational activities in the area to fill a weekend or more.

Total mileage: Approximately 95 miles

Marshall House

Streets, a block behind the courthouse. The elder Marshall was the county's first clerk of court, a position that passed to his son Thomas Jr. in 1781. During the 1860s, the house belonged to Judge Green Berry Samuels, who served on the Virginia Supreme Court and was also a United States congressman.

The man who was perhaps the town's most legendary resident was one of its first. John Peter Gabriel Muhlenberg came to Woodstock as a preacher in 1773; his father, Henry Melchior Muhlenberg, is considered the father of the Lutheran Church in America. The younger Muhlenberg's church was built of logs, like most structures of the day. It stood in the middle of what is now the intersection of Main and Court Streets, almost in front of the courthouse. It is thought that the church was already there when the town was laid out. Some believe that is why Main Street was so much wider than other streets of the time.

Politically active from the start, Muhlenberg was elected to the Virginia House of Burgesses in 1774, at the age of 28. He soon became involved in local patriots' meetings. By January 1776, the Virginia House of Delegates had made him a colonel in the Eighth Virginia Regiment (also called the German Regiment) of the Continental Army.

Later that same month, during an impassioned sermon in his little Woodstock church, he made a dramatic appeal to the congregation. After citing the Bible ("There is a time for every purpose . . . a time for war, and a time for peace"), he declared it was time for the colonists to fight. One account described his actions this way: "As a bugler at the door sounded a rousing blast, he threw aside his priest's mantle to reveal a colonel's uniform of the Continental Army." He then called for volunteers to join him in war.

He and his men—mostly German settlers from the Valley—went first to defend Charleston, then to various places throughout South Carolina and Georgia. Muhlenberg later fought at Yorktown and rose to the rank of major general. His German Regiment went on to assist George Washington at Brandywine, Germantown, Valley Forge, and Monmouth.

The Shenandoah County Courthouse dates to the early 1790s and is the oldest courthouse in continuous use west of the Blue Ridge. Made of locally quarried limestone, it has been altered and enlarged on several occasions; its columned portico was added in 1920.

The weather vane on top of the courthouse cupola may look like an Indian from a distance, but closer inspection reveals that the man in a feathered hat and topcoat holding a spear is a different figure altogether. The meaning of this figure remained a mystery for many years. In 1927, Shenandoah Valley historian John Wayland heard about a monument that had been erected in Lucerne, Switzerland, to the memory of Swiss Guards who were massacred in Paris in 1792, during the French Revolution. The Swiss Guards were, for the most part, mercenary soldiers from Switzerland who served the French monarchy.

On a hunch, Wayland wrote a letter to Lucerne's mayor and requested a list of their names. The surnames on the list were the same as those of several early Valley residents: Bowman, Kibler, Kaufman, Miller, Hoover, Senseney, Suter, Walker, and others. From this research, Dr. Wayland surmised that the murdered Swiss Guards may have been related to some of this area's settlers, who probably designed the weather vane as a memorial.

Turn left off Main Street on to Court Street at the courthouse to see the Woodstock Museum, located at 137 West Court. The museum is open Thursday through Saturday from May through September. Staffed by local volunteers, it includes artifacts, furniture, quilts, maps, tools, Civil War memorabilia, and many interesting items of everyday life in the past—even a 19th-century still.

The museum also owns the Dick Wickham House, located across the street and directly behind the courthouse. The house dates to the 1770s. The current weatherboarding covers the original log construction. Many old houses in Woodstock and elsewhere in the Valley were originally log cabins that have since been covered with other materials—a practice that gave the homes a more finished look as well as helped keep out cold drafts. The Dick Wickham House can be toured when the Woodstock Museum is open.

Return to Main Street and turn left to see several homes of historic interest.

The Effinger House, at 201 North Main, was named for a Hessian soldier who fought with the Americans during the Revolutionary War and served for a time as George Washington's bodyguard. Local legend claims that the logs in the front of this house came from the church where Peter Muhlenberg preached.

The Clower House is at 237 North Main. It was named after Revolutionary

Weathervane on top of the Shenandoah County Courthouse

Silhouette of the figure on the weathervane

Wickham House

War soldier George Clower, who lived here until his death in 1822. The original part of the house is a 1700s log cabin.

The Tollgate Keeper's House, at 409 North Main, was also built of logs. A tollgate stood in front of the house during the days when this road was the Valley Pike—one of the first macadamized roads in the country, dating to the late 1830s. The tollgate keeper lived in this house.

Turn around, head back into the downtown area, and continue past the courthouse. At 403 South Main is the Hester Brown House, thought to be one of the oldest homes in town. Its weatherboarding conceals a log home, and a breezeway connects the main part of the house to what was once a separate kitchen with a large fireplace for cooking.

Continue south on Main Street past the military academy. At the traffic light, turn right on to Route 42. The tour continues on Route 42 for about 10 miles. You'll cross I-81 and pass through several hamlets before reaching the intersection with Route 703 just before Conicville. Turn right on Route 703 and drive about 0.5 mile to see the small stone structure known as the Rinker House.

Rinker House

This area was settled by Jacob Rinker, a Swiss immigrant, around 1749. He built this two-room home around that same time. It was constructed over a spring, providing a convenient source of water, a common practice in those days. The stone construction suggests that the house may have served as an fort to protect local families from Indian attacks.

This was later the home of Rinker's son, also named Jacob, who served as a lieutenant in Muhlenberg's famous Eighth Virginia Regiment during the Revolutionary War. In addition to his military endeavors, which included service with George Rogers Clark in the Illinois Territory, Jacob Rinker, Jr., was a well-respected county magistrate and surveyor. He was also a member of the Virginia convention that ratified the United States Constitution.

Old Conicville schoolhouse

Turn around, return to Route 42, turn right, and drive into **Conicville**. The village sits on a ridge that provides great views of mountains in all directions. Conicville grew in the years after the Civil War and eventually had three stores and two churches. The schoolhouse on the right at the far end of town was built in 1911 to replace a one-room schoolhouse that had served the community since 1873.

Continue on Route 42 to **Hudson Crossroads**, *the next hamlet down the*

road. A wonderful old stone house built by pioneer Thomas Hudson sometime in the mid-1700s still stands in the village. Look for it on the left as the road winds toward the two white frame churches that sit to the right of the crossroads. (The house is easier to see once you get to the crossroads and look back.) Be sure to note the slits in the walls at the basement level. These served two functions—they provided light and air to the lower level and also provided a protected area from which to respond to Indian attack. The house's longevity can be attributed to the huge timbers used in its construction and the quality of the stonework.

A Lutheran church has existed in Hudson Crossroads since before 1850. Its church building was also used by a Reformed congregation until a Reformed church was built across the street in 1852.

Follow Route 42 for another 2.2 miles, then turn right on Route 263 West (Orkney Grade Road). This road, which originates at the southern end of Mount Jackson, had its beginnings as Howard's Lick Turnpike, a privately built and maintained toll road that once took travelers over Great North Mountain and into Hardy County, West Virginia, to the towns of Lost City and Mathias.

Route 263 soon begins to wind down into an unexpected green valley with dramatic views of Great North Mountain. As it levels out, you'll reach the village of **Basye** *and the entrance to Bryce Resort.* If you want to make a side trip to the resort—which is open to the public and offers skiing, golf, boating, swimming, and tennis—turn right at the entrance sign after crossing the bridge over Stony Creek.

Continue on Route 263 for 1.5 miles to **Orkney Springs**, *where the road ends.* Orkney Springs has been a travelers' destination since the first pioneers arrived in the late 1700s; Indians apparently visited the springs many years before that. The area was first called Yellow Springs, because the minerals in its springs colored the moss-covered rocks a bright yellow.

The area's first settler was Dr. John McDonald, who bought more than 300 acres of land here in 1774. His wife was a daughter of Jost Hite, one of the early Valley settlers. In 1805, the McDonalds' son sold the land to a major in the Revolutionary War, Peter Higgins. Not long after that, the first of two or three small log "hotels" was built at the springs.

In 1850, the owners of the property founded the Orkney Springs Mineral Company. By 1853, the Maryland House (which still stands) was built, and Orkney Springs was on its way to becoming one of Virginia's most popular and enduring mineral springs resorts. The various types of springs here were reputed to have curative powers for a variety of complaints, including mental and physical exhaustion.

The source of the village's name is uncertain. Dr. McDonald is thought to have come to America from the Orkney Islands, off the coast of Scotland. Another theory is that George Washington, who helped survey this area for Lord Fairfax, named it after the earl of Orkney, the first Royal governor of Virginia. For a short time, the village was known as VanBurenville, after Martin Van Buren, who visited here during his campaign for the presidency in the late 1830s.

The main hotel building today is, and long has been, the Virginia House, built between 1873 and 1876. Even by modern standards, it is large, measuring 100 feet wide by 265 feet long and standing four stories high. In its early days, it boasted 175 guest rooms, a 40-by-155-foot dining room, and a 50-by-100-foot ballroom. The names of the various cottages built later on the grounds provide clues to the guests' probable hometowns: Philadelphia,

Hotel at Orkney Springs

Washington, Baltimore, Richmond, Norfolk, Charleston, Savannah. The hotel and its cottages could accommodate up to 750 guests.

Most guests were families who came for a month's stay in the summer to escape city heat and humidity. The men would commute on weekends from their jobs. Guests from Washington, D.C., would take the train to Mount Jackson and then travel by horse-drawn stagecoaches (which ran twice a day) down an old Indian road—now Route 263—to the springs. The trip takes 25 minutes today but required at least four hours back then. In the 1850s, stages also ran from New Market to Orkney Springs three times a week. Today's visitors can only wonder how the horses managed to pull buggies loaded with guests and their trunks up the steep, unpaved, winding road out of Basye on the return trip to Mount Jackson.

The resort was just as popular with local residents. In *A History of Shenandoah County, Virginia*, John Wayland wrote, "Before cars, a procession of buggies used to mark the road up Mill Creek [Route 263] and across the hills to Orkney on Sunday and Saturday afternoons. It was the ambition of almost every rural swain to take his best girl to Orkney."

Postcards from the resort's peak period—1870 to 1890—show well-dressed men and women (most of the latter carrying opened parasols) sitting on the hotel's many balconies and porches or strolling the grounds with their children. In those days, the roof of the main building was in the French mansard style, which gave it an elegant appearance. The largest swimming pool in the South at the time (90 by 50 feet) was built here in 1890. Many other sports and activities were offered, including horse races.

By the 1920s, the resort's success began to fade because of the advent of automobile travel. People were no longer limited to places where the railroads could take them. Around that time, the Episcopal diocese of Virginia built a retreat called Shrine Mont next to resort. In 1979, it bought the entire 950-acre Orkney Springs resort. It restored the property in 1987.

Orkney Springs has been home to the Shenandoah Valley Music Festival since 1963; for a few years before that, it hosted summer workshops of the American Symphony Orchestra League. Every summer since 1979, the Fairfax Symphony has put on a series of popular and classical music concerts on summer weekends in the open-air pavilion behind the hotel. Several other musical events take place here at other times of the year.

The Virginia Springs Resorts

At least 75 mineral springs resorts have come and gone in Virginia over the past 200 years or so. They peaked in popularity around the mid-1800s as cool summer getaways and "restorers of health" for city dwellers. Most guests came by rail and stayed for a month or longer. Some resorts were run strictly for their so-called health benefits and offered only the basic amenities. But others were fashionable places to stay, where social contacts and business deals were part of the attraction.

Many of the resorts were damaged during the Civil War and never reopened. Later, advances in medicine and the advent of the automobile hastened the demise of most that remained. Many hotels burned down around that time, with arson suspected in more than a few cases. Orkney Springs still has its original buildings intact and is one of the few mineral springs resorts left in operation.

When you are ready to leave Orkney Springs, turn around, head back up Route 263 to Basye, and turn left on Route 717 (Alum Springs Road) just before the Community Store. It is 0.7 mile to a sign for Chalet High, a resort rental company. The Alum Springs Hotel began operating nearby in 1852. It became quite popular by the 1870s, evidently as much for its elegant restaurant as for the healing powers of its springs. It ceased operations many years ago.

In 0.6 mile, look on the left for the ruins of Myers Furnace. Also called Alum Springs Furnace and Henrietta Furnace, this facility was built along Beetle Run by Samuel Myers, who ran it from 1855 to 1865. Myers was killed in the Civil War, and the furnace never operated again.

Continue 5.3 miles to where Route 717 intersects Route 703. Turn left toward **Jerome**. The road through Jerome, which was settled as early as 1785, curves around a picturesque white church perched on a hilltop. Built in 1892, St. Paul's Lutheran replaced an 1854 structure. Before then, the congregation met in a nearby schoolhouse.

In 0.4 mile, the road becomes Route 701 (Liberty Furnace Road). Stay straight. In 1.8 miles, you'll see a white mansion high on a hill to the left. The ruins of Liberty Furnace and an old gristmill lie below. Turn left just beyond the Liberty Furnace sign on to Route 691 (Cold Spring Road).

Old mill at Liberty Furnace

Walter Newman, whose family had been in the area since the 1760s, built and began operating this furnace in 1822. He turned it over to his son in 1842. In 1886, after changing hands a few times, both Liberty Furnace and Columbia Furnace (visited later in this tour) were bought by a Philadelphia company and renamed the Liberty Iron Company. A 12-mile narrow-gauge railroad was built to connect the furnaces to the main railway in Edinburg. But by 1907, the iron-ore industry in the Valley could no longer compete with cheaper sources in the West, and the Liberty Iron Company shut down its furnaces. The railroad tracks are long gone as well, pulled up and sold as scrap metal during World War II.

After passing through a mile of dense forest, with Laurel Run rushing alongside on the right, Route 691 turns sharply to the left and becomes Judge Rye Road; this is where the tour will later meet Cold Spring Road again. Don't turn here; instead, stay straight on what is now Route 789 (Sam Clark Road) for 0.4 mile until you reach Route 675 (Wolf Gap Road). Turn left. You will soon enter **Wolf**

Gap Recreation Area, *managed by the United States Forest Service and the Virginia Game Commission. The road winds up the mountain for 1.7 miles to the park campground and picnic area; this is also where the Tibbet Knob Trail and the Mill Mountain Trail meet. You'll cross the West Virginia line and enter Hardy County at the crest of the mountain.*

Although Wolf Gap may have been named after an animal once prevalent in the area (before settlers were paid handsome bounties for wolf heads), it was probably named for Jacob Wolfe, who bought 400 acres of land south of here in 1754. The elevation at the gap is 2,250 feet.

In less than 4 miles, you'll come out of the forest and enter **Perry**, *West Virginia. There, you'll pass the Perry General Store, which operates a zoo of sorts.*

It is 3 miles to the ruins of another iron furnace; look carefully to the right to see it. In another 1.4 miles, look for the brown sign pointing left to **Trout Pond**; *turn left on to this road. In 6.4 miles, you will reach the entrance to* **Trout Pond Recreation Area** *in George Washington National Forest. This park has camping and picnic areas, short trails, the two-acre Trout Pond, and the 17-acre*

Rock Cliff Lake

Rock Cliff Lake. The small white-sand beach on Rock Cliff Lake is especially popular with families in the summer months. No food is available here; if you need supplies, be sure to stop on your way to the park.

Trout Pond came by its name honestly. One early traveler, Taverner Beale, claimed he saw ten thousand trout in the pond. Although there may not be as many trout here today, the pond is still a popular fishing spot. Trout Pond also has the distinction of being the only natural lake in West Virginia.

From the turnoff into Trout Pond Recreation Area, continue down the mountain for 4.7 miles into **Lost River**, *where the road intersects Route 259. Turn left on to Route 259.*

Lost River General Store

The village of Lost River dates back to the 1750s. A battle in the French and Indian War took place here in 1756. The town has a few points of interest for visitors, including the Lost River General Store (to the right near the intersection of Route 259 and Trout Pond Road), the Lost River Craft Cooperative, and the Lost River Museum (both to the left on Route 259 as you head south). These attractions are generally open daily except Wednesdays and Thursdays from May through October.

Continue south for 2.5 miles on Route 259 to **Lost City**. *If you want to take the side trip to Lost River State Park (see the sidebar on page 95), you'll continue straight on Route 259 for another 4.3 miles.*

To complete the tour, turn left off Route 259 on to Route 20 (Lower Cove Run Road) at the crest of a hill. Lower Cove Run Road runs by Lost City Baptist Church. You'll soon reenter George Washington National Forest. You'll come to an intersection in 2.8 miles, but continue straight toward Columbia Furnace as the road becomes Route 691. You'll be driving on gravel for the next 6.5 miles. Although you don't need a four-wheel-drive vehicle, this road is not for the faint of heart. It's narrow in parts, and there are no safety rails. But on a clear day, the views are as dramatic as those from Skyline Drive. Every so often, the road widens to provide a place to pull off and take pictures or just admire the view. You may see white-tailed deer. In June, these woods are full of the pale pink blossoms of mountain laurel.

Continue to the intersection with Route 789 (Sam Clark Road). Turn right, drive 1.5 miles to Route 717 (Liberty Furnace Road), and turn left. From here, it is 5.7 miles to **Columbia Furnace**. *The road becomes Route 675 as it ap-*

proaches that community. Big Stony Creek is on the right much of way.

From 1780 to 1880, iron making was important to the development of this part of the Valley. Columbia Furnace was the heart of industrial activity in Shenandoah County. Built around 1804, it continued operations under various owners until 1907, despite being burned three times during the Civil War.

The iron-smelting industry, however, took its toll on area forests. Until coke was introduced as a more efficient fuel in the late 1800s, charcoal was needed to create the hot fires in the iron furnaces. Charcoal was made by burning small pine trees in kilns, or "pits." It's been estimated that each furnace required cutting down about 150 acres of woodland a year. The mountains eventually became stripped and bare in parts.

Other problems also contributed to deforestation. For example, between 1880 and 1890, most of the yellow pines in the Valley were killed by an insect infestation. And the chestnut blight affected the northern end of the Valley (and much of the eastern United States) beginning in 1914. Today,

Lost River State Park Side Trip

If time allows, you may want to make a side trip to Lost River State Park. This attractive park offers 19 hiking trails, rental cabins, a restaurant (in the summer season), a swimming pool, tennis and volleyball courts, a softball field, and horseback riding.

Drive south from Lost River on Route 259 for 4.3 miles; in Mathias, watch for the brown state park sign just before Route 12. The large log cabin facing Route 259 at the intersection is the Mathias Log Homestead, built in the 1790s. A state historical marker here notes that Confederate general Thomas Jonathan "Stonewall" Jackson's great-grandparents settled in this area around 1750, and that his grandfather was born here. Shortly afterward, the family moved to Clarksburg, where Stonewall Jackson was born in 1824.

Turn right on to Route 12 and drive 4 miles to the park. This area was known as Howard's Lick in the early 1800s. The Lee family had a summer retreat here. Henry "Lighthorse Harry" Lee was given a part of Lord Fairfax's landholdings as a reward for his service in the Revolutionary War. The cabin he built is now a museum in the park. One of his sons, Charles Carter Lee (Robert E. Lee's brother), built a boardinghouse and cabins here for guests who came to "take the waters" from the sulfur springs. The property was later sold, and the new owners expanded the resort and renamed it Lee White Sulphur Springs. After the hotel burned down in 1910, the resort closed.

The western end of the old Howard's Lick Turnpike, which began in Mount Jackson and led past Basye over the mountains, is a short distance south and across Route 259 from Route 12; it is now known as Upper Cove Run Road.

another natural disaster is in the making—a small insect is killing off many of the grand old hemlock trees in these forests.

By the 1900s, people realized the damage that had been done and began efforts to regenerate the forests. By the 1930s, thousands of seedlings were being planted by the United States Forest Service and the Civilian Conservation Corps. Conservation efforts continue, and the Valley's forests no doubt have more trees now than they did during much of the 1800s. Today, almost all of the mountain forests that form the western boundary of the Valley are part of George Washington National Forest or Thomas Jefferson National Forest, both of which are managed by the United States Forest Service, an agency of the Department of Agriculture. For more information, contact one of the ranger-district offices listed in the appendix.

The tour ends at Columbia Furnace. The road veers to the right and passes over a low concrete bridge. After crossing the bridge, go to the stop sign at the main road (Route 42) and turn left to return to I-81 near Woodstock.

Road along Great North Mountain ridge

TOURING THE SHENANDOAH VALLEY BACKROADS

View from Great North Mountain

These Ancient Mountains

Great North Mountain is the first ridge in the Alleghenies, which stretch about 500 miles from northern Pennsylvania to southwestern Virginia. The Alleghenies are the westernmost range of the Appalachians (the other two ranges being the Blue Ridge and the Cumberlands).

The mountains that surround the Shenandoah Valley are among the oldest on earth, much older than the Rockies, the Alps, and the Himalayas.

Mountain-building processes had already been going on here for 200 million years when the Appalachians came into being. They were formed when tectonic forces caused the landmass we know today as Africa to push into eastern North America 250 to 300 million years ago, buckling the rocky land into a series of high ridges. Later, all the earth's continents moved together to form the supercontinent that geologists call Pangaea. The young Appalachians were located in the interior of this massive continent for 50 million years or so. At one time, these mountains may have been as high as the Himalayas are today, but the forces of erosion have long been at work, wearing down their height and softening their sharp peaks for millions of years.

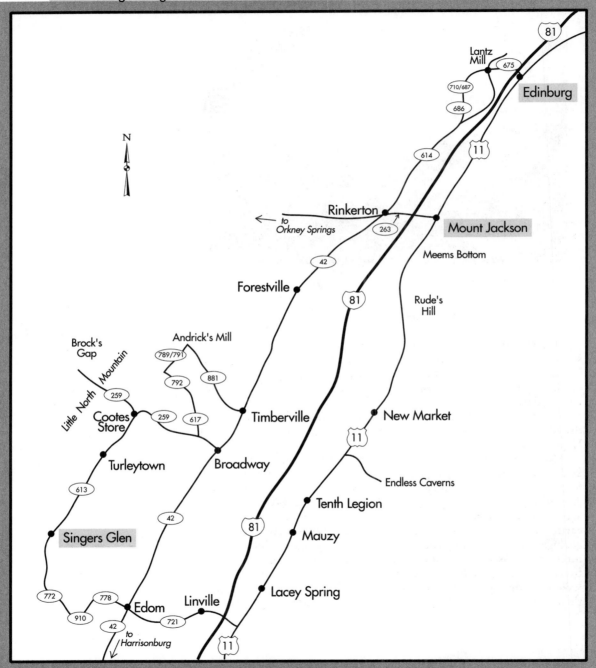

The Edinburg to Singers Glen to Mount Jackson Tour

The Edinburg to Singers Glen to Mount Jackson Tour

This tour begins and ends on the historic Valley Pike, today's U.S. 11. It passes through scenic farmland of the central Shenandoah Valley in the foothills of Massanutten Mountain, Great North Mountain, and Little North Mountain, following routes used in colonial times and even earlier. The tour begins in Edinburg and passes through Lantz Mill, Forestville, Turleytown, Singers Glen, Edom, Lacey Spring, Tenth Legion, and New Market. It ends just a few miles south of where it began, on U.S. 11 at Mount Jackson.

Highlights include several Civil War sites (including the famous New Market battlefield), a farm where Indians staged a brutal attack on settlers in the 1750s, a perfectly preserved 19th-century village that influenced American religious music publishing and education in the 1800s, several restored mills, the place where Abraham Lincoln's father was born, portions of a trail George Washington used to return to Mount Vernon from western Virginia, and one of the last covered bridges in Virginia.

Total mileage:
Approximately 65 miles

*The tour begins at the town of **Edinburg**, which is about midway between Winchester and Harrisonburg. Take Exit 279 off I-81 and follow Route 185 East (Stony Creek Boulevard), which ends at U.S. 11 (Main Street) in less than 1 mile. Turn right at the stop sign to see the Edinburg Mill, on the right a short distance down U.S. 11.*

George P. Grandstaff began building this mill in 1848. It is one of only a handful of pre–Civil War mills that survived Union general Philip Sheridan's campaign of destruction—known as "The Burning"—in the central and northern Shenandoah Valley in 1864; this tour visits three others as well. The Grandstaff Mill, as it was known then, was set on fire at least twice by Sheridan's forces, but the townspeople—mostly women and children, since it was wartime—saved it on both occasions by setting up bucket brigades stretching to nearby Stony Creek.

Legend has it that on one of those occasions, two of the miller's daughters begged General Sheridan to spare the mill, which was vital to the town's survival. Swayed by their pleas, Sheridan instructed his soldiers to help douse the fire. One version of this story claims that Sheridan asked the girls for a small favor in return: that they name their dog after him. Nellie Grandstaff, a good Southern girl, sharply refused the general's request.

The mill operated continuously until 1978 and has been used from time to time as a restaurant and gift shop. Efforts are under way to turn the building into a historical and cultural center.

Edinburg Mill

Edinburg's Geology

Edinburg is interesting geologically as well as historically. Like much of the Valley, it lies over limestone formed millions of years ago, when the entire region was under a vast sea. The many caves and underground streams in the area were formed when drainage water dissolved the limestone. Some believe that Edinburg lies above a large underground lake, stream, or cavern. Over the years, residents have reported hearing the sound of rushing water beneath their homes after a heavy rain. There have also been reports of local people trying to tap sticks or poles into the ground and then watching them either disappear or descend to as far as 16 feet below the surface. Sinkholes are fairly common throughout the area.

The Edinburg Inn, the white-and-green Victorian house to the left of the mill, was built in 1850 and served as the miller's house until 1983, when it was sold and turned into a bed-and-breakfast.

Across the street from the mill at 211 South Main Street is the Mary and Pres Grandstaff House. Mary and Pres were brother and sister, children of Philip Grandstaff; they raised four foster children in this house. A shed behind the house served as Union headquarters during the month-long siege of Edinburg in 1862.

From the mill parking lot, turn left and go back into town. Just after you cross the bridge is a white clapboard house on the right that was built by George P. Grandstaff sometime before 1835. Many Grandstaff descendants still live in the Edinburg area.

Early settlers in Edinburg were typical of those who came to this section of the Shenandoah Valley in the 1700s and 1800s. Most were Protestants from Pennsylvania. Many were members of the Mennonite faith, which began as a Swiss sect of the Anabaptists, who had been persecuted in Europe because they believed in adult, rather than infant, baptism. The settlers originally came from three regions of Europe: the Rhineland in Germany (also known as the Palatinate), Alsace (once part of Germany but today part of France), and Switzerland. From Pennsylvania, most headed south down the old Indian trail that later became the Valley Pike and today's U.S. 11 in their search for cheap, fertile land and freedom from religious oppression. In the Shenandoah Valley, many found what they were looking for, and more; the rolling valleys and soft hills and mountains are said to have reminded them of their homeland.

The town began as a German settlement in the late 1700s. One of its early settlers was George Grandstaff. As a boy of 16, Grandstaff was captured near what is now Luray during an Indian attack on settlers in the 1760s. He managed to escape about three years later and return to the Valley. By 1814, members of the Grandstaff family had built a dam on Stony Creek to provide water power for a sawmill, a carding mill, and a boring mill for a rifle factory. The rifle factory, begun by George and Philip Grandstaff, provided rifles for the War of 1812 and later for the Civil War.

The community was originally called Stony Creek and then Shyrock. By the 1840s, Swiss settlers arrived in the area and began to call the town

Edenburg, presumably a tribute to the town's picturesque setting—their long-sought Garden of Eden. The spelling somehow changed, and the town was incorporated as Edinburg in 1852. It was fairly prosperous in those days, thanks to the several mills along its creek and its position on the Valley Pike, which was by then a macadamized toll road between Winchester and Staunton.

Leave Edinburg the way you came in, by turning back on to Route 185 and following the signs toward I-81. Instead of getting on I-81, continue under the interstate; the road now becomes Route 675. Continue for 0.7 mile, then turn left on Route 809 (Union Forge Church Road). The road winds down to Stony Creek, which you may be able to see (depending on the time of year) on your left far below.

This area was the site of the Union Forge Iron Company, which began making iron around 1820, primarily for a cannon company in Richmond. The company built the white frame Union Forge Church down the road on the right, as well as a school for its workers' children. Throughout the 1800s, the supply of iron ore fueled industry in this part of the Valley.

As you approach the intersection with Swover Creek Road at the bottom of the hill, stay on Route 809 as it curves sharply to the left; follow the small sign pointing to Lantz Mill. In 0.1 mile, you'll see the ruins of Lantz Roller Mill, on the left.

The **Lantz Mill** area was settled in 1740 by Jacob Wolfe but was named for another German immigrant, Hans George Lantz. Lantz came to the Shenandoah Valley from Frederick County, Maryland. He acquired land in this area in the 1760s and built a gristmill, a sawmill, and a granary. His sons and grandsons continued the family business until the late 1880s. All the original Lantz properties were burned by Union soldiers. The impressive old Victorian house across from the mill, known today as Campbell Farm, was built after the Civil War by Jacob Lantz, a great-grandson of the original settler.

Lantz Mill

Archaeologists believe that the area around Lantz Mill was occupied by Indians between 6000 B.C. and 400 A.D., based on a 1996 survey that uncovered more than 600 artifacts here.

Louis Michel, a Swiss visitor to the Edinburg area in 1706, noted in his journal that "all this country is uninhabited except by some Indians." Around

1754, the Indians living in the Valley suddenly disappeared, moving west into the Ohio Valley to join other tribes there. That move, historians believe, was instigated by the French, who were at odds with the British over claims to the land west of the Alleghenies. When the French and Indian War began that same year, it became obvious that the French had recruited the Indians' help in their fight against the British.

General Edward Braddock's defeat by the French at Fort Duquesne (today's Pittsburgh) in 1755 was a sign of bad times to come. Soon, forts were being erected every 20 miles or so along the frontier. These forts were built under the direction of the young George Washington (see The Middletown to Winchester Tour, pages 47–48). But the forts couldn't stop the raids. Groups of Indians, often led by a Frenchman or two, began conducting terrorist-style attacks on settlers. Women and children were rarely spared.

In the Lantz Mill area, the tale is told about how Jacob Wolfe built a fort—a fortified house, really—to protect his family and neighbors during Indian raids. He was walking on his property one night when his dog began acting strangely. Samuel Kercheval related the story in his *History of the Valley of Virginia*, published in 1833. The dog, he wrote, "repeatedly crossed

Indians in the Shenandoah Valley

Long before Europeans settled Virginia and the Shenandoah Valley, native people were living along the rivers and creeks here. Scientists have uncovered evidence of settlements in Virginia dating from 9500 to 8000 B.C. One of the most significant prehistoric sites in eastern North America is Thunderbird, south of Front Royal off U.S. 340. Paleo-Indians lived and quarried jasper for tools there for almost 2,000 years.

The people who lived in the northern Shenandoah Valley between 400 B.C. and 200 A.D. built hundreds of low stone burial mounds throughout the area. Later, from about 950 until the late 1600s or so, another culture built much larger earthen burial mounds in the Valley, some of them almost 20 feet high. Those mounds are largely gone today, destroyed by three centuries of plowing and flooding.

During the early 1700s, the Valley was common hunting ground for several tribes, including the Shawnees, the Susquehannocks, and the Iroquois. Only a few native settlements remained in the Valley at that time. Possible reasons for the Indians' departure include tribal warfare, the introduction of European diseases, and conflicts with settlers.

[Wolfe's] path, endeavoring to obstruct his walk; would raise himself up, and place his feet on his master's chest, and strive to push him back; would run a few steps toward the fort and then return whining." Wolfe took the hint and headed quickly back to his house, narrowly avoiding attack by an Indian lying in wait behind a nearby tree. Many years later, Wolfe couldn't bear to put the beloved dog to a merciful death when it became old and sick.

Leaving Lantz Mill, turn left on to Route 710 (Hamburg Road), which crosses the creek over a low concrete bridge. Shortly, you'll cross a second concrete bridge. When you reach the intersection with Route 687, go straight; you are now on the unpaved Route 687. This road winds among cedar forests, old homes, and farmland until it meets Route 686 (South Ox Road). Turn right. Route 686 parallels I-81 for a short distance and provides a great view of Massanutten Mountain on the left and Great North Mountain ahead and to the right.

Drive 0.4 mile on Route 686 to a stop sign; take a right on South Middle Road (Route 614 South). Like U.S. 11, this road was once an old Indian trail. In the 1800s, it was used by drovers taking their livestock to market after the Valley Pike was macadamized. The sharp rocks used to "pave" that road hurt the animals' feet. Middle Road was still a dirt trail and thus easier on the sheep and cattle.

Drive about 1.8 miles to a red-roofed white barn on the right with the words "Indian Fort Stock Farm" painted in large letters on the side. Immediately past this barn, a stone chimney stands alone near the road. Fort Painter, a large log house owned by early settler George Painter, stood just beyond it. This was the site of one of the worst Indian raids on Valley settlers during the French and Indian War. The cemetery on the hill above the barn contains the remains of some of the victims.

One summer day in 1758, the warning went out that about 50 Indians and four Frenchmen were in the vicinity. Many area residents sought protection at Fort Painter. In the ensuing attack, George Painter was killed, and the rest of the settlers surrendered. At that point, the Indians murdered four infants, burned the house and stable, and took 48 prisoners over the Alleghenies. Only three people evaded capture: two of Painter's sons and a young man who had hidden nearby. That night, two of the boys ran 15 miles west to Fort Valley for help. But when the members of the rescue

Fort Painter

party learned how many Indians had attacked, they gave up hope of pursuit.

About three years later, some of the victims, including Mrs. Painter and a son and two daughters, were able to return home. Three other daughters remained with the Indians, including Mary Painter, who was nine years old at the time of the raid. She was found by an American trader 18 years later. He married her and brought her back to the Valley. But by then, she had forgotten her German. For the rest of her life, she primarily spoke the Indian language she had learned as a child.

In the years following the attack, a stone house and barn were built (possibly by one of the family's surviving sons) near the site of the burned log house for defense against further Indian raids. The lone chimney near the road is all that remains of those structures.

Many attractively restored homes and barns line the road past Indian Fort Stock Farm. Massanutten Mountain rises into view on the left, offering a good view of New Market Gap. Great North Mountain and the Alleghenies in West Virginia can be seen in the distance ahead and to the left. The long metal buildings you'll see at farms along this road and elsewhere in the area are poultry houses, a major part of the agricultural scene in Shenandoah County, and even more so in Rockingham County, which lies a few miles ahead. Llamas are among the farm animals kept in this area. You may see some of these exotic-looking animals grazing in fields along the road.

Drive about 3.5 miles past Indian Fort Stock Farm to the ghost town of **Rinkerton***.* On the left is Otterbein United Methodist Church, built in 1913. The current church building replaced Otterbein Chapel United Brethren in Christ, which was constructed in 1845. The church is practically all that is left of a once-bustling community at the intersection of South Middle Road and Orkney Grade Road (Route 263). If you look closely on the left at the intersection, you can see the crumbling stone foundation of Colonel Levi Rinker's large brick mansion. Built before the Civil War, the home burned to the ground in 1920—by which time Rinkerton was already deserted.

Rinkerton may have been the site of the first mill in the Shenandoah Valley, built by John Pennywitt after he came to the area from Alsace around

1747. Jacob Rinker, Sr. (1726–97), a Swiss immigrant from near Zurich, may have been the first member of his family to arrive here; John Pennywitt's mill eventually became known as Rinker's Mill. Many more buildings stood here in the 1800s—a flour mill, a sawmill (both on Mill Creek along Orkney Grade Road), a store, a blacksmith shop, and a shoe shop. The settlement was also a popular speaking stump for local politicians.

Continue straight on Route 614 toward Forestville. The large hill ahead and to the left is called Third Hill. During the Civil War, it was used as a signal station. Its name is a mystery—no First or Second Hill is anywhere around.

Turn left at the stop sign at **Forestville** *and drive a short distance to the lovingly restored Zirkle Mill, located on the right on Holman's Creek behind an old frame farmhouse.* This mill was built sometime before 1760 by German settler Andrew Sircle; the spelling of this common area name became Zirkle or Zerkel over the years.

Zirkle Mill

The mill was one of the few in the Valley to escape Sheridan's torch in the Civil War. During the time of "The Burning" in the Valley in 1864, miller Samuel Hockman noticed that a nearby mill was in flames. He quickly hoisted a Union flag on top of his mill, found the officer in charge, and convinced him of his Union sympathies. Hockman's actions saved his mill but cost him the respect of his customers.

Since Hockman's establishment was the only area mill that remained in operation, local farmers had no choice but to depend on his services. When they begged him for credit, he coldly turned them down. When they asked how they were going to survive, the story goes that he replied, "You will have to bake cakes." Whether that was a common saying of the time or simply a variation on Marie Antoinette's famous retort is not clear.

Soon after the war, other mills in the area were rebuilt. Once competition returned, the local farmers boycotted Hockman. Now strapped financially, Hockman is said to have asked his former customers, "What am I going to do?" Their answer, of course, was "You will have to bake cakes."

The mill was sold to a new owner in 1867. It operated into the 20th century.

Return to the intersection in Forestville. This community apparently got its name because the surrounding area was covered by dense forest when settlers arrived in the 1700s. By the mid-1800s, the town was prospering, no doubt helped by its location on what was then known as either the Woodstock and Harrisonburg Road or the Alexandria-Tennessee Road (now U.S. 42). By 1919, the town had to build its third school, which has recently been restored and sits on the hill across from the Zirkle Mill.

Turn left on to Route 42 South/Route 614 South (Senedo Road), heading toward Timberville. This road straddles Timber Ridge. In spots, it offers an unbeatable view of Massanutten Mountain (to the left) and Little North Mountain and the distant Allegheny ranges in West Virginia (ahead and to the right). Much of the land in this area is so rocky that it can be used only for grazing. The outcroppings that cover the fields are limestone formations that geologists refer to as karst topography.

Drive about 5.4 miles to the "Welcome to Timberville" sign. About 0.7 mile past the sign, turn right on to Route 881 (Orchard Drive) just as the road begins to curve left; if you go into the town, you've gone too far. This tour bypasses **Timberville**, which lies on the North Fork of the Shenandoah River and was a settlement as far back as 1750. Much of this area was burned by Sheridan's forces during the Civil War.

Drive west on Route 881 toward the base of Little North Mountain. In 1.9

Forestville School

miles, you'll pass the Bowman Apple Storage Facility, which serves the many orchards in the area. About 0.5 mile past the facility, turn left on to Andrick Mill Road (Route 789). Andrick Mill is on the right almost immediately after the turn. Perhaps this mill's out-of-the-way location saved it during the Civil War.

Follow Andrick Mill Road (which becomes Route 790) to the stop sign at Route 792 (Crossroads Lane). Turn left. In 1 mile, Route 792 ends at a stop sign; turn right on Route 617 (Spar Mine Road). In 1.4 miles, you'll reach Route 259 (Brock's Gap Road) on the outskirts of the town of **Broadway**. *Turn right.*

This road leads into West Virginia through the ancient mountain opening called Brock's Gap, thought to have been used by buffalo and Indians in early times as they traveled into the first range of the Alleghenies. The North Fork of the Shenandoah River, which has its source not far from here in the mountains to the west, follows the right-hand side of the road.

Route 259 crosses several feeder creeks—first Cedar Creek in 1 mile, then Turley Creek 1.5 miles farther along. About 0.5 mile past the Turley Creek bridge, you'll see a sign pointing left to Singers Glen. Turn left on to Route 613 (Turleytown Road) at the tiny community called **Cootes Store**.

In 1870, merchants began using the Shenandoah River from Brock's Gap to Cootes Store for transporting goods and passengers on flatboats, also called "floatboats" or "gundalows." Other parts of the Shenandoah River were put to similar use, but the long-held dream of making the river fully navigable (George Washington was an early proponent) was finally put to rest when railroad lines were completed throughout the Valley in the late 1800s.

George Washington noted in his diary that he passed through Brock's Gap on horseback early in the morning on September 30, 1784, as he returned from a trip to the Ohio Valley. He planned to spend the night with his friend Thomas Lewis, who lived near what is now Port Republic (see The Harrisonburg to Port Republic Tour, page 140). He turned on to Turleytown Road (known in those days as Back Road) and followed a route similar to the one you are currently traveling. Washington noted in his journal that he rode about 40 miles that day and reached Lewis's house at sundown.

Like Middle Road, Turleytown Road was used by farmers in the 18th and 19th centuries to drive their livestock to market and to summer

Chimney Rock/Fulks Run Grocery Side Trip

A few miles west down Route 259 past the tour's turnoff at Cootes Store are two interesting stops.

The first—a little over 1 mile down the road, at the intersection with Route 612—is an unusual rock formation known as Chimney Rock. The best way to view the formation is to turn right on to Route 612 and look to the right. Chimney Rock is immense but is sometimes partially hidden because of tree cover. It is not to be confused with Natural Chimneys near Mount Solon (see The Harrisonburg to Port Republic Tour, pages 130–31).

Continue 2.6 miles past Chimney Rock on Route 259 West to Fulks Run Grocery, the second stop. This wood-floored grocery sells award-winning sugar-cured Turner Hams. The hams are cured in a smokehouse behind the store.

pastureland in Highland County, southwest of here.

Drive 2 miles past Cootes Store to the Neff Lumber Mill. The last surviving industry in once-thriving **Turleytown**, the mill is on the site of an earlier combination flour mill and sawmill on Turley Creek. In the early 1900s, the Neff Lumber Mill sawed logs of walnut from nearby West Virginia and sent the wood to furniture makers in Baltimore. During World War II, it provided timber to the army and navy while also making chicken coops for Valley farmers.

The area's first settler was Giles Turley, who was traveling to points south when he decided to settle here in 1804. The town grew largely because of its location on the drovers' road. Within a few years, Turley built a wayside inn and tavern.

Turley Creek, also called Brock's Creek, is a powerful stream that supported five gristmills, a hominy mill, one or two sawmills, a carding mill (used to prepare wool for spinning), a mill that rolled hemp (once an important Valley crop) for ropemaking, a foundry, a tanyard, and other businesses. The ruins of the Turley Roller Mill, built in 1880, still stand near the bridge over the creek about 0.2 mile past the lumbermill.

Continue 0.7 mile past the old mill to the unusual-looking stone house on the right. This home was obviously built from rocks from the large quarry below.

Follow Turleytown Road through tranquil green hills and lush valleys to the town of **Singers Glen**, *which welcomes visitors with a sign calling it the "Birthplace of Sacred Music in the South." At the stop sign, turn right to remain on Route 613, which is now called Singers Glen Road.*

This town, first called Mountain Valley, was settled in 1809 or 1810, when Joseph Funk built a small log house here. He and many other local settlers were descendants of German Anabaptists who came to Virginia from Pennsylvania in the late 1700s. Funk was born in Berks County, Pennsylvania, in 1777; his grandfather was the first Mennonite bishop in America. His parents settled in nearby Sparkling Springs in 1786.

Joseph Funk raised a large family and became the community's self-appointed teacher. He placed a heavy emphasis on music in his lessons. Around 1816, he published a volume of hymns that became popular among rural congregations throughout the country. By 1847, Funk's music publishing business had grown to the point that he and his sons were able to establish their own printing shop and bindery in town. For the next 30 or so years, they published many music books and periodicals that gained nationwide circulation. In 1861, they began a school for teachers of vocal music, which became the Singer's Glen School for Advanced Scholars in Literary Studies and Music.

The elder Funk died in 1862, but one of his grandsons, Aldine Kieffer, and Kieffer's sister's husband, Ephraim Ruebush, continued the business. In 1878, they moved the publishing operation to Dayton, near Harrisonburg, where it became the Ruebush-Kieffer Company, a well-known music publishing company in the South. The school of music also grew, eventually moving to Dayton and becoming the Shenandoah Conservatory of Music. It moved once more, to Winchester, and is known today as Shenandoah University.

This peaceful little town of Singers Glen seems frozen in time. Many descendants of the original families still live here in the restored homes of their ancestors.

As you enter town on Singers Glen Road, you'll see the post office—the red-and-yellow frame building on the left. This was the town's store from the time it was built in 1890 until 1974; the post office has occupied space in the building since 1914.

Singers Glen Post Office

On the other side of the street, across from Donovan Memorial United Methodist Church, is the Swank-Ruddle House, which dates to 1826. This home was built at a different location—back up Turleytown Road near the cemetery on the outskirts of town—as the home of Jacob Freeze. The Funks bought it, took it apart, and moved it to the present location in 1885 for use as a lumber planing mill. It was later used as a carriage factory. In 1903, S. Henton Swank bought it for use as a residence.

In the next block, you'll see Singers Glen Baptist Church on the right. Next to the church stand four Funk homes. The first, known as the Funk-Acker House, belonged to Joseph Funk's son, Timothy, who built it in 1850. Its next resident, John Acker (1845–1923), was active in county political affairs and served as a state senator. The two white Victorian gingerbread houses next door were built in the 1890s by Funk grandsons. Next to those is the original Joseph Funk dwelling, constructed around 1810, a small, unassuming house with a green tin roof. Its log construction was long ago covered by weatherboarding. A great-granddaughter of Joseph Funk owns the house, which is a registered National Historic Landmark.

Leave town by continuing south on Route 613. In 1 mile, you'll reach a small sign pointing to Sparkling Springs Road, on the right. If you have 10 minutes to spare, follow this road past a beautifully maintained white-brick farmhouse to one of Virginia's many popular old resort springs. These springs, located at the base of Little North Mountain, were a Mennonite facility that began around 1898. Today, the cottages are privately owned, but the place retains the feel of a peaceful summer retreat tucked into the side of a mountain.

Continue south on Route 613 for 1.5 miles, where you'll see St. Johns Lutheran Cemetery on the left just before the road begins to curve to the left. Almost immediately after the cemetery, make a left turn on to Route 772 (Greenmount Road). You'll come to a stop sign at Snapps Creek Road in 0.6 mile; keep going straight for 1.1 miles to the intersection with Sky Road. (That's Peaked Mountain, at the south end of the Massanutten range, that you see in the distance ahead.) Turn left, then make an immediate right to stay on Route 772. In another mile, you'll reach the intersection with Route 910 (Grist Mill Road). Turn left, proceed 1.4 miles to Route 779 (Acker Road), and turn right. This road quickly becomes Route 778 (Brenneman's Church Road); continue straight for 0.6 mile.

On the left side of the road is the old Turner Mill, once known as Brenneman's Mill. It was built of bricks and limestone around 1800 and, like other mills on this tour, was among the few to survive General Sheridan's burning during the Civil War. The mill was saved, according to local legend, because Union soldiers were sympathetic to reports of illness in the mill owner's family. The more likely story is that the family was able to extinguish the flames in time.

Turner Mill is especially interesting because it was operated continuously for nearly 200 years, thanks in part to the single-handed efforts of J. Howard Turner, who bought the mill in 1933 and ran it by himself until he died in 1988, at the age of 88. At the time, Turner Mill was the last stone mill operating in Rockingham County.

Route 778 intersects U.S. 42 (Harpine Highway) in 0.9 mile. Turn left on to U.S. 42, drive 0.7 mile, and turn right on Route 859 (Jesse Bennett Way). This is the town of **Edom**. Its main street was named for the Edom man who performed the first successful Cesarean operation in North America. In 1794, Dr. Jesse Bennett's pregnant wife became ill, and she and her unborn child were facing almost certain death. Dr. Bennett tried to convince a colleague and teacher of medicine in Staunton to perform surgery on his wife, but the man refused. Dr. Bennett courageously went ahead with the surgery by himself and saved the lives of both his wife and daughter, who lived to be 77.

As you drive into town, you'll see, back from the road on the left, the ruins of another old mill, this one unusual because it was made of limestone. Overgrown and abandoned for many years, this is the Edom-Burrus Mill, built around 1867 at the site of an earlier mill burned during the Civil War. In the early 1900s, the Edom-Burrus Mill produced 50 barrels of "Famous White Rose Flour" a day and was the hub of the town's activities. It burned in 1960.

The man who built the mill, John K. Beery, was obviously speaking from experience when he offered future builders of stone structures this rule of thumb: "First of all, haul twice as much stone as you think you will need, then double that, and you may have half enough."

At the first intersection in town, turn right on to Route 721 (Linville-Edom Road). Continue east toward Linville. Notice the lovely arched stone bridge to the right as you cross Linville Creek—it looks old but was built in the early 1900s.

It is 0.1 mile to a charming old brick house on the creek just before the Linville-Edom School. Known as the J. Owen Beard House, it was constructed in two stages. Joseph Wenger (J. Owen Beard's grandfather) built the original home in 1819. In 1835, a new house was built next to it. The intention was to tear down the earlier structure, but instead, the owners decided to join the two. They added a second floor to the original structure so the rooflines would meet, but in doing so, they had to leave a three-foot space between the buildings. This bricked-up area came in handy years later as a place to hide valuables from looting Yankees during the Civil War. Notice the unusual round brick pillars supporting the porch in back.

The Linville-Edom School was built in the early 1900s at this compromise location—the exact midpoint between the two towns.

Across the street is a lovely old red-brick house, Farmingreen, built by

Lincoln Homestead Side Trip

Follow Route 42 about 2.5 miles north from Edom if you care to see the painted two-story brick house known as the Lincoln Homestead, located on the right. The home was built around 1800 by Captain Jacob Lincoln. A state historical marker stands in front of the house (now a private home), which is reached via a short access road off Route 42. An earlier house located nearby was where President Abraham Lincoln's father, Thomas, was born in 1776. That branch of the Lincolns moved to Kentucky when Thomas was only six years old. Many members of the Lincoln family remained in this area of the Valley, however; a graveyard containing the remains of five generations of Lincolns sits on the hill above the house.

J. Owen Beard House

Henry Wenger, whose family had emigrated to Lancaster County, Pennsylvania, from Switzerland in the late 1720s. A barn built on the estate around 1790 survived the Civil War but burned to the ground in 1895. The main part of the house was constructed in 1825; the frame and brick additions on the right date to the 20th century.

Daniel Boone's family traveled through the Linville area around 1750 on its way to the Yadkin Valley in North Carolina. Daniel was a teenager at the time. His parents were friendly with the Bryan family, who lived in the area. It was during this visit that he may have met Rebecca Bryan, who became his wife about five years later.

*The next intersection is at Kratzer Road in the town of **Linville**. To stay on Route 721, turn left, then make an immediate right. Route 721 now becomes Long's Pump Road.*

The three-story house on the left at the corner is the Sipes-Davis House, sometimes called the Stone House. Now used as apartments, the structure was built as a barn in 1811 by German immigrant Christian Kratzer. It was turned into a residence following the Civil War. At various times after that, it housed a general store, a cheese factory, and the town's post office.

Drive 1.4 miles on Long's Pump Road as it curves past dairy farms and rolling fields. Turn left on to Route 619 (Simmers Valley Road). It is 2 miles to where the road passes Landwirt Winery. This is one of the Valley's small but well-regarded wineries. Landwirt is a German word meaning "the farmer's vineyard," a reflection of both its purpose and its owner, who is of German descent.

*About 0.3 mile past the winery, stay straight even though Route 619 curves left. You are now on Route 806 (Lacey Spring Road), which leads 2 miles to **Lacey Spring**, and U.S. 11. Turn left on U.S. 11 and head north toward New Market.* Soon after you turn, you'll see a state historical marker on the right. It notes the location, some 4 miles west, of the Lincoln Homestead (see the sidebar on page 111) and mentions the existence of an inn owned by members of the Lincoln family at this spot. The inn was destroyed by fire in 1898.

You are driving along one of the oldest and most-traveled roads in America, although it may not look like it today. For about a century, from the 1740s to the mid-1800s, what is now U.S. 11 was the primary road for settlers traveling from Pennsylvania to points south and west. According to historian Carl Bridenbaugh, "In the last sixteen years of the colonial era southbound traffic along the Great Philadelphia Wagon Road [one of the road's many earlier names] was numbered in the tens of thousands; it was the most heavily traveled road in all America and must have had more vehicles jolting along its rough and tortuous way than all other main roads combined."

The road was macadamized in the late 1830s and became known as the Valley Pike. It was later heavily used by Civil War soldiers of both sides. Many battles took place along it, including one just a short distance ahead. After that time, the road took another name: the Long Gray Trail.

By the mid-1960s, I-81 was built, leaving most of the 1940s- and 1950s-vintage motor hotels and tourist courts along U.S. 11 to go out of business. Many of those buildings still stand, in varying states of decay, as lonely reminders of the road's past importance.

Continue 1.8 miles from Lacey Spring to the old stagecoach stop once known as Sparta or Spartopolis and now called **Mauzy**, *located just before U.S. 11 crosses I-81.* On the left side of the road is a red-roofed building with porches running along the length of both floors. Now a private residence, this was once a popular wayside tavern known as the Mauzy House. It was built by William Pickering around 1800. The building is unusual because it seems to have been created by joining two six-room houses.

Mauzy House

Continue on U.S. 11 to the next village, **Tenth Legion**. Local historians claim that its unusual name was inspired by Thomas Jefferson, who is said to have called this part of the Shenandoah Valley his "Tenth Legion of democracy" (a reference to Julius Caesar's loyal Tenth Legion). The people living here had great respect for Jefferson and were strong supporters of his beliefs on religious freedom.

As you enter Tenth Legion, note the stone building on the left next to a larger brick church. The stone structure is Bethlehem Church, named in honor of Moravian brethren from Bethlehem, Pennsylvania. The Moravians left behind a journal that mentioned this area during their "toilsome journey" through Virginia to Winston-Salem, North Carolina, in 1753. The church was built around 1844 as the second Quaker meeting house on the site. It served as a hospital during the Valley Campaign in 1862. After the Civil War, the Quakers merged with another local church. In 1952, the new church was built next door.

The old-fashioned gas station across the street from the church has

Old gas station on U.S. 11

*Rockingham County,
"Turkey Capital"*

operated continuously at this spot since 1928.

Drive about 0.8 mile past Tenth Legion. Set far back from the road on the left is the Martz-Harrison House. Like so many old homes in the area, it consists of an old log dwelling, built about 1750, that has been weatherboarded and a later frame structure, also weatherboarded. The original building is a classic Colonial salt-box design. J. Houston Harrison, the author of *Settlers of the Long Grey Trail,* a history of Rockingham County, was born in this house.

Continue about 0.3 mile to the impressive white mansion on the right, Mooreland Hall, once known as Court Manor. It looks every bit the Southern plantation home. The house was built by Reuben Moore around 1800 of bricks made on the grounds. In 1925, it was bought by Dr. Willis Sharpes Kilmer, who bred and trained racehorses here. The house is surrounded by beautiful lawns and stately old trees today.

The road to one of the Valley's many unusual limestone-formation caves, Endless Caverns, is 1.7 miles ahead. If you care to make a brief side trip, follow the lovely tree-lined drive for 1.8 miles to the caverns; campground facilities and a bed-and-breakfast are located off the road. The caverns were discovered in 1879 by two boys who were hunting rabbits with their dog. The dog chased a rabbit behind some limestone boulders. When the boys moved the boulders aside, they discovered a large dark opening leading to the caverns below.

Another old farmhouse lies to the left of U.S. 11 about 1.2 miles past the road to the caverns. This is Hardscrabble Farm, built around 1776 by William McDowell, a merchant and tavern keeper. It was named Hardscrabble by its next owner, Major Peter Higgins, who bought it in 1806 and soon discovered that the farm's soil had been exhausted by poor farming practices. For a time during the Civil War, the house served as the headquarters of two Union generals, John P. Gordon and Robert Toombs. After the Battle of New Market, which took place a few miles up the road, the home was one of many in the area that served as makeshift hospitals.

Just down the road, you can't miss seeing the large stone marker with a bronze statue of a turkey on top. It marks the Rockingham County line. Rockingham County is called the "Turkey Capital" for good reason—it ranks second among all the nation's counties in poultry production.

Continue less than 1 mile past Hardscrabble Farm to where you'll see three state historical markers on the left. One of them notes that at this point, U.S. 11 crosses the old Fairfax Line, which was the southern boundary of Lord Fairfax's immense landholdings in northern Virginia in the 1700s. (See The White Post to Millwood to Berryville Tour, pages 54–55, for more about Lord Fairfax.) When Peter Jefferson and Thomas Lewis surveyed the Fairfax Line in 1746, they referred to the trail as the "Old Indian Road." Another historical marker notes the nearby birthplace of John Sevier. The son of New Market innkeeper Valentine Sevier, John Sevier was a six-time governor of Tennessee. The third marker notes that the Battle of New Market took place to the north.

In 0.5 mile, just as you enter **New Market***, you'll pass The Shenvalee.* The name was created from the words *Shenandoah, Virginia,* and *Lee.* This hotel and public golf course, long popular with Valley residents for its scenic location near the base of Massanutten Mountain, has been around since 1926. During World War II, the State Department took it over for more than a year to house Italian prisoners of diplomatic rank.

It is another 0.5 mile to the downtown section of New Market. The beginnings of the town go back to the late 1700s. The town grew because of its location at the junction of the Valley Road (in the days before it was a turnpike) and the road that ran between Massanutten Gap (to the east) and Brock's Gap (to the west). In fact, the settlement's early name was Cross Roads. The town was later renamed after New Market, England, for reasons unclear.

Several old structures along Congress Street (U.S. 11) are of historic interest.

Portions of the Calvert House, on the left at 9485 Congress Street, date back to the 1770s. The home once belonged to Major John S. Calvert, who served as secretary of the treasury for the Confederacy. He met with an untimely and unusual death in Richmond in 1870, when the Capitol dome collapsed. He was a descendant of the Calverts who founded Maryland.

New Market achieved prominence in the 1800s as a printing and publishing center. The building that housed the Henkel Press is on the left at 9445 Congress Street. The press began when Ambrose Henkel, the 16-year-old son of a local preacher, decided to walk to Hagerstown, Maryland, to

DOWNTOWN NEW MARKET

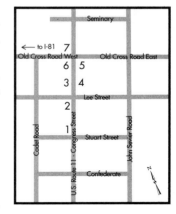

1 Calvert House
2 Henkel Press
3 Solomon Henkel House
4 Dr. C. C. Henkel House
5 Lee-Jackson Hotel
6 John Sevier Trading Post
7 Abbie Henkel House

learn the printing trade. In 1806, his on-the-job training complete, he bought a printing press in Reading, Pennsylvania, and brought it back to New Market to begin his business. Because the surrounding area was so heavily settled by German immigrants and their descendants, most of the printing he did before 1830 was in German. Henkel's first newspaper, *Der Volksberichter*, was printed here between 1807 and 1809.

Many other newspapers and books followed during the more than 100 years the family owned the press. Among them was an English-language newspaper called the *Shenandoah Valley*. That newspaper survives today; after being combined with another old newspaper, it is now published in Woodstock as the *Shenandoah Valley Herald*. Elon Henkel, grandson of the founder, sold the press in 1925. It ceased operations in 1975.

The Solomon Henkel House, on the left at 9417 Congress Street, was built in 1802 and now serves as the town's library. Solomon Henkel was a physician and druggist. Note the metal plate tacked to the front door; it is said to cover up damage made when Union soldiers, trying to barge in, struck the door with their bayonets and rifle butts. They gave up after a group of women poured hot water on them from the upstairs window. The shutters on the house are said to be original.

Dr. C. C. Henkel House

The impressive brick house across the street at 9400 Congress Street was built by Dr. C. C. Henkel, who was a surgeon for the Army of Northern Virginia during the Civil War.

Three interesting structures are located at the town's main intersection, where Congress Street crosses U.S. 211 West.

At the southeast corner stands a building dating back to the early 1800s. It has seen many uses—as a store, as a site where Stonewall Jackson reviewed his troops in 1862, as General Jubal Early's headquarters in 1864, and as the Lee-Jackson Hotel in the early 1900s. Today, it houses a private museum and a shop that sells antiques and pottery.

John Sevier trading post

John Sevier had a trading post in town perhaps as early as 1765. It was located behind the current log cabin (said to have been built using some of the original timbers from Sevier's store) on the southwest corner of the intersection.

One of the oldest buildings in the area, perhaps built before the Revolutionary War, is the structure of gray stone and brick on the northwest corner. Now a bank, it is known as the Abbie Henkel House. In the 1830s, Abe Neff and Samuel Funkhouser ran a store in the building.

The town is still a busy crossroads, partly because New Market Battlefield State Historical Park receives a steady stream of visitors year-round. This tour does not visit the state historical park, though it does visit the battlefield itself. If you care to make a side trip to the state historical park, turn left on to U.S. 211 West; the park is located down the first side road to the right on the far side of I-81. The Virginia Military Institute operates the Hall of Valor Civil War Museum on the site; the New Market Battlefield Military Museum is on the same road. Also located off U.S. 211 West just as you pass beneath I-81 are the privately run Cavalry Museum and the headquarters of the Shenandoah Valley Travel Association, which is open seven days a week and provides information about points of interest and accommodations for the entire Shenandoah Valley.

Hall of Valor Civil War Museum

From the main intersection in New Market, continue north on U.S. 11 for about 1 mile to see the fields where the Battle of New Market took place on a rainy Sunday in May 1864. On the way, you'll pass an impressive-looking old brick mansion set back from the road on the left. Once known as the Rice House, it was built in 1834 by Dr. John A. Rice, who served in the Mexican War and was an early president of the Valley Turnpike Company. It is said that Union general Banks used the house as his headquarters for a time in 1862. It is now a residence home.

The Battle of New Market is briefly described on the historical marker and signs on the left side of U.S. 11. General John C. Breckenridge (who had been United States vice president under President James Buchanan from 1857 to 1861) was in command of 4,500 Confederates facing Union general Franz Sigel's 6,000 men. With nowhere else to turn for help, Breckenridge called on the Virginia Military Academy in Lexington for reinforcements. Of the 300 young men in the cadet corps there at the time, some 250 were sent to New Market.

On their arrival, the cadets assumed reserve positions, but about midafternoon, they joined the fight. The legend goes that Sigel, in a panic, lapsed into speaking orders in his native German, confusing his troops and contributing to the Union's humiliating defeat at the hands of a much smaller force. When the battle was over, 600 Confederate and 800 Union soldiers were dead, and Sigel's troops were chased down the Valley Pike past Mount Jackson. Ten V.M.I. cadets lost their lives. This battle was the last Confederate victory in the Valley.

Soon afterward, General Grant replaced Sigel with General David Hunter and instructed him to "make all the valleys south of the Baltimore and Ohio road a desert as high up as possible." He further told Hunter to "eat out Virginia clear and clean as far as they go so that crows flying over it for the balance of the season will have to carry their provender with them." Grant was determined to cut off the large supply of food that Valley farmers provided to the Confederate army.

The summer of 1864 saw widespread devastation in the Valley, as Union troops looted, burned, and destroyed every barn, bridge, and railroad in sight, an event that came to be known as "The Burning." Union general Sheridan, assisted by General Custer and others, later bragged that by October 4, they had burned more than 2,000 barns filled with wheat and hay, more than 70 mills filled with wheat and flour, and 3,000 sheep. Many homes and fields were also torched. By the fall of 1864, the Valley north of Staunton had become a wasteland.

As you continue driving U.S. 11, you'll be following the path of Sigel's retreat toward Mount Jackson. After 3 miles, you'll pass another Civil War site, Rude's Hill, just before the signs pointing to I-81. General Stonewall Jackson set up camp here for two weeks in early April 1862 after fighting at Kernstown, before moving his force of 11,000 men to battles to the south and west. Rude's Hill was then quiet for two years, until Confederate general Jubal Early paused here as he retreated south in October 1864 after his defeat by General Sheridan at the Battle of Opequon, near Winchester. Two months later, Early was back at Rude's Hill, being attacked by Sheridan again. This time, Sheridan's forces were turned back.

A short distance farther down U.S. 11, just beyond the I-81 turnoff and behind the barn on the corner, is a nondescript asbestos-sided house. This is the Rude House, used by Jackson as his headquarters while he camped here in 1862.

Just beyond Rude's Hill along U.S. 11 is a flat stretch of farmland called Meems Bottom, named after an early owner of the property. This especially fertile stretch has been enriched over the centuries by the flooding

Shenandoah River, which flows around and through it.

During Stonewall Jackson's retreat up the Valley in the spring of 1862, Confederate colonel Turner Ashby's beautiful white stallion was struck by a Union bullet during a skirmish at Meems Bottom. Legend says that the horse carried his master off the field of battle and, head held high, walked down the pike with the retreating soldiers before finally falling and dying about a mile past New Market, near Hardscrabble Farm.

Archaeologists believe that the Senedo Indians had a permanent settlement here until they were wiped out by another tribe, possibly the Catawbas. Early Valley historian Samuel Kercheval recorded that in the mid-1700s, a local man was frequently visited by an elderly Indian, who told him that, many years earlier, a group of invading Indians from farther south had killed his entire nation except for himself and another child. Historians have estimated that the massacre occurred between 1650 and 1700. The peaceful Senedos may have been caught up in an ongoing battle between the Catawbas and the Delawares. Early settlers reported seeing tribes passing up and down the Valley on the old Indian trail that extended from New York to South Carolina, part of which is today's U.S. 11.

On the left side of the road is a state historical marker for the covered bridge at

Meems Bottom covered bridge

Meems Bottom. Turn left 0.2 mile past the marker, on to Wissler Road. Lined with Norway maples planted in 1910, this road leads less than 0.5 mile to the longest covered bridge remaining in Virginia. The small parking area to the left just before the bridge is a good place to stop and take pictures.

During the 1800s, there were hundreds of covered bridges in Virginia, but only eight are left today. Of those, only five are accessible to the public. This one, featuring a single-span Burr arch truss, is 204 feet long. It was built in the early 1890s. Burned by arsonists in 1976, it was rebuilt three years later. At least two other bridges once crossed the Shenandoah at this point. One was burned during the Civil War, and another was destroyed by a flood in 1870.

Retrace your route to U.S. 11. In the distance across the road is Mount Airy Farm, which began as an old stone mansion built around 1799 by Baron Steenbergen. John G. Meems bought the estate in 1841. The house was then purchased and rebuilt in 1909 by Daniel Kelleher, whose wife was a Meems granddaughter. Owners since then have included a member of the famous Vanderbilt family, Harold S. Vanderbilt.

Turn left on U.S. 11 and drive 0.7 mile toward the bridge over the Shenandoah River into **Mount Jackson**. Before you cross the bridge, look for the small house on the left behind the trees and bushes. This structure is what remains of an old tollhouse, one of many that used to line the Valley Pike every 5 miles between 1840 and 1918, when the toll-taking ended and the state took over maintenance of the road.

Continue across the bridge into Mount Jackson. Settled in the 1730s, the town was originally called Mount Pleasant but was renamed in 1826 to honor Andrew Jackson, hero of the War of 1812. In the center of town is Union Church, built around 1825 and surrounded by an old cemetery. The term *union* meant it was a "free" church, to be shared by various denominations and used for community functions. It was used as a hospital in the Civil War.

Continue north along U.S. 11. It is 0.9 mile from Union Church to a Confederate cemetery and a monument to Confederate soldiers, located on the left.

Directly across the street from the cemetery, the Confederacy built a large hospital complex consisting of three two-story buildings that could accommodate 500 soldiers. The hospital was run by a local physician, Dr. Andrew

Russell Meem, whose staff tended sick and wounded soldiers who arrived by train from places like Gettysburg and Manassas. Colonel Levi Rinker, mentioned earlier in this tour, donated the land for the hospital and cemetery. After the war, the hospital was torn down and the lumber used to build a military installation at Rude's Hill. That installation was used by Union forces during Reconstruction.

The cemetery was begun in 1861 and contains the bodies of 400 Civil War soldiers from 11 states.

The tour ends here. To return to I-81, follow the signs pointing left off U.S. 11 just beyond the cemetery.

Confederate Cemetery

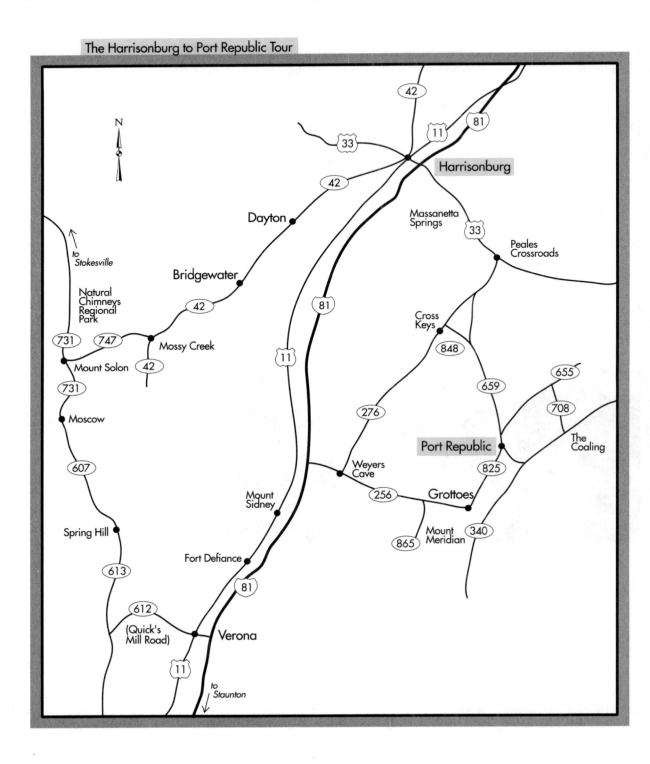

The Harrisonburg to Port Republic Tour

The Harrisonburg to Port Republic Tour

*The tour begins at Courthouse Square in downtown in **Harrisonburg**. From I-81, take Exit 247B, which will put you on U.S. 33 West. In 1.9 miles, you will reach Courthouse Square; you'll see the green-domed courthouse building as you approach the downtown area. Park on the square and walk to the first few attractions in this tour.*

Known as Rocktown in its early days because of the prevalence of limestone in the area, Harrisonburg officially became a town in 1780. It was named after its founder, Thomas Harrison, who was born to English immigrants on New York's Long Island in 1704. When Harrison was in his early thirties, he, his father, and four brothers traveled to Virginia, drawn by the prospect of plentiful and fertile farmland. The tract that Harrison selected for himself makes up the heart of downtown Harrisonburg today. It was centered on a large spring that still flows under the copper-covered gazebo (an exact replica of the original domed springhouse built in 1832) at Courthouse Square.

Harrisonburg is the county seat of Rockingham County, which was created in 1778 by splitting off a portion of Augusta County. It was named for the marquis of Rockingham, Charles Watson Wentworth. Five courthouses have stood at this square since the first log one was built in 1781. The present limestone building was completed in 1897.

The town began here, at the site of the old crossroads of the Spotswood Trail (now U.S. 33) and the Indian Trail (later known as the Valley Pike and now as U.S. 11). As travel on these roads grew, so did the town. Stagecoaches began stopping here on their way between Winchester and Staunton

This tour begins in Harrisonburg and follows historic country roads that pass early Valley settlements and Civil War sites. It stops at the Shenandoah Valley Folk Art Museum and Heritage Center in Dayton, then takes scenic Route 42 through the college town of Bridgewater and to Mount Solon and Natural Chimneys Regional Park. From there, it winds through hilly central Virginia farmland until it meets historic U.S. 11 in Verona. The tour then proceeds north to the historic Augusta Stone Church and into the town of Mount Sidney. Past Mount Sidney, it crosses I-81 and proceeds into the 1890s boom town of Grottoes, long famous for its Grand Caverns. The next stop is the peaceful hamlet of Port Republic, the scene of Civil War action during Stonewall Jackson's Valley Campaign. The tour ends near where it began in Harrisonburg.

Total mileage:
Approximately 84 miles

Rockingham County Courthouse

Thomas Harrison House

Virginia Quilt Museum

in the 1820s, and traffic increased after the Valley Pike was built in the 1830s. Another important early road through Harrisonburg evolved into today's Route 42. It was built in the 1800s as a turnpike to the resort areas in and around Warm Springs to the southwest.

Several Civil War battles were fought in and around the city. The Battle of Harrisonburg took place at Chestnut Ridge southeast of town on June 6, 1862. General Turner Ashby was killed during that battle; a monument to him stands off Port Republic Road about 0.5 mile east of that road's interchange with I-81. The nearby Battles of Port Republic and Cross Keys are described later in this tour.

The intersection of U.S. 33 (Market Street) and U.S. 11 (Main Street) at Courthouse Square remains the main crossroads in Harrisonburg today. From the square, walk two blocks south on Main Street to Bruce Street. Around 1750, Thomas Harrison built a stone house that still stands as the rear portion of the building at 30 West Bruce, across from Asbury United Methodist Church. This is the oldest structure in the city and is on the Virginia Landmarks Register. The building's historical marker mentions that it was the place where Methodist bishop Francis Asbury (the man who almost single-handedly established the Methodist Church in America) held the first Methodist conference west of the Blue Ridge in 1794. Harrison's original stone structure became the rear wing of a brick house that was built in the mid-1800s.

The old brick house on the corner of Bruce and Main Streets across Main from Asbury United Methodist Church was completed in 1849 by the town's first mayor, Isaac Hardesty; it later served as an inn.

Continue south on Main Street to the Virginia Quilt Museum, at 301 South Main. This museum has a permanent collection of more than 60 quilts and features changing exhibits of local and international quilts. Begun in 1995 with donations from quilt guilds all over Virginia, it is one of only four museums in the nation devoted to preserving the heritage of quilt making. It occupies an 1856 residence known as the Warren-Sipe House. The museum is open daily except Tuesdays and Wednesdays.

Walk back to Courthouse Square to resume the driving tour. Follow U.S. 33 West for 3.5 miles. After you pass the town limits sign for Dale Enterprise, turn left on to Route 701 at the small sign pointing to Dayton.

The large hill on the right after the turn is Mole Hill, one of two known extinct volcanoes in the state of Virginia. (Trimble Knob in Monterey, described in The Monterey to Hot Springs Tour, is the other). Molten lava from the eruption at Mole Hill more than 50 million years ago has been found 10 miles away at Natural Chimneys. Today's hill, which rises about 500 feet off the Valley floor, has eroded greatly over time. Local lore says that citizens celebrated the end of the War of 1812 atop Mole Hill. There, they barbecued an ox, whose final act was to walk up the hill.

On Route 701, you may catch sight of one of the area's many Old Order Mennonites in a horse and buggy. This area was settled by Mennonites, often called German Quakers in the early days. Mennonites believe in living a simple life, often shunning modern conveniences. They began as an Anabaptist sect in 16th-century Switzerland. Anabaptists believe in adult, rather than infant, baptism and were persecuted in Europe for that and other beliefs. Like the Quakers and the Amish (a denomination that split from the Mennonites in the late 1600s), Mennonites do not believe in military service, which caused them problems during both the Revolutionary War and the Civil War.

Silver Lake, with Mole Hill in the background

James Madison University

Harrisonburg is the home of James Madison University, which had its beginnings in 1908 as the state-established Normal and Industrial School for Women. *The main part of this ever-growing campus (in 1998, it had 13,500 students) faces U.S. 11 less than a mile south of the Virginia Quilt Museum, past a neighborhood of lovely old Victorian homes.*

The university maintains a 125-acre arboretum on the eastern side of the campus. It features forested walking trails, 14 gardens, and many rare and endangered plants native to the mid-Appalachian area. *The arboretum is on University Boulevard a half-block east of the Port Republic Road interchange with I-81. From Port Republic Road, turn left at Forest Hills Drive, turn left on Oak Hill Drive, and then turn right on to University Boulevard.*

This part of Rockingham County, with its rolling fields and picturesque farms, reflects the county's longstanding importance as an agricultural center. It ranks second in the nation in poultry production and is one of the country's top 20 agricultural counties.

Continue on Route 701 to **Dayton**. Before entering town, you'll see Silver Lake on the right. This lake was formed when a dam was built on Cooks Creek to provide water power for two mills that operated here as early as the 1820s. The mill that stands today, known as Upper Mill, was built in the 1870s to replace two earlier mills; one burned in 1855 and was rebuilt the following year, only to be burned nine years later by Union troops during their campaign of destruction in the Shenandoah Valley in 1864. The existing mill was operated by the Rockingham Milling Company until the mid-1990s.

After you pass the lake, turn left at the next intersection on to Route 732, then turn right on to Route 42 Business (Main Street), where you'll see Fort Harrison (also known as the Daniel Harrison House) on the right. Daniel Harrison, one of the Harrison brothers mentioned earlier, was Dayton's first settler. He arrived in the area in 1745 and built the front portion of this stone house in 1749.

Stone houses like this one were often called forts, because their thick walls served to protect area families against Indian attacks, which were frequent in the Valley during the mid-1700s. Early settlers in Dayton were especially vulnerable because they were near the old trail leading to Warm Springs, a favorite Indian destination. The settlers built an underground passage that led to a spring by Cooks Creek, providing them with access to water in case they were confined for a long period. The house is open on weekend afternoons from May through October.

As early settlement here grew, the community came to be known as Rifetown or Rifesville after Daniel Rife, who owned much of the land the town occupies. It was formally established as Dayton in 1833. By then, the town had become important because of the many mills in the areas and the ironworks at Mossy Creek, visited later on this tour. No one is sure why the name Dayton was chosen.

From Fort Harrison, continue on Main Street to the next intersection, Mill Street, and turn right. Go one block and turn right on College Street.

Take a Hike

A scenic hiking trail, the Cliff Trail, maintained by the Dry River Ranger District of George Washington National Forest, is about 14 miles west of Dayton. *To get there, turn right on Mason Street (Route 257) as you leave Dayton, drive 11 miles to Forest Road 62, then follow the sign about 3 miles to the campground.*

For more information, call the Dry River Ranger District office in Bridgewater (see the appendix).

Many of the old homes and businesses on College Street have a connection to the town's past as a center for music education and publishing. In 1878, the publishing firm of Ruebush-Kieffer moved here from Singers Glen (see The Edinburg to Singers Glen to Mount Jackson Tour, pages 108–10). Dayton was also home to the institution that later became the Shenandoah College and Conservatory of Music; founded in 1875, it is now known as Shenandoah University and is located in Winchester. Ephraim Ruebush, a president of the college, lived in the Victorian house at 315 College Street. He and Aldine Kieffer were grandsons of Joseph Funk of Singers Glen, whose interest in music and education led him to establish both the publishing company and a school for music educators.

Some of the old college buildings are still in use as homes and businesses. At 325 College Street is the Kieffer Memorial, which served as a gymnasium and auditorium. The oldest school building, constructed at the turn of the century, is the one at 340 College Street. The building at 355 College Street dates to 1930 and once housed the school's administrative offices.

After three blocks on College Street, turn left on Route 732 (Bowman Avenue), then go left on High Street to reach the Shenandoah Valley Folk Art and Heritage Center. The center is operated by the Harrisonburg–Rockingham County Historical Society. The main level contains a gift shop that specializes in local folk arts and crafts, as well as books and publications. The museum contains permanent and changing exhibits about local history and folk art, including a large map and a film that tell the story of Stonewall Jackson's Valley Campaign of 1862. Upstairs, the society manages a genealogical research library. The center is open daily except Tuesdays.

Shenandoah Valley Folk Art and Heritage Center

From the parking lot at the Heritage Center, turn left on to High Street and go two blocks to Mill Street; turn left and go three blocks to Main Street. Turn right, drive to the stop sign at Mason Street, turn left, then turn right on to Route 42 South (John Wayland Highway). In about 0.2 mile, you will reach the Dayton Farmers Market, on the right. The building houses a collection of shops and a cafeteria-style restaurant and bakery run by area Mennonites. The Dayton Farmers Market is open Thursdays, Fridays, and Saturdays.

Continue south to **Bridgewater**, *where Route 42 becomes Main Street.*

One of the area's early settlers was a man named Alexander Herring. He married one of Daniel Harrison's sisters, Abigail. Their daughter, Bathsheba, married a man from the Linville Creek area named Abraham Lincoln; one of their children, Thomas Lincoln, was the father of the future president. Until a few years ago, the house Herring built stood on Cooks Creek between Dayton and Bridgewater. It has since been moved log by log to a spot about 11 miles west.

Bridgewater was first called Bridgeport. The area was settled by Scots-Irish immigrants as early as 1740. By the early 1800s, many Pennsylvanians of German descent were moving to the area as well. The many mills in the area sent their flour and other products to market on flat-bottomed boats on the North River, which flows through the southern end of town. Of the eight bridges that have spanned the river here since 1820, the most famous was a 240-foot covered bridge said to have been the longest single-span wooden bridge in the world at the time.

After Union soldiers burned the bridge that stood here during Stonewall Jackson's Valley Campaign, the Confederates came up with an inventive way to cross the river into Bridgewater. It was reportedly suggested by Jedediah Hotchkiss, Jackson's mapmaker and the founder and former superintendent of Mossy Creek Academy (see below). They laid wagons side by side across the water, then placed wooden planks between them to form a temporary bridge.

Today, the town is home to Bridgewater College, a private school operated by the Church of the Brethren. It was established in 1880 at Spring Creek as the Virginia Normal School and was later moved here. The college is home to the Reuel B. Pritchett Museum, which contains 10,000 historical, cultural, and religious items that were part of a private collection of Pritchett, a minister and farmer from Tennessee. The museum contains more than 175 rare books and Bibles, including a copy of the Venice Bible published in 1482. Other items on display include antique guns and swords, jugs, glassware, and carpentry tools. The museum is on the lower level of Cole Hall and is open Monday through Friday afternoons.

Many interesting old homes line Main Street. A former mayor of Bridgewater owned the Barbee House on 403 North Main, built in 1818. This brick house was later turned into a tavern; after the Civil War, it became a girls' school. It is claimed that Henry Clay and Andrew Jackson slept here.

J. G. Brown, a captain in the Civil War, built the imposing white house with columns at 111 South Main in 1849.

Dinkle Tavern

At least six of the town's doctors have lived at the T. H. Brown Home at 115 South Main, which was built about 1838.

The Dinkle brothers, John and Jacob, were two of the town's early settlers. They operated a sawmill and a gristmill here around 1810. In 1815, Jacob built the Dinkle Tavern at what is now 215 South Main, just before the North River bridge. The tavern became a popular stopping place for travelers going from Washington, D.C., to Warm Springs before the Civil War. At that time, Route 42 was known as the Harrisonburg–Warm Springs Turnpike.

Follow Route 42 across the North River bridge and drive 3.2 miles. At **Mossy Creek**, *Route 42 veers sharply to the left just after passing a beautiful old stone-and-brick house on the left. Don't turn here; instead, stay straight on Route 747 (Mossy Creek Road), following the signs toward Natural Chimneys.* The stone-and brick-house at the junction was once known as the Miller House and is one of the oldest homes in Augusta County. The stone portion was built in 1784 by Henry Miller, who founded a large ironworks nearby. Miller was a cousin of Daniel Boone and is thought to have learned iron making from Boone's father, Squire Boone.

Miller House

On the right after 0.7 mile on Route 747, you'll see a brick entranceway leading to a handsome red-brick house with two white pillars. Known as the George Craun House, it was built near the site of Mossy Creek Academy. Mossy Creek Academy was established by Jedediah Hotchkiss around 1853. Hotchkiss was an engineer and teacher who later played an important role in the Civil War as General Stonewall Jackson's topographical engineer and mapmaker. The school is said to have produced many promising young people. It shut down once the Civil War began and was used for a while as a Confederate hospital. A fire destroyed the building soon after that war.

The farmland across the road from the academy once was the site of a lake, created by a dam built on Mossy Creek to provide power for the ironworks and mill; the ruins of the dam are almost concealed by plant growth next to the small roadside pull-over just past the intersection of Routes 42 and 747. The lake had a pavilion and dance hall and was a popular weekend gathering spot from the mid-1800s until the early 1900s, bringing day-trippers from Harrisonburg on the Chesapeake and Western Railroad. After the ironworks and mill ceased production in the early 1900s, the lake was drained and returned to farmland.

Continue 0.8 mile to Mossy Creek Presbyterian Church, beautifully situated on a hill to the left. This church was founded in 1768 by early Scots-Irish settlers. It is one of several early Presbyterian churches in this part of the Valley.

As you continue toward Mount Solon, you'll pass the area where Stonewall Jackson's army camped after the Battle of McDowell in Highland County (see The Monterey to Hot Springs Tour, page 180).

It is 1.9 miles to the stop sign on the outskirts of Mount Solon. Turn right on to Route 731 (Natural Chimneys Road). Before you turn, note the white frame building directly across the street. This old mill is now a VFW post, but during the Civil War, it was where Generals Jackson and Ewell met to lay out a plan to pursue Union general Banks.

Natural Chimneys

After about 0.7 mile on Route 731, you'll seen a green-and-yellow sign marking the entrance to **Natural Chimneys Regional Park**. The park has picnic tables and shelters, a campground, and a swimming pool. It is operated by the Upper Valley Regional Park Authority, which charges a small admission fee.

Directly behind the parking lot are the seven limestone "chimneys," the highest of which measures 120 feet. They are about 500 million years old, formed from the sediment of an ancient sea that covered the Shenandoah Valley. Once part of a huge cavern, the chimneys are what was left behind after the roof caved in. The stone markers scattered around the area tell the geological story of their formation.

William Jennings Bryant described the Natural Chimneys in his book *Picturesque America*, published in 1872. He said they resembled ancient castle ruins. As such, they provide a perfect backdrop for the park's most famous activity—the Natural Chimneys Jousting Tournament, which the park claims is the oldest continuously held sporting event in America. Participants re-enact the sport of knights, but instead of knocking each other off horses, they try to guide their lances through small suspended metal rings while galloping.

The games began here in 1821 as a way for two local men to settle their claim on the young woman both wanted to marry. Today, riders come from surrounding states to compete in a sport that originated—in a more dangerous form—in France in the 11th century. The tournament is held on the third Saturday in August. Call the park authority for more information; the number is listed in the appendix.

From the park, head back to Mount Solon. When you reach the stop sign at the intersection, stay straight on Route 731.

Mount Solon has been around since the 1700s and is said to have been named for the ancient Greek lawgiver. As you pass through the town, you'll see several old buildings. Just past Mount Solon Grocery (on the right at the far edge of town) is a beautifully restored home, the J. Marshall McCue House. Here, on the evening of May 17, 1862, Mr. McCue entertained Stonewall Jackson and members of his staff at dinner, while Jackson's men camped in the area.

Continue on Route 731 out of Mount Solon. In 2.3 miles, you'll come to a stop sign at Route 42 at **Moscow***; continue straight on what is now Route 607 (Mount Solon Road). This road changes numbers several times; stay on the main road (which you can tell by its yellow centerline). On the 5 miles to* **Spring Hill***, the road leads through rolling farmland with dramatic views of the Blue Ridge Mountains to the east and south. Less than 4 miles past Spring Hill, look for Pleasant View Lutheran Church on the left. Shortly after you pass the church, turn left on to Quick's Mill Road (Route 612). A short distance down the road, Massanutten Mountain and the Blue Ridge range will come into view as you descend toward U.S. 11 and the town of* **Verona***, well known for its many antique shops. Turn left on to U.S. 11.*

The city of Ann Arbor, Michigan, was named for an early settler who once lived in the Verona area, Ann Allen. She left here in 1824 to join her husband, John, who had moved west—as many Valley residents did during that period. He and another man, Elisha Rumsey, settled at a place in the Michigan Territory that they named Ann's Arbor, after both their wives. Several years later, Ann Allen's husband left Ann Arbor to make his fortune in the California gold rush and was never heard from again. She later returned to Verona and died here; her tomb is at Augusta Stone Church, visited later on this tour. The Allen family's home still stands; it is on the

Stokesville Side Trip

If you turn right as you leave the entrance to Natural Chimneys Regional Park, you'll end up in Stokesville, about 4.5 miles west. This was the terminus of the old Chesapeake and Western Railroad—called the "Crooked and Weedy" by locals of the time. The line began in Dayton in 1895 and primarily transported lumber from Mount Solon to Elkton. When the lumber supply became exhausted in the 1930s, the line ceased operations. The Stokesville Campground office occupies the restored train station today; a cheery red caboose sits nearby. The village was named after local millionaire W. E. D. Stokes, who helped finance the rail line from Mount Solon.

Mount Solon Grocery

left side of U.S. 11 just after you cross the concrete bridge over the Middle River as you leave Verona.

About 2 miles past the Middle River bridge, look for a state historical marker on the left side of the road. It notes the location of an early travelers' stop known far and wide as the Willow Spout.

Sometime after 1785, Peter Hanger, a German immigrant who owned a 500-acre plantation that included what is now Gypsy Hill Park in Staunton, bought land in this area and built a stagecoach stop, a hotel, and a distillery. A later owner fashioned the Willow Spout in 1848. The spout was designed to bring spring water up to road level through the trunk of a willow tree, allowing horses to drink from a trough without having to be unreined. For years, this ingenious source of water was appreciated by stagecoach passengers and their horses, as well as by soldiers on both sides during the Civil War.

Continue north on U.S. 11 for 1 mile to **Fort Defiance**. Look to the left to see the abandoned buildings of the Augusta Military Academy. Charles S. Roller, a Confederate veteran and state delegate, founded the school in 1879 to teach the classics. Perhaps because so many of his students were Confederate veterans, he also ran the school partly as a military academy. It later became a traditional military academy and was a well-respected school for more than a hundred years. In 1920, it formed the first Junior Reserve Officers' Training Corps in the country. It was operated by Roller's descendants until it closed in 1984 because of financial difficulties.

Just past the military academy is Augusta Stone Church, also on the left. The original part of this church—which is the oldest Virginia church building west of the Blue Ridge and the oldest Presbyterian church in continuous use in the state—was built in 1749. Its grounds and cemetery, set in a grove of towering old oak trees, are well worth a stop. The main church building was enlarged in the early 1920s, but the original walls and roof remain.

Augusta Stone Church

The area's first settlers were Scots-Irish who were searching for land of their own and for religious freedom. Over the years, they and their ancestors had moved from Scotland to Ireland, then from Ireland to America. Settling first in Pennsylvania, they found they didn't fit in well with the established German and Quaker settlements. In the 1700s, many came to the central and southern part of the Shenandoah Valley, areas that were largely unsettled at the time.

In 1738, a group of Scots-Irish formed a "Christian society" here. They worshiped in a log cabin located on the site of what is now the church cemetery. Their first minister, John Craig, arrived from Ireland via Delaware in 1740. He made an observation about the Shenandoah Valley, calling it "a wilderness in the proper sense, and a few Christian settlers in it with numbers of heathens travelling among us . . . . [The local people] generally march about in small companies from fifteen to twenty, sometimes more or less. They must be supplied at any house they call at, with victuals, or they become their own stewards and cooks, and spare nothing they choose to eat and drink." The Reverend Craig obviously had his work cut out for him.

For many years, he was also the minister (every other Sunday) at another early Presbyterian church, Tinkling Springs (see The Staunton to Steeles Tavern Tour, pages 168–69). Craig's Sunday-morning sermons lasted from ten o'clock to noon, and his afternoon service lasted from one o'clock to sundown. A local history, *The Annals of Augusta County*, notes that the latter service was "sometimes so late that the clerk found it difficult to read the last Psalm."

During the French and Indian War, many area settlers feared for their lives and moved out of the Valley. The Reverend Craig felt strongly that residents should stay, not flee, and was a strong supporter of fort building in the Valley. He and his congregation—men and women alike—constructed Augusta Stone Church and its surrounding stockade with their own hands, to provide families with a safe haven when Indians were in the area. Such structures were probably the source of the name Fort Defiance.

Continue to the next town up the road, **Mount Sidney**. In the late 1700s, this was the only stage stop between Keezletown at the base of Massanutten Mountain (to the east) and Staunton (to the south). Many of the town's lovely old homes and buildings house antique shops today.

A farm near the town was the birthplace of Dwight D. Eisenhower's mother, Elizabeth Stover, in 1862. Her grandfather, William Link, raised her; he was a grandson of Mathias Link, who came to the area in the 1750s. Elizabeth Stover moved to Kansas in 1883, where she met and married

The "Ungainly" Parson Speece

The fourth minister of Augusta Stone Church began his tenure in 1813. He was an educated and colorful character named Conrad Speece, whom a local historian described as follows: "Parson Speece chewed tobacco excessively, even sleeping with a quid in his mouth. He was tall, heavy, and ungainly; and his clothes, always too large for him, hung loosely on his large frame. His voice was loud, deep, and resonant. He was very sociable and an able conversationalist, sprinkling his remarks with droll and curious phrases. He was a bachelor, whether from choice or because Shenandoah women could not discern his sterling worth beneath his rough and ungainly exterior, the records do not state."

David Eisenhower. President Eisenhower visited Mount Sidney in 1952 to see the farm where his mother grew up.

This section of U.S. 11 was not part of the original Indian Trail. Historians believe the trail left what is now U.S. 11 near Mauzy, north of Harrisonburg, and rejoined it above Mount Sidney. Most of the old route followed the path of today's Route 276, which is called the Indian Trail in some places.

As you leave Mount Sidney, turn right on to Route 750 (Keezletown Road), which passes over I-81 and intersects Route 256 (Weyers Cave Road) in 3 miles. Turn right and continue toward Grottoes. The mountains you see to the left are the southern end of the Massanutten range; to the right and ahead are the Blue Ridge Mountains, topped by Skyline Drive. The tallest peaks here range in height from 3,300 to almost 3,600 feet.

About 3.3 miles down the road, look for a sign pointing right to **Mount Meridian***. Turn right on Rockfish Road (Route 865), drive 0.4 mile, and turn right on to Snowflake Mill Road, which dead-ends at an old iron bridge across the Middle River.* An unusual octagonal barn is just beyond the bridge. A Virginia Historic Landmark, this barn was built in 1867 by Samuel Harnsberger, whose ancestors were Swiss-Germans who came to the Valley in the early 1700s. He apparently was inspired by the octagonal house in Grottoes built by his brother (see below). During the barn's construction, its design reportedly stumped local carpenters. An outside expert had to be called in to help them fit everything together. The barn was restored in 1978.

Mount Meridian provided a place for Stonewall Jackson's army to rest for a peaceful five days in mid-June 1862, "the men reposing under the shade, or bathing in the sparkling waters of the [river], and the horses feeding in the abundant pastures," as a Major Dabney recorded.

Retrace your path to Route 256, turn right, and drive 2 miles to Grottoes. Grottoes is located just across the South River, which joins the North River at Port Republic in about 3 miles to form the South Fork of the Shenandoah River.

Before you cross the South River bridge, you'll pass a state historical marker on the left. It notes that in 1811, artist George Caleb Bingham was born in a frame house nearby. Bingham was well known for his paintings of the American West, where his family moved when he was a boy.

Grottoes was named for the large caverns now known as Grand Caverns. Located at the foot of the Blue Ridge, the caverns were discovered in 1806 by a young man named Bernard Weyer (the source of the name of another local town, Weyers Cave). They contained deposits of potassium nitrate, used in making gunpowder, a product that was in great demand in the early 1800s and again during the Civil War. The caverns were originally called Madison's Cave, for John Madison, the first clerk of Augusta County, who lived in nearby Port Republic.

Both George Washington and Thomas Jefferson visited the caverns. Jefferson described them in his book, *Notes on the State of Virginia*: "It is in a hill of about 200 feet perpendicular height. . . . It extends into the earth about 300 feet, branching into subordinate caverns." The largest of these caverns is Cathedral Hall, which is 280 feet long and more than 70 feet high, making it one of the largest cavern rooms on the East Coast.

The caverns were put to recreational use in 1836, when the owners opened the Grand Ballroom chamber for use as a dance hall. Tourists could view all the caverns on one day each year, when each room was lighted with candles. During the Civil War, Stonewall Jackson's troops camped in the caverns, and just like tourists through the ages, they wrote their names on the walls. By 1889, permanent lighting was installed.

To reach Grand Caverns Regional Park, turn right at Dogwood Avenue (Route 825) just past the softball field as you enter town. The caverns are open daily from April through October and on weekends in March. Tours run every half-hour and last an hour. The park has campgrounds, a swimming pool, hiking and biking trails, playgrounds, and picnic shelters. Call the Upper Valley Regional Park Authority (see the appendix) for more information.

To continue into Grottoes from the caverns, turn around and follow Dogwood Avenue across Route 256. The gridlike layout, with numbered streets intersecting avenues named for trees, reflects the grand plans the town's founders had for it during its heyday in the 1890s.

For a short time, business prospects looked promising. Besides the tourist appeal of the caverns, the area was rich in mineral deposits and iron ore. The railroad also made it a convenient shipping point for the many agricultural products that this part of the Valley produced in the late 1800s. Grottoes grew after a group of investors (including Jedediah Hotchkiss, mentioned earlier in this tour) organized the Grottoes Company of the Shenandoah in 1888. Like land developers elsewhere in the Valley at the time, they hoped to establish a thriving new city. They improved the caverns, built a large hotel (which burned to the ground after just four years of operation), and planned factories. Their dream for Shendun (their new name for the town) included a 30-mile-long streetcar system that would use mules for power. The first leg of the line began running in 1892. A year later, the company went into receivership.

The boom went bust for various reasons: the panic of 1893, rapidly declining land values, the abandonment of plans for an east-west railway, and the discovery of cheaper-to-mine iron ore in Minnesota. By 1912, the town's population dropped to about half its 1891 high of 709. That same year, the townsfolk took back their old name of Grottoes.

Route 663, which runs east out of Grottoes up into the Blue Ridge, was the original part of the old Brown's Gap Turnpike, the most direct route between Harrisonburg and Charlottesville in the early 1800s and an important route from the Valley over the mountains into eastern Virginia during the Civil War. The turnpike was closed when Shenandoah National Park was created.

Harnsberger House

Turn left off Dogwood Avenue on to 14th Street. Go all the way to the end, to Holly Avenue, and turn right at the yield sign. Almost immediately on the left is an octagonal house built in 1856 by Stephen Harnsberger, a member of the Harnsberger family mentioned earlier. The home is listed in the Virginia Landmarks Register. Harnsberger based it on a plan he found in an 1853 book on octagonal houses, which were something of a fad in the mid-1800s. It's now a restored private home.

To continue the tour, return to Dogwood Avenue (Route 825 East) and turn left. You'll reach **Port Republic** *in about 1 mile. At the stop sign, turn left on to Route 659 (Port Republic Road).*

After you cross the South River bridge just after the turn, you'll see the Port Republic Museum, located in the Frank Kemper Home (also known as the Turner Ashby House), the small tan frame house with green shutters at the corner of Port Republic Road and Water Street. The house has been turned into a museum by area volunteers and is open on Sunday afternoons. It is listed with the Virginia Landmarks Commission and is on the National Register of Historic Places.

The body of beloved Confederate general Turner Ashby was brought to this house after he was killed during a skirmish with Union troops at Chestnut Ridge, southeast of Harrisonburg. His death occurred shortly after his horse was shot from under him; without hesitation, he continued to lead his men on foot and was soon killed by enemy fire. General Stonewall Jackson and others are said to have come to this house to pay their last respects. (A monument to Ashby is located near the site of his death, off Port Republic Road a short distance before it intersects I-81 in Harrisonburg.)

Port Republic Museum

Across Port Republic Road from the museum, on the other side of Water Street, is Bradburn Memorial Park, where you can have a picnic lunch along the South River and see the area where much of the original town stood. It was here that Union forces forded the river to invade the town in 1862.

The area around Port Republic has attracted settlement for at least 300 years. Shawnee Indians are said to have lived here in the early 1700s. A German immigrant named Jacob Stover received an 800-acre tract of land from the king of England in 1733 that included the area that later became Port Republic. As was the practice in those days, land grants were issued on the condition that the grantee settle a certain number of families on the land within a given period. Although the story was never proven, local wags of the day claimed that Stover, after failing to meet this requirement and not wanting to lose the land, gave fictitious human names to each of his horses, cows, hogs, and dogs, and even a few chickens. He supposedly drew up a report that designated these animals as heads of households and sent it to the king. The grant was approved, after which Stover divided the land into small parcels and sold them.

Today, Port Republic retains an old-time feeling. Its layout remains much as it was in 1802, and its streets are lined with houses spanning three centuries. A pamphlet describing a walking tour of the town is available at the Port Republic Museum; copies are kept in the small mailbox near the front door when the museum is closed.

From the park, drive west to the end of Water Street. Turn right, go one block to Main Street, and turn left. Go a short distance and turn right on to Route 605. Madison Hall once stood on the site now occupied by the

---

1916 Victorian-style farmhouse you'll see on Route 605. Madison Hall was built here in 1751. It originally belonged to John Madison, a cousin of President James Madison. John Madison's son, James, was the first Episcopal bishop in Virginia and was president of William and Mary College for many years.

During the Civil War, Stonewall Jackson used Madison Hall as a temporary headquarters during the Battles of Cross Keys and Port Republic. Traveling along what is now U.S. 11, Jackson arrived in the Port Republic area in June 1862 after winning important battles in Front Royal and Winchester. At the time, he was being pursued by two Union armies, one led by General John C. Frémont and the other by General James Shields.

While staying at Madison Hall, Jackson barely escaped enemy capture. He had planned to attend church on Sunday morning, June 8, 1862, but around eight o'clock, the sound of guns and cannons announced the presence of Union cavalry, who had crossed the South River into town. Jackson found himself separated from his army by the raging North River, swollen by recent spring rains. He and several of his staff officers made a mad

A Shenandoah River Port

Today, little is left of the once-bustling river port of Port Republic, partly because of General Sheridan's campaign of destruction in the Valley during 1864 and partly because of two destructive floods in the 1870s.

Port Republic was established in 1802. After the South Fork of the Shenandoah was made navigable, the town began to grow in the 1820s and 1830s. The boats that merchants used had flat bottoms that curved up at each end. They were called floatboats or gundalows—most certainly after the Italian word *gondola*—and were constructed of heavy timbers. They carried lumber, iron ore, flour, and other items downriver—meaning northward on the Shenandoah—to Harpers Ferry, from where they could be transported down the Potomac River and the C & O Canal to Georgetown and Alexandria. Because the boats could not make the return trip against the current, they were broken

apart and sold as lumber. It is said that much of the town of Harpers Ferry was built of wood scavenged from these boats.

It took some clever navigating to get the boats north. Prominent Valley historian John Wayland recorded in *The History of Rockingham County* how the boats were moved down the Shenandoah, a river that is shallow and quite rocky in places: "The floatboats used were made of heavy undressed lumber, and were guided by rudders at each end. At the dams in the river, next to the shore, chutes were placed, constructed of strong timber, for the passage of the boats. When the rise in the river was sufficient, the boats would go over the dam."

The boats measured about nine feet wide by 80 to 90 feet long. They could carry up to 12 tons of iron, 12,000 feet of lumber, or 110 barrels of flour—if the water was high enough. The boatmen were paid from 14 to 18 dollars to make the dash on horseback across the river's covered bridge, attracting enemy fire as they ran. When they came out the other side, they found themselves face to face with Federal troops. Some members of his staff were captured, but Jackson somehow was able to rejoin his troops. Later that day, the Confederates regained the town.

On that same harrowing day, Richard Ewell, one of Jackson's generals, and his 5,000 men defeated General Frémont's army of 10,000 at Cross Keys, 4 miles northwest of here.

That night and early into the next day, June 9, Jackson moved most of his army to a location called "The Coaling" above the Shenandoah River east of town. This was an area used to burn wood for making charcoal, which was the fuel for the local iron furnaces. Union general Shields had placed a division of men to hold that strategic spot high above the surrounding fields, while waiting for Frémont to move his troops there from Cross Keys.

Jackson knew he had to capture the hill before Frémont's troops arrived. During heavy fighting that morning, the Union lost and then rewon the

trip; after reaching Harpers Ferry, they had to walk home. One report noted that a typical trip took five to seven days—three or four days on the boat, then two or three days to walk back. The fact that it took less time to walk the route reveals something about the difficulties involved in navigation.

Wayland's book contains an eyewitness report of a local man who, as a boy in the late 1800s, watched the boats on the Shenandoah near Luray:

> We got in sight just in time to see the first boat go thro, strike a great rock, split in twain, and the whole cargo of pigiron went to the bottom. Each boat was manned by six men, and when the boat broke those on it were carried to such deep water that they had to swim. There were 18 boats in this fleet, and soon the men began to wade in and gather the iron together in a pile. The broken boat was taken to the bank and repaired, reloaded, and started on its way again. . . .

Nearly all the boats were provided with tin horns about 8 feet long, and when they would start from the stations on the River, all would blow. War songs were the favorite tunes, and the music they made would make your hair stand on end. These horns could be heard for 5 miles.

Floatboats were a common sight on many parts of the Shenandoah and North Rivers throughout much of the 1800s (see The Natural Bridge to Lexington Tour, pages 198–200). Early town names revealed the importance of river trade: Bridgewater, on the North River, was once Bridgeport; Timberville, on the North Fork of the Shenandoah, was first known as Williamsport.

The days of flatboats on the Shenandoah came to an end by 1890; they were put out of business by the growing network of railroads in the Valley.

hill twice before the Confederates managed to take it for good. By the time Frémont's army arrived, Jackson's troops were in an advantageous position to deal with them. The fighting began shortly after daybreak, and by ten-thirty that morning, the bloody battle was over. Federal casualties totaled 1,100 and Confederate casualties 1,000.

In the end, the victorious Confederates chased the Federals to Elkton, to the north. The Battle of Port Republic was the last engagement in Jackson's brilliant Valley Campaign, during which he successfully diverted Union forces from other parts of the state and from taking the Confederate capital of Richmond.

Retrace your route to the park. To visit the Port Republic Battlefield at "The Coaling," turn right on to Route 659, go across the bridge the way you came into town, and drive 1.4 miles to the intersection with U.S. 340 (East Side High-way). Turn left and drive 1.1 miles, where you'll see a battlefield marker on the left side of the road. Continue 1 mile to the brown historical-site road sign near U.S. 340's intersection with Route 708; turn right after the sign on to Route 708 (Ore Bank Road).

A stone marker sits in a parking area just below a white frame church. To the left is a self-guided walking trail through the battlefield. The trail goes up a fairly steep hillside maintained by the Blue and Gray Education Society and the Association for the Preservation of Civil War Sites.

When you are ready to leave "The Coaling," follow Route 708 across Route 340; stay on Route 708, which becomes Lynnwood Road. Continue 0.5 mile to Lynnwood, located just past the railroad crossing and set far back from the road on the right. This white-painted-brick mansion was built by the son of the original landowner, Thomas Lewis, in 1812. Lewis's earlier white frame home was George Washington's destination on the night of September 30, 1784, after he spent the day riding 40 miles through the Valley from Brock's Gap (see The Edinburg to Singers Glen to Mount Jackson Tour, page 107).

Lewis bought the surrounding 530 acres (much it part of the Stover grant mentioned earlier) from a Pennsylvanian named Christopher Franciscus in 1751. He named the house after his mother, Margaret Lynn Lewis. Lewis was one of four distinguished sons of John Lewis, the early Scots-Irish Valley settler and founder of Staunton. Thomas Lewis worked with Peter Jefferson (Thomas Jefferson's father) to survey the Lord Fairfax grant in the

1750s. In 1788, he became the first surveyor of Rockingham County.

Continue a short distance up the road and across the Shenandoah River bridge to another historic mansion, Bogota. This beautiful English-style white-painted brick home sits behind a stand of pine trees on a bluff on the right. It was built in the mid-1840s by Jacob Strayer, who for reasons unknown named it for the city in South America. In 1862, the Strayer family watched the Battle of Port Republic from the balcony. Clara Strayer, the 19-year-old daughter of the owner, recorded her impressions of the battle, which soon descended on the house itself:

Bogota

> A rifle shell passed about 15 feet from the southwest corner of this house, another fell through the roof of a cabin on the upper edge of the orchard, within two feet of old Uncle Daniel who had been on the retired list. He yelled lustily, being more scared than hurt as the shell did not explode. . . .
>
> They next came to the house in search of Rebels. . . . [Union soldiers] poured in every door, and such clanking of sabers, ransacking of presses, trying to break open doors, I never saw. They came into our chamber, when I remarked, "This is a lady's chamber and as such will be respected by *gentlemen*." The leader, a big bluffy Dutchman [the local term for German immigrants], replied, "Yah, yah! If dere be any Dutch gentlemen! Come boys, let's go to town!"

This property was originally purchased in 1751 by Gabriel Jones, a descendant of settlers from Wales who was born in Williamsburg and educated in London. Jones built a house just a few hundred feet south of where Bogota stands now. When Rockingham County was created in 1777, Jones was named deputy attorney for the county; he had served as the head of the Augusta County Court since 1746. George Washington dined with Jones here as he passed through the area in 1784.

Continue 0.5 mile on Route 708 until it meets Route 655 (Lawyer Road, named after Jones by the local people because it was the route he took on his frequent trips to court in Harrisonburg). Turn left, drive 2.2 miles to Route 659 (Port Republic Road), and turn right. Heading north, you'll pass much of the area where the Battle of Cross Keys took place. In about 1.9 miles, look for a large barn on the left; if you think you see a camel among the farm animals, be

---

Cross Keys Tavern

The Geology of Massanutten Mountain

Past Cross Keys, the tour passes the southern end of Massanutten Mountain, which divides the Shenandoah Valley for 50 miles from Strasburg south to this point. Massanutten Mountain is geologically quite different from both the Blue Ridge to the east and the Alleghenies to the west. Unlike those mountains, the Massanutten range is composed of hard, slow-to-erode sandstone, the remnant of a huge sand shoal that lay beneath the ancient Iapetus Sea, which covered the Valley some 430 million years ago.

assured that you are not imagining things. About 1 mile past the barn, you'll see an antique shop on the right. In 0.2 mile, turn left on Route 848 (Artillery Road). After 2 miles, Route 848 intersects Route 276 (Keezletown Road). Turn right. This is the village of **Cross Keys**. *To see the falling-down old tavern that gave the town its name, turn left just after the Cross Keys town sign.*

The tavern, or what's left of it, stands behind a school-bus parts and supply store. The structure was built around 1800 and served as a post office, then as a store run by the Rodham Kemper family from 1823 to 1845. Like so many homes and buildings in the area, it was used as a hospital during the Civil War. A member of the Kemper family says the name came from an old bookstore in London; the sign above the tavern door probably bore a picture of two keys crossed.

Return to Route 276 and continue north. The southern end of the Massanutten range, named Peaked Mountain by early surveyor Peter Jefferson, will come into view on the right.

Local legend holds that gold was buried on Peaked Mountain by a wealthy early settler who then returned to Germany. In the early 1800s, treasure hunters tore up the side of the mountain searching for it.

One day, the story goes, a local Irish tailor decided to take advantage of the treasure hunters. He told them he had recently traveled to Ohio, where he had visited a factory that made spyglasses that could look into the earth. Having noticed their lack of success, he offered to return to Ohio and purchase one of those helpful instruments for them—with their money, of course. They pooled their resources and sent the tailor to Ohio. A few months later, he returned. He said he had bought a wonderful spyglass but had lost it, along with most of his possessions, while crossing a swift-running creek. When he offered to go back for another one, the trusting locals once again came up with the required amount. This time, the tailor left the area and was never heard from again.

Continue 1 mile to the traffic light at the intersection with Port Republic Road. Less than 0.5 mile later, you will pass Meadow View Farm, on the left. This red-brick house with white trim was built by Edward Kemper in 1870. He was not the first to enjoy this picturesque spot, though. For hundreds of years, Indians traveling through the Valley camped here, as evidenced by the many arrowheads that have been uncovered in the surrounding fields. A house stood on the property as early as 1745. One of the land's early owners, John Stephenson, built a horse-racing track across the road around 1780. It is thought to have been the first west of the Blue Ridge.

Continue 1.8 miles past Meadow View Farm to **Peales Crossroads**, *where Route 276 meets U.S. 33.* The old red-brick house on the right was built by Jonathan Peale in 1844; the Peales acquired the land in 1811, having come here from England by way of Pennsylvania. This home may have been used as a headquarters by Stonewall Jackson before the Battle of Cross Keys. Mrs. Peale used to tell stories about entertaining Jackson and his staff during the war; she claimed that she once fed and housed 60 men here. The house was the center of the community's social activities for many years, but by the 1930s, it had been converted into a guesthouse. Today, it is a private home.

Turn left off Route 276 on to U.S. 33. It is 1.6 miles to the turnoff for **Massanetta Springs**, *on the left.* These hot springs were originally owned by the Taylor brothers, Jonathon and William, who bought the land in 1814. The property has been owned by many others since. In 1888, it was purchased by Dr. Burke Chrisman, who owned a mineral water company. He named the springs Massanetta, combining his wife's name, Henrietta, with Massanutten. He bottled the water from the springs and sold it throughout the East as a cure for various ailments. The water's popularity brought people to the springs, so Chrisman constructed a small hotel to accommodate them. A later owner built a large brick hotel and turned the grounds into a popular summer resort. Since 1922, the property has been owned by the Presbyterian synod of Virginia; it is used as a national Bible conference center.

Continue for about 3 miles on U.S. 33 to I-81 in Harrisonburg, where the tour ends.

Peaked Mountain

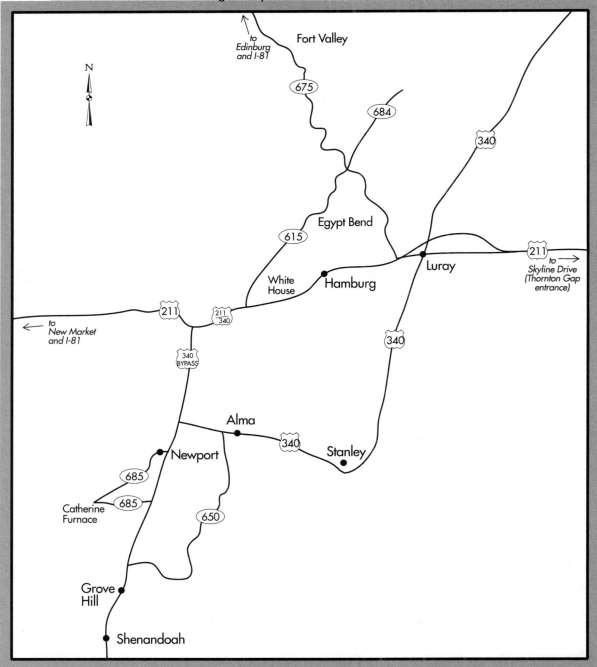

The Massanutten Mountain-Page Valley Tour

The Massanutten Mountain–Page Valley Tour

This tour begins by climbing the western range of Massanutten Mountain near Edinburg and descending into Fort Valley at Kings Crossing. In a few miles, the road traverses the eastern range of Massanutten and then descends into Page Valley and the town of Luray.

Page Valley was one of the earliest settled areas in the Shenandoah Valley—by Late Woodland Indians around 950 A.D. (and probably by Paleo-Indians thousands of years earlier), then by Swiss and German immigrants in the early 1700s. If you've ever stood along the Skyline Drive overlooks near Loft Mountain or Big Meadows and faced west, then you've seen Page Valley. Two of the first Europeans to reach the top of the Blue Ridge and look west did so from near those same spots.

The tour visits a Civil War site, the ruins of an old iron furnace, and the 1800s industrial town of Shenandoah before ending with a scenic drive along the Shenandoah River.

Total mileage:
Approximately 60 miles

To begin the tour, take Exit 279 off I-81 and turn on to Route 185 East toward **Edinburg** at the bottom of the ramp. Drive 1 mile to the stop sign at Main Street. Turn left on to U.S. 11 North and go through the town (described in The Edinburg to Singers Glen to Mount Jackson Tour, pages 99–101). Just after you pass the car dealership on the edge of town, turn right on to Route 675 (Edinburg Gap Road), following the signs toward Kings Crossing, Fort Valley, and Camp Roosevelt.

The road crosses the North Fork of the Shenandoah River and then winds through Edinburg Gap (and George Washington National Forest) over the western ridge of Massanutten Mountain. It soon descends into Fort Valley, a scenic and secluded "valley within a valley," the northern part of which is covered in The Strasburg to Fort Valley to Front Royal Tour. This tour passes through Fort Valley's southern section on the way to yet another valley within the larger Shenandoah Valley—Page Valley, bordered by the Massanutten range on the west and the Blue Ridge on the east.

In 5.4 miles, Route 675 intersects Route 678 (Fort Valley Road) at **Kings Crossing**. Turn right toward Luray and follow the signs to Camp Roosevelt. The road forks almost immediately after the turn; keep to the left to stay on Route 675, now called Camp Roosevelt Road. In 3.4 miles, past the signs for Camp Caroline Furnace, the road meets Moreland Gap Road and curves sharply to the left. Be sure to veer left to stay on Route 675. The entrance to Camp Roosevelt is up the road a short distance on the left.

No one can be sure which family or families first settled the Shenandoah Valley, because no written records have survived—or perhaps were ever made—of their arrival. Historians often point to a German immigrant named Adam Miller (Mueller) from the Rhineland town of Schriesheim (near Heidelberg) as the first settler for whom proof can be established. His request for citizenship, dated March 1741, stated that he had lived in the Valley for 15 years, which puts the year of his arrival at 1726 or 1727. Miller lived near what is now Bear Lithia, south of the town of Shenandoah and just north of Elkton. Settlers apparently arrived in the Luray area about the same time.

The land here was extremely attractive to settlers because it was ready-made for planting—the Indians had long ago done the hard work of clearing the fertile Massanutten fields of trees, brush, and rocks.

This was the first of 1,500 Civilian Conservation Corps camps established in the United States in the 1930s. During the Depression, the federal government created the CCC with two aims in mind: to provide paying jobs for unemployed young men and to restore and conserve dwindling national-forest resources. During that decade, the CCC built roads, blazed trails, planted trees, controlled erosion, and developed recreation areas and parks, including Shenandoah National Park. Today at Camp Roosevelt, you can see the foundations of that first CCC camp. A campground, a picnic area (with toilets), and hiking trails are available to visitors.

From Camp Roosevelt, continue on Route 675 as it begins to climb the eastern range of Massanutten Mountain. In about 1.5 miles, you'll be treated to panoramic views of Page Valley below. As the road levels off, you'll reach a stop sign at the intersection where Route 615 (Egypt Bend Road) goes to the right and Route 675 (now called Fort Valley Road) goes to the left. Turn left, go 0.4 mile, then turn right, continuing on Route 675 across the Bixler's Ferry bridge toward Luray.

The land along the Shenandoah River in Page Valley was one of the earliest settled areas in the Shenandoah Valley. Around 1726 or 1727, Jacob Stover, a Swiss immigrant, was granted several thousand acres here and began to sell tracts to Swiss and German settlers who came from the Lancaster, Pennsylvania, area. Most were Mennonites or Lutherans. Originally known as the Massanutten Patent, this land grant stretched 10 miles up and down the Shenandoah River from near what is now Luray.

South of the Bixler's Ferry bridge is an area along the river called Egypt Bend. One of the early settlers, Abraham Strickler, called this land Egypt, apparently comparing the settlers' flight to Virginia from religious persecution in both Europe and Pennsylvania to the Israelites' flight to Egypt. The surnames of other early settlers—which can still be seen on area mailboxes and businesses—include Miller (Anglicized from Mueller), Long, Kauffman, Burner, Brubaker, and Ruffner.

For many years, these early settlers faced the prospect of surprise Indian attacks. A tragic tale is told of a man named John Roads (later spelled Rhodes). Roads was a Swiss Mennonite minister whose family lived peacefully in a log cabin beside a river bend near here for more than 30 years. One day in August 1766—three years after the official end of the French and Indian War—eight Indians and "a worthless villain of a white man" (as described by 19th-century Valley historian Samuel Kercheval) came looking for the family's hidden money.

The attackers shot and killed the reverend and his wife immediately. They also brutally murdered several of the couple's children. One of the family's older daughters grabbed her toddler sister and escaped by running to safety at a neighbor's house. One son was kidnapped by the Indians but managed to return to the Valley about three years later. The attackers never found the money, which was stashed in a cellar wall, so they set the home on fire before they left.

Mimslyn Inn

One of the family's grandsons later built a log-and-stone house on the site using some of the charred timbers from the original structure. That home, called Fort Rhodes, survived well into the 20th century, only to burn down several years ago.

After crossing the Bixler's Ferry bridge over the Shenandoah River, you'll enter the outskirts of **Luray***.* To the right just across the bridge, in a field beyond the Shenandoah River Inn (which once served as a stagecoach stop), is the Old Stone House, also called the Daniel Strickler House; the Old Stone House is difficult to see from the road. Built around 1790 by Abraham Heiston, it was later purchased by Daniel Strickler, a descendant of one of the early settlers. It remained in the Strickler family for many years. Compared to the typical log houses of the time, this stone structure was a substantial and impressive home.

Aventine Hall

Three miles past the bridge, the road crosses over U.S. 211. In another 0.5 mile, turn right on to Lee Street, then go 2 blocks to the stop sign at Main Street and turn left. Directly across Main Street before you turn is the Mimslyn Inn, a 1931 brick building on 14 acres. It is not the first structure to stand on this hill. Aventine Hall was built here in 1852 by Peter Bock Borst, the commonwealth attorney for Page County at the time. During the Civil War, soldiers were housed in Aventine Hall. In the 1920s, it was the main building of Luray College. After the Mimslyn Inn was built, Aventine Hall was taken apart and reassembled a few blocks away, where it stands today.

To see this unusual old home, go one block to Main Street and turn right on to South Court Street. The house is at 143 South Court, on the left past the Page County Courthouse and partially hidden behind the tall shrubs lining the

Page County Courthouse

street. Aventine Hall was named for one of Rome's seven hills and was built without nails; every piece of wood in the house was mortised and pinned with pegs. Marble mantels from Italy top the seven fireplaces in the house. It remains a private home and is listed on both the National Register of Historic Places and the Virginia Landmarks Register.

The Page County Courthouse, which you passed on the way to Aventine Hall, was constructed in 1833 by the same men who built the University of Virginia for Thomas Jefferson.

Beginning in the late 1700s, area citizens lobbied the Virginia legislature to form a new county. For years, they had to cross Massanutten Mountain (as this tour did, but on roads that were nothing more than rough trails) to get to Woodstock, the county seat of the then-much-larger Shenandoah County. It took awhile, but 20 years after town founders optimistically laid out the new town of Luray to serve as the county seat, the assembly finally agreed, naming the new county for former Virginia governor John Page.

The county administrative building, located directly across the street from the courthouse, was built as Luray High School in 1880 and was one of the early public high schools in Virginia.

No one is sure how the town came to be called Luray. One theory is that the name was derived from the Indian word—Anglicized as Lorrain—for Hawksbill Creek, which runs through the town. Another suggests that the grandfather of one of the town founders, William Staige Marye, came to America from Normandy, which has a village named Luray. The most amusing theory is that the town was named after early lot owner Lou Ramey, a well-known blacksmith. But records show that the town had already been named several months before Ramey bought property here. The best thing about this theory is that it explains the local pronunciation of the town's name—"Loo-ray."

Return to Main Street and turn right to pass through the downtown area. Several local buildings date to the 1800s. The Luray Visitor Information Center is on the right past the traffic light at the intersection with U.S. 340.

Continue east on Main Street. Cross the railroad tracks, go past the large cemetery on the right, and prepare to turn right at the next traffic light. The Barbee Confederate Monument, dedicated in 1898, is ahead and to the right. Well-known sculptor Herbert Barbee was born in Luray, the son of William Randolph Barbee, a famous sculptor of the 1800s. Herbert, following in his father's footsteps, studied art in Florence, Italy. He later established studios in New York, Baltimore, St. Louis, Cincinnati, and Washington, D.C. The soldier depicted in the monument is standing next to a wall made of stone, a symbolic reference to the beloved Stonewall Jackson.

Barbee Confederate Monument

At the light, turn right on to Reservoir Avenue, then make an immediate right turn on to First Street. Continue on First until it intersects Luray Avenue across from Luray High School. Turn right on Luray Avenue. At the stop sign at Amiss Avenue, turn right again. In two blocks, turn left at the stop sign at Cave Street. Turn left again at the next street, Zerkel Street.

The log building to the left of the Page Public Library is a restored one-room schoolhouse. Known as the Massanutten School, it was moved to this location in 1972 and restored by the Page County Heritage Association. It contains 16 original desks, an old cast-iron stove, an 1880 schoolhouse bell, and other historical objects and photos. Check with the Luray Visitor Information Center for hours of operation.

Inn Lawn Park, across the street from the library, was originally the grounds of the massive (153 feet by 160 feet) Luray Inn, constructed in 1883 by the Luray Cave and Hotel Company. It was a grand place built in the English Tudor style, designed to lodge the hundreds of tourists who came by train from Eastern cities to view the Luray Caverns. Like so many of the other Valley hotels of the time, it burned to the ground, in 1891.

Massanutten School

Luray's growth as a town took off with the coming of the railroad and the discovery and development of Luray Caverns west of town in the early 1880s. But an economic depression hit the nation in 1884, and by 1885, the Shenandoah Valley Railroad (which began running in 1867 and eventually connected Hagerstown, Maryland, with Roanoke, Virginia) went bankrupt. It was auctioned off in 1890. Its 238 miles of track, 48 locomotives, 29 passenger cars, and 961 freight cars were purchased by the Norfolk and Western Railroad.

The town's railroad station was located across the street from the inn. If you look behind the old schoolhouse, you can see the now-abandoned passenger terminal building, for years a hub of activity as horse-drawn coaches met tourists and took them across town to the caverns.

Return to Cave Street and turn left; you'll pass Luray's second statue to Confederate soldiers. Turn right at the yield sign (this is U.S. 340, although it is not marked as such), then turn left at the traffic light on to Main Street. As you pass out of the downtown area, Main Street becomes U.S. 211 West. On the edge of town, you'll see a large stone tower on the right. Turn right on Northcott Drive. This is the Luray Singing Tower, which houses a carillon containing 47 bells that are played using a keyboard.

Carillons are popular instruments in Europe, where they originated more than 400 years ago; the bells for the Luray carillon were cast in England. The largest bell weighs more than 7,000 pounds and the smallest just 12.5 pounds. The tower was built as a memorial to Belle Brown Northcott by her husband, T. C. Northcott, and their daughter in 1937. Recitals are given on weekend afternoons during the fall and spring and on weekend evenings in the summer.

Colonel Northcott was born in Virginia but later moved to Illinois, where he served in the Union army. He bought Luray Caverns in 1900 and moved to town. He built a home he called Limeair on the grounds of the caverns. Northcott came up with the idea of cooling the house in the summer by bringing in the 54-degree air from the caverns, making Limeair by some accounts the first "air-conditioned" home in America. It burned down in 1940, and Northcott died at age 97 a year later.

Proceed to the entrance of Luray Caverns.

The caverns were discovered in 1878 by Andrew Campbell, a local tradesman, and Benton Stebbins, a 50-year-old man from Maryland who had recently arrived in Luray seeking a new home for his photography business.

As Russell Gurnee relates in his 1978 book, *Discovery of Luray Caverns, Virginia*, Stebbins had learned about an underground cavern in Cave Hill, on the edge of town. Knowing that the railroad was going to come through Luray, he wondered about the possibility of developing it into a tourist attraction. He became acquainted with Campbell, who felt that the known cave was too small for development. They began to look for a bigger and better cave and after a few weeks of intense searching found the huge underground complex they named Luray Caverns.

They kept their discovery quiet until they could buy the land above the caverns—coincidentally, land that was about to be auctioned by the county

Luray Singing Tower

TOURING THE SHENANDOAH VALLEY BACKROADS

to pay the debts of the current owner. Successful in their bid, Stebbins, Campbell, and their partners immediately began illuminating and building trails, floors, and stairs in the caverns, all the while admitting visitors to help finance development. Tourists began arriving in large numbers within the year, thanks to the publicity that began appearing in newspapers and magazines in New York and elsewhere.

Representatives of the Smithsonian Institution visited the caverns in 1880 and included in their report this statement: "It is safe to say there is probably no cave in the world today more completely and profusely decorated with stalactitic and stalagmitic ornamentation than that of Luray." That endorsement alone soon put Luray on the map.

While the development of Luray Caverns continued, the previous owner of the property, William Biedler, became painfully aware of what he had lost. He brought a lawsuit against Stebbins and Campbell, stating that the sale was fraudulent, since they had prior knowledge of the existence of the caverns.

In 1879, the case came before the county court, which ruled in favor of Stebbins and Campbell. Biedler then appealed to the state supreme court in Richmond, which two years later overturned the lower court's decision, giving the land back to Biedler. Biedler paid off his debtors and wasted no time in selling the property to a company that built the Luray Inn.

Stebbins and Campbell were left with nothing for their three years of investment and hard work. Campbell remained at the caverns as a tour guide, but Stebbins moved his family to the nearby town of Stanley, then called Marksville. There, he spent the remaining years of his life futilely attempting to develop an ocher mine (ocher was in demand as an ingredient in paint) and later a copper mine. Both endeavors failed. Stebbins died in Stanley in 1906.

Luray and several other caverns in the Shenandoah Valley proved to be popular tourist attractions throughout the 1900s, thanks first to the railroads and later to automobile travel; way back in 1925, for example, Luray Caverns had about 100,000 visitors.

From Luray Caverns, continue west on U.S. 211. In 1.6 miles, turn right on to Route 766 directly across from the Parkhurst Inn. You will soon enter **Hamburg**. Most of this town's early residents were Mennonites from Switzerland and Germany.

Old gazebo in Hamburg

On the right a short distance down the road is an old log structure, Mauck's Meeting House, originally called Union Church. Built around 1770, it has been restored by the Page County Heritage Association and is a National Historic Landmark. The tin roof is a later addition, having replaced the original chestnut shingles.

Across the street from the meeting house is Calendine, a house built around 1852 by Townsend Young, who operated a general store and post office here. Calendine was later purchased by William Barbee, the sculptor mentioned earlier, who used the general store as his studio. The structure now houses a museum operated by the Page County Heritage Association.

Return to U.S. 211 and turn right. In 1.3 miles, you will see a Virginia Civil War Trails roadside monument in a small parking area on the right. The historical marker commemorates the Shenandoah River bridge and the old structure known as the White House, located to the right of the bridge just beyond the farmhouse.

The bridge across the Shenandoah here has long been known as White House Bridge. Confederate general Stonewall Jackson and his army crossed the bridge on May 21, 1862, on their way to Strasburg to try to outflank

Mauck's Meeting House

General Banks's troops. Two days later, Jackson defeated Banks in Front Royal and then turned south to escape the Federal forces pursuing him—General Shields, who was coming down Page Valley, and General Frémont, who was heading down the Valley Pike to the west.

The White House

To prevent the two Union forces from meeting in the main part of the Valley, Jackson ordered Turner Ashby to burn the bridges over the Shenandoah (which at the time was rising because of heavy rainfall) at the White House and at Columbia Mills near Alma, just east of here. The Confederates carried out the burnings early on the morning of June 2. With the bridges gone, Shields's troops were delayed in crossing Massanutten Mountain and uniting with Frémont. As a result, Jackson was able to defeat Shields and Frémont in separate battles in early June at Cross Keys and Port Republic (see The Harrisonburg to Port Republic Tour, pages 138–40).

Historians believe the White House was built in 1760 by Martin Kauffman II—the son of one of the area's first settlers—as a residence and Mennonite meeting house. Both Kauffman and his father were Mennonite ministers. Many of the Mennonites in this area became Baptists by the end of the 1700s, largely due to the efforts of the Reverend John Koontz of Front Royal. Martin Kauffman II was one of Koontz's early converts; he became a Baptist minister. One of Kauffman's 10 children, Martin III, later accompanied several members of White House Church to Ohio, where they established a Baptist church in the early 1800s.

Continue driving west. In 0.6 mile, look on the right side of the road for a 1929 monument to the early Massanutten settlers. Follow U.S. 211 West for another 2.3 miles, then turn left on to U.S. 340 South. The area along U.S. 340 was another part of the original Massanutten settlement. In later years, this road was known as the New Market and Gordonsville Turnpike, which cut through Fishers Gap to connect eastern and western Virginia in this part of the state.

Monument to Massanutten settlers

Continue 4 miles to the village of **Newport**. *Turn right on to Route 685 just before Kite's Store.* This road leads through an area of old barns, smokehouses, and springhouses to the once-bustling Catherine Furnace. Kite's Store, a general store, service station, and camp store (for the popular riverside campground across the street) has operated at this location since 1929 and is an area landmark.

The story of the many iron furnaces near the Shenandoah River can be traced back to George Washington, who had the river surveyed to determine its suitability for commercial navigation. His plan was to build a gun factory at Harpers Ferry, to which pig iron could be shipped by Shenandoah River flatboats (also called floatboats or gundalows). Eventually, the river was cleared, dredged, and opened to commercial boating. The people of the Valley at last had a better and faster way of getting local products to and from markets to the east, via Harpers Ferry and the C & O Canal. During the mid-1800s, pig iron from Catherine Furnace, Shenandoah Iron Works, and other iron furnaces and forges was among the materials being shipped to Harpers Ferry.

In 2.2 miles, Route 685 curves sharply to the left. To reach Catherine Furnace, stay straight and go down the unpaved road marked "Katherine Furnace Road" (a misspelling). In less than 0.5 mile, you'll see the ruins of the furnace to the right, across a low concrete bridge over Cub Run, a scenic trout stream.

Catherine Furnace was built by brothers Daniel and Henry Forrer around 1836; they apparently named it after their mother. The stone structure that remains on the site was just one part of a large complex of structures and machinery needed to operate the furnace. A bridge connected the top of the furnace to the top of the hillside above it. Workers would dump iron

Catherine Furnace

ore (mined less than a mile away), limestone (in plentiful supply throughout the Valley), and charcoal (made by burning timber, also plentiful) into the top of the fiery furnace. The resulting product was large blocks of pig iron, which were then taken to a forge for shaping into nails, horseshoes, tools, kettles, and other products.

It is said that Catherine Furnace produced metal used to make ammunition for the war with Mexico in the 1840s; two decades later, it provided iron for the Confederacy during the Civil War. About the same time, the Forrers built a complex of structures called Shenandoah Iron Works just down the road in what was to become known as Shenandoah City.

Return to Route 685 (Newport Road) and turn right. In a little over 1 mile, the road meets U.S. 340 South; turn right again. As you approach the town of **Shenandoah**, *which is 4.5 miles away, you will pass through the community of Grove Hill. Shortly after you pass St. Peter's Lutheran Church in Shenandoah, turn right on to Virginia Avenue, following the sign to the business district. At the bottom of the hill, turn left on to First Street.*

The business district sign is an overstatement today. Although several nice residential areas surround the town, the "downtown" section of Shenandoah is virtually a ghost town, with just a handful of businesses lining the streets. Most buildings are boarded up. But at its peak in the late 1800s, this community was a major rail and industrial center—and the largest town in Page County.

In 1866, the Forrers sold their businesses to William Milnes and his partners, who were coal operators from Pennsylvania. In 1870, the growing town and the ironworks had to be rebuilt after a devastating flood that wiped out 60 commercial buildings and numerous homes.

Around that same time, Milnes began working with other Valley investors to bring a railroad through the area. When the line that would eventually extend through the Valley to Roanoke was finally begun in Hagerstown in 1880, Milnes borrowed money to expand his ironworks and build what he called the Shenandoah Iron, Lumber, Mining, and Manufacturing Company.

The Shenandoah Valley Railroad arrived in town in 1881. The next year, the enormous Gem Furnace was built. The site had 24 boilers and a brick stack rising 100 feet. This furnace—fueled by the more efficient coke—produced over 100 tons of iron a day and employed up to 400 people, far exceeding the 40-person, 10-ton-a-day Catherine Furnace.

In 1882, the town's name was changed to Milnes; some citizens admiringly called it "the Pittsburgh of the Valley." But the town's prosperity was short-lived. The depression of 1884 caused William Milnes's business to go into receivership. By 1885, the Shenandoah Valley Railroad also failed.

The town of Milnes—later renamed Shenandoah City—recovered during the boom years of the early 1890s, like so many other towns in the Valley. By that time, the offices of the Shenandoah Land and Improvement Company were bustling, buying up land and selling lots. People were optimistic—one citizen predicted that the town would one day have 10,000 residents. But by around 1905, the entire ironworks operation shut down, put out of business by the discovery of far richer iron deposits in Michigan.

The railroad helped keep the town on the map for the next four de-

The People of the Park

Beginning in the mid-1700s, people gradually began settling in the hollows, mountainsides, and ridges of what is now Shenandoah National Park. Some took refuge there to avoid military service for religious reasons during the American Revolution and the Civil War. Others were tenant families who tended cattle for Valley farmers who owned meadowland on top of the mountains.

In the years after the Civil War, life became difficult for these mountain families, and many began to leave. The area had been overlogged and overhunted, and large game was scarce. Families who operated water-powered mills at the base of the mountains were put out of business by steam-powered mills in the 1880s. After that, some residents began to sell tanbark to supply the tanneries in the Valley; others collected and sold bushels of chestnuts. But in the early 1900s, the chestnut blight began killing those grand old trees, and tanneries stopped using tanbark.

When Shenandoah National Park was established in 1935, about 465 families still resided within the park boundaries, and fewer than half owned the property they lived on. In an attempt to resettle these people, the federal government built seven communities outside the park, in which the families could buy farms below cost and with no money down. About 170 families eventually moved to those communities, one of which was Ida, a few miles east of Alma, south of Luray; in 1934, the government built 18 farms there. None of the original Ida families remains, although many of the homes are still there.

Only 43 people were allowed to live out their lives in the park; the last person to do so died in 1979.

cades. The yard at Shenandoah was located at the midpoint of the line between Hagerstown and Roanoke. Its engine repair shops and other operations employed more than 400 men during the first half of the 1900s, peaking during World War II.

When you reach the end of First Street, turn left on to Maryland Avenue. The unusual-looking house on the left at Second Street is Stevens Cottage, which is listed on the Virginia Landmarks Register. It was built in 1891 as offices for the Shenandoah Land and Improvement Company. The architect was William M. Poindexter, who also designed the state library in Richmond. When Shenandoah's boom went bust, the building was sold to two sisters, Mary and Edna Stevens. Mary Stevens was a much-loved schoolteacher here for 50 years; she died at the age of 93 in 1968. A relative sold the house to the Shenandoah Heritage Center in 1974.

Stevens Cottage

Continue up Maryland Avenue to the traffic light at U.S. 340, turn left, and retrace your route to **Grove Hill**. This area is the site of an Indian mound measuring 75 feet long and 20 feet wide, one of the many mounds found in Page County. The local farmer who discovered it unearthed 17 bodies that had been placed head to head like spokes in a wheel; tools and other artifacts were also found. The flood of 1870 uncovered between 200 and 300 fire beds near the river, evidence of an Indian village here.

An 1894 expedition by the Smithsonian Institution found 24 mounds and several village sites in Page County—far more than in any other county it had investigated in the Potomac and James River Valleys.

After you pass through Grove Hill, look for a small sign for Route 650 just before the Shenandoah River bridge. Turn right on to Route 650 (Grove Hill River Road).

This road follows the bends of the North Fork of the Shenandoah River, which is quite wide here, with rapids in places when the water is high. Vacation cottages line the hills above this peaceful tree-lined road. Portions of Shenandoah National Park extend almost to the river in places.

If you were to climb the mountains on the right side of the road, you would eventually arrive in the vicinity of Big Meadows in Shenandoah National Park. Just south of Big Meadows is Milam Gap. Some historians believe that it was the point where Governor Spotswood's first official expedition across the Blue Ridge descended into the Shenandoah Valley in 1716. Others think that he descended several miles south, at Swift Run

George Washington National Forest has a visitor center at the top of Massanutten Mountain on U.S. 211; the center is located 12 miles west of Luray at the top of New Market Gap. There, you can pick up a leaflet that describes several self-guided interpretive trails. The Discovery Trail, which begins at the center, is quite short—only 0.2 mile—and is wheelchair accessible. The 0.5-mile wildflower trail, which also begins at the center, follows Stonewall Jackson's route over New Market Gap and ends at a picnic area.

A short distance up the road from the center, off U.S. 211, is Forest Road 274 (which may not be marked as such but is the only road in the area leading off U.S. 211). This road, which soon becomes unpaved, passes the trailhead for the Massanutten Story Trail after about 1.5 miles. This trail is also suitable for wheelchairs.

Eight miles farther, Forest Road 274 passes the trailhead for the Lions Tale Trail. This 0.5-mile loop trail was specially designed for the blind and visually handicapped by the Lions Clubs of Virginia.

Forest Road 274 ends near Caroline Furnace at Route 675, which is the road you took through Fort Valley near the beginning of this tour.

Gap, where U.S. 33 crosses the Blue Ridge today. (Most historians agree, however, that Spotswood's party ascended the Blue Ridge from the east at Swift Run Gap.)

Alexander Spotswood, the Royal governor of the Virginia colony and a proponent of increased westward settlement, organized the trip to claim this unknown area for England. At that time, only a few Europeans had seen the wilderness on the other side of the mountains. The first to do so and record what he saw was John Lederer, a German physician and scholar sent to explore the area in 1669 by Governor William Berkeley. Lederer made three trips to the Blue Ridge and probably (based on his general descriptions) reached Big Meadows and Milam Gap. His last expedition took him to Chester Gap or Manassas Gap, near Front Royal.

Spotswood and 63 men, along with 74 horses, began their trip from Germanna, west of what is now Fredericksburg. When they discovered the Shenandoah River—which they described as wide, deep, and northward flowing—they named it the Euphrates. That evening, they set up camp on the riverbank and proceeded to celebrate their successful journey over the mountains. One of the men recorded the raucous evening in his journal:

> The governor buried a bottle with a paper enclosed on which he wrote that he took possession of the place in the name of and for King George the First of England. . . . We had a good dinner, and after it we got the men together and loaded all their arms, and we drank the King's health in champagne, and fired a volley, the Princess's health in Burgundy, and fired a volley, and the rest of the Royal family in claret, and a volley. We drank the Governor's health and fired another volley. We had several sorts of liquors, viz: Virginia red wine and white wine, Irish usquebaugh, brandy shrub, two sorts of rum, champagne, canary, cherry punch, water, cider, etc.

The men of this expedition later became known as the Knights of the Golden Horseshoe. Because of the rocky terrain they had to cross, horseshoes were needed to protect their horses' feet—a practice often not necessary in the soft soil of eastern Virginia. After the expedition, Governor Spotswood gave each man a small horseshoe made of gold and encrusted with jewels. The gifts were inscribed in Latin. "This will enable you to cross the mountains," was written on one side, and "Knights of the Golden Horseshoe" on the other.

Because the mountains were so difficult to cross, settlement from the east was slow for many years to come. But the route from the north was relatively flat and easy. That is why the Valley came to be inhabited by Swiss, German, and Scots-Irish immigrants from Pennsylvania. They followed the old Indian route that later developed into the Great Valley Road, one of the many names used for what is now U.S. 11.

*Route 650 passes through the hamlet of **Honeyville** before it ends at U.S. 340 Business just south of **Alma**. Turn left on Business 340 South at the stop sign.*

General Stonewall Jackson's army camped near Alma in June 1862 on its way to fight battles at Cross Keys and Port Republic to the south.

The area above the bridge near Alma was once known as Columbia Mills. In the mid-1800s it was a busy place. Traffic on the river here was bustling by 1868, when the local newspaper reported the following: "During the last week in February, 41 gondola boats passed Columbia Mills in different groups with the following freight: 8 boats with flour, 85 barrels each, 11 with lumber, 80,000 feet, . . . 22 with bloom and pig metal, ten tons each."

Columbia Mills was the site of a family tragedy during the disastrous Shenandoah River flood of 1870. Noah Kite (who operated the mills), his wife, and four of their children were swept away and drowned by some of the worst floodwaters the area has ever experienced.

*The tour ends here. Continue on U.S. 340 Business until you see the signs to U.S. 211. Turn right, which will put you on U.S. 340, and drive 2.8 miles to the intersection with U.S. 211. **To return to I-81**, turn left; this will take you across New Market Gap and into the town of New Market in about 7 miles. In New Market, follow the signs to I-81.*

***If you are returning to the Baltimore-Washington area, you have two options.** You can turn right on to U.S. 211/U.S. 340 North heading toward Luray; from Luray, continue on U.S. 211 East, which crosses Skyline Drive at Thornton Gap and then passes through Sperryville, Warrenton, and Gainesville, where it meets I-66 East. Or you can continue through Luray on U.S. 340 North to Front Royal, where it meets I-66 East.*

The Staunton to Steeles Tavern Tour

The Staunton to
Steeles Tavern Tour

This tour begins in Staunton, settled by Scots-Irish immigrants in the 1730s. Staunton has several attractions of historic interest, including the house where President Woodrow Wilson was born, several old schools and churches, many beautiful old homes, a restored historic wharf and railroad depot, and the Museum of American Frontier Culture. The tour continues to Waynesboro, an early Valley settlement that dates to the late 1700s. From there, it heads west, past the P. Buckley Moss Museum, through Stuarts Draft, and then south down one of the prettiest roads in the Valley through the 1800s towns of Middlebrook and Newport. It passes by an old working gristmill near Raphine before ending near Steeles Tavern at the Cyrus McCormick Farm.

Total mileage:
Approximately 70 miles

*The tour begins in **Staunton**. Take Exit 225 off I-81, marked "Woodrow Wilson Parkway/Staunton/Route 275," and stay to the right at the end of the ramp. Follow the signs for the historic downtown district. In 1.6 miles, turn left on to U.S. 11 South/Route 250 East.* After you turn on to U.S. 11, notice the large estate on the right side of the road. The lovely old home with four tall white columns is called Merrifield and is more than 200 years old.

In about 0.5 mile, the road splits; stay to the right on U.S. 11 South, following the signs toward the Woodrow Wilson Birthplace Museum. In another 0.7 mile, the road splits again; this time, stay to the left, following the signs for downtown Staunton. In about 1.5 miles, you'll begin to see the campus of Mary Baldwin College on the right; you'll pass the Woodrow Wilson Birthplace Museum another 0.4 mile down U.S. 11 (Coalter Street). Continue straight on Coalter Street past Beverley Street and Kalorama Street to Commerce Road at the bottom of the hill. Turn right. Go through two traffic lights. You are now on Johnson Street. You'll soon see a large parking lot on the left that charges tourist-friendly rates; park here.

Staunton (pronounced "Stanton") is one of the Valley's earliest towns. It was incorporated in 1761 on land that was part of a 1736 grant to William Beverley of Essex County, who called the tract Beverley Manor. He built a mill and a house here on the site of an old mansion called Kalorama.

Another of the town's fathers was Irish immigrant John Lewis, who moved from Pennsylvania with his family and settled near what is now Staunton in 1732. Lewis built a house called Bellefonte about 2 miles east of the

Mad Ann Bailey—whose nickname supposedly reflected her quick temper—came to the Staunton area from Liverpool, England, as an indentured servant in the mid-1700s. Her happy marriage to James Trotter at age 23 came to a sad end nine years later when Trotter was killed by Indians at the Battle of Point Pleasant. Leaving her only child in the care of others, Mad Ann began to scout against the Indians, promising to avenge her husband's death. She scandalized Valley settlers of the time by wearing men's clothes and living the life of a frontiersman. But she did make good on her promise—legend has it that she "put more than one Indian out of the way."

At the age of 49, she was still at it, saving the day for the besieged Fort Lee in what is now West Virginia. She rode her horse through Indian territory to Fort Union (now Lewisburg) to fetch needed gunpowder, then returned with it to Fort Lee.

For a time, she lived alone in a cabin near Falling Spring, where a plaque honors her memory today (see The Monterey to Hot Springs Tour, page 188).

present downtown area. He had four well-known sons. One of them, Thomas, later became the official surveyor for Augusta County and later for Rockingham County; in 1747, Thomas Lewis surveyed and platted Staunton. (For more about the patriotic Lewis family, see The Monterey to Hot Springs Tour, pages 183–84.)

Augusta County was formed in 1738 and named for Princess Augusta, the wife of Frederick, prince of Wales. At the time, Augusta County stretched westward to include parts of what are now Illinois, Indiana, Ohio, and Kentucky. In 1745, the first courthouse was built in the newly designated county seat, Staunton. The town is thought to have been named for Lady Rebecca Staunton, the wife of Royal Governor William Gooch.

By the 1790s, Staunton had grown to a town of 800 people and 200 dwellings. The first volunteer fire department in Virginia was created here in 1790. By the early 1800s, the development of roads in the area helped establish Staunton as a transportation hub. The first graded road in the county was the Staunton and James River Turnpike, which led to Scottsville on the James River south of Charlottesville; completed in 1824, it gave farmers an improved route to markets in the eastern part of the state. The Valley Pike—the macadamized version of the Great Philadelphia Wagon Road and the precursor of today's U.S. 11—connected Staunton to Winchester, 95 miles north, by 1840. Also around that time, construction began on the Staunton-Parkersburg Turnpike—what is now U.S. 250. Finally, the Middlebrook and Brownsburg Turnpike—parts of which followed what is now Route 252, traveled later in this tour—began carrying traffic in 1851.

Staunton also became an educational center. Its three schools for women—the Presbyterian-founded Augusta Female Seminary (later called Mary Baldwin College), the Episcopalian Virginia Female Institute (later called Stuart Hall School), and the Methodist Wesleyan Female Institute, which no longer exists—were founded in the 1840s with the goal of truly educating young women, not just serving as finishing schools.

By the Civil War, Staunton had grown to a town of 4,000 people, 400 houses, and 80 businesses. But when Union major general David Hunter took the town the day after the Union victory at the Battle of Piedmont in 1864, it was the beginning of the end for the Southern cause. While headquartered at the Virginia Hotel (which still stands), Hunter proceeded to

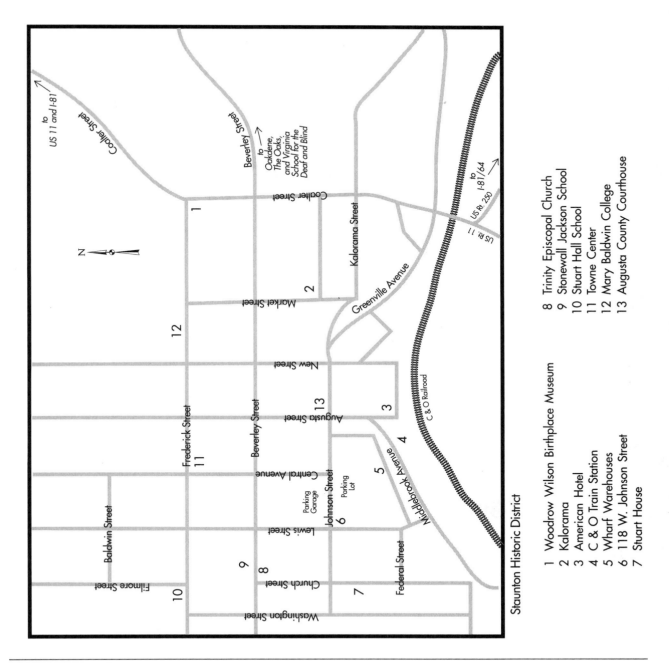

Staunton Historic District

1 Woodrow Wilson Birthplace Museum
2 Kalorama
3 American Hotel
4 C & O Train Station
5 Wharf Warehouses
6 118 W. Johnson Street
7 Stuart House
8 Trinity Episcopal Church
9 Stonewall Jackson School
10 Stuart Hall School
11 Towne Center
12 Mary Baldwin College
13 Augusta County Courthouse

destroy everything in Staunton that could help the Confederates, sparing only the area's charitable and educational institutions. The railroad station, shops, factories, mills, and foundries were turned to rubble.

The town recovered fairly quickly after the war, however. By the 1870s, a boom began that lasted until the bust of the 1890s. Staunton had streetcars (drawn by mules), an opera house, a YMCA, a public library, a municipal park, and a professional fire department.

Today, Staunton's compactness makes it a great town for a walking tour. An abbreviated tour is provided in the following paragraphs. For information on additional historic sites, pick up the free brochure entitled "The Walking Tours of Historic Staunton," available at the visitor center and in many of the shops and businesses in the downtown area; the visitor center offers free one-hour guided walking tours on Saturday mornings from June through October.

The walking tour begins at the historic wharf buildings, which face the public parking lot and Johnson Street. Most have been renovated and restored to their original appearance.

Behind the wharf area is Staunton's restored railroad station, which now houses shops, restaurants, and a modern Amtrak station. To get there, walk behind the wharf buildings down Augusta Street (located to your left as you face the wharf buildings from the parking lot). The coming of the Virginia Central Railroad in 1854 spurred the town's rapid growth.

Staunton Station

Return to the parking area on Johnson Street and turn left, continuing one block down Johnson to Church Street. Turn left. One of the oldest brick-and-stone homes in Staunton—and one of the first truly large homes in the Shenandoah Valley—is located at 120 Church Street. Built in 1791 by Judge Archibald Stuart, it is still home to members of the same family. After the Revolutionary War, Judge Stuart was a law student in Thomas Jefferson's office; some think this house was influenced by Jefferson's architectural preferences. It is said that Jefferson often visited here, as did Robert E. Lee. Stuart was the judge of the General Court of Virginia for 39 years.

Stuart House

Turn around and walk one block back up Church Street to Beverley Street to see the historic Trinity Episcopal Church. This 1855 building is the third church on the site. The first was built here in 1763; brick from the first church was used in the keystone of the present building. The church is worth a visit for both its historic value and its 13 Lewis Tiffany stained-glass windows. The Madonna-and-child window was signed by Tiffany himself. The cemetery at Trinity Episcopal has many old tombstones, the oldest of which marks the grave of Roger North, who died in 1776.

The original church building served as the meeting place for the Virginia General Assembly for two weeks in June 1781, after the members fled here to escape attack during the Revolutionary War. During the Civil War, the church once again served as a safe haven, this time for the Virginia Theological Seminary, whose students and teachers fled here from Alexandria.

Across Beverley Street from Trinity Episcopal Church is the unusual-looking Stonewall Jackson School. This building housed the city's first public school beginning around 1887 and now operates as a private school.

Stonewall Jackson School

Turn left off Church Street on to Beverley Street. After one block on Beverley, turn right on Washington Street. Walk one block to Frederick Street. Straight ahead is Stuart Hall School's "Old Main," at the corner of Frederick and Filmore Streets. This 1846 building was originally known as the Virginia Female Institute. Before the Civil War, two of Robert E. Lee's daughters went to school here; following the war, Lee served on the institute's board of trustees. In 1907, the school was renamed to honor its headmistress from 1880 to 1899, Flora Stuart, the widow of Civil War general J. E. B. Stuart.

Turn right on Frederick Street and walk three blocks to Augusta Street. The attractive brick building on the corner, now called Towne Centre, was built in 1914 as the town's YMCA, thanks to a generous donation from the estate of Cyrus McCormick, the man who invented the mechanical reaper. (McCormick's farm is visited later in this tour.)

Stuart Hall

Continue one block down Frederick Street to see the lovely main building of Mary Baldwin College, at the corner of Frederick and New Streets. This institution had its beginnings as the Augusta Female Seminary, a Presbyterian school, in 1842. An early graduate of the school was Staunton native Mary Julia Baldwin. Miss Baldwin, who came from a well-to-do local family, used her own money to start a free school for the town's poor children. She later became principal at the seminary. In the 1870s, the seminary became independent of the Presbyterian Church. Two years before Baldwin's death in 1897, it was renamed for her.

Mary Baldwin College

Woodrow Wilson Birthplace Museum

Continue down Frederick Street past Mary Baldwin College to the Woodrow Wilson Birthplace Museum, at the corner of Frederick and Coalter Streets; the Staunton Welcome Center is located behind the museum.

Woodrow Wilson, the nation's 28th president, was born in this house at 24 North Coalter in 1856. His father was the pastor of First Presbyterian Church at the time. The Wilson family had recently moved into this new house, which was built as the manse for the church. Wilson spent the first two years of his life here, until the family moved to Augusta, Georgia.

Wilson became president in 1912. Following World War I, he helped establish the League of Nations, the forerunner of the United Nations. The museum contains Wilson family photographs and possessions, including the president's Pierce-Arrow limousine. The house is a National Historic Landmark and has been owned by the Woodrow Wilson Birthplace Foundation since 1938. It is open daily.

Retrace your steps down Frederick Street for three blocks to Augusta Street; turn left on Augusta and walk two blocks to the Augusta County Courthouse, at the corner of Augusta and Johnson Streets. The first courthouse in Staunton, made of logs, was built on this site in 1745. This building, constructed in 1901, is the fifth to serve as the courthouse.

Turn right on Johnson Street and walk one block to the parking lot in the wharf area to conclude the walking tour. To leave Staunton, turn back down Johnson Street the way you came into town and proceed to the intersection of

The Stonewall Brigade Band

Still going strong today, the Stonewall Brigade Band had its beginnings as the Mountain Sax Horn Band in 1855; it changed its name after five of the band's members served in the Stonewall Brigade during the Civil War.

After the Confederate surrender, Union general Grant allowed the band members to keep their instruments, rather than forcing them to turn them over as spoils of war. Indebted to Grant after this kind act, the band later participated in his presidential inaugural parade as well as at the dedication of his tomb in New York City.

Today, Staunton claims that the Stonewall Brigade Band is the oldest continuously performing band in the nation. In the summer, the band gives free concerts on Monday evenings at Gypsy Hill Park, the lovely city park just west of the downtown area.

Commerce Road and Coalter Street. Turn right, pass under the railroad bridge, and make a left turn at the next light, following the signs for I-64 and U.S. 250 East. In 1.7 miles, you'll see the entrance to the Museum of American Frontier Culture on the right.

This unique museum consists of four representative farms—18th-century German, 19th-century Ulster Irish, 17th-century English, and 19th-century American—that provide a realistic look at the people who settled the Shenandoah Valley. Each farm features costumed interpreters who offer demonstrations and answer questions about the daily life of the place

The Oaks

Oakdene

Beverley Street

Beverley Street is Staunton's main shopping street, as you may have noted on the downtown walking tour. If you have time, you may want to venture a few blocks east of the shops and businesses, across Coalter Street, to Beverley Street's area of gracious old homes.

The home at 324 East Beverley once belonged to the engineer who built bridges for General Stonewall Jackson during the Civil War, Claiborne Rice Mason. The house was probably completed sometime before 1848. Mason was a self-taught engineer who worked on the C & O Railroad before the war. He was legendary for getting jobs done quickly. The story goes that General Jackson once told him that draftsmen were planning to work through the night to draw up plans for a bridge. The next morning, Jackson asked Mason if he had received the plans. Mason supposedly answered, "The bridge is finished. I don't know if the pictures are or not."

The Oaks, at 437 East Beverley, was once owned by Jedediah Hotchkiss, who served as General Jackson's mapmaker. Hotchkiss was a longtime educator who founded Mossy Creek Academy northwest of Staunton in the 1850s (see The Harrisonburg to Port Republic Tour, page 129). He added the unusual front portion to his house in 1888.

Oakdene, at 605 East Beverley, is an elaborate Victorian home built in 1893 by Virginia's lieutenant governor at the turn of the century, Edward Echols.

Across and just down the street from Oakdene is the Virginia School for the Deaf and Blind, which was established by the state legislature in 1838. The porticoed main building was completed in 1846. This school served as a military hospital during the Civil War; during that period, the students were moved to what is now Stuart Hall School.

and period. The authentic farmhouses were brought here from Germany, Ireland, England, and Botetourt County, Virginia, between the late 1980s and the mid-1990s. This open-air museum may be visited daily except Thanksgiving, Christmas, and New Year's. The visitor center has exhibits and a 15-minute film. To see the farms, you'll follow a self-guided walking tour that takes an hour and a half to two hours; motorized chairs are available for those who can't make the walk.

The old brick buildings you pass on the way into the museum grounds once belonged to Western State Hospital, which is now housed in newer facilities across the highway. In 1825, this became the second state mental hospital established by Virginia; the first was started in Williamsburg in 1773. The Staunton hospital was one of only five in the United States at the time.

From the museum entrance, continue on U.S. 250 East, passing under I-81. Although the tour does not visit it, one of the oldest churches in the Valley, Tinkling Springs Presbyterian, is located about 1.3 miles south of **Fishersville** on Route 608. The first log church was built there in 1748, by a congregation that was formed in 1741. The members shared their first

Irish farmhouse, Museum of American Frontier Culture

TOURING THE SHENANDOAH VALLEY BACKROADS

Folly Side Trip

Folly

Folly, one of the area's most interesting and little-mentioned old homes, is a short trip from downtown Staunton. Follow the directions for leaving Staunton presented in this chapter, but instead of turning left at the light on to U.S. 250 South, continue straight on U.S. 11 South after you pass under the railroad bridge. Drive almost 5 miles until you see a sign for a roadside table. The house is some distance from the road on the right side; pull over at the roadside table for a better view.

Folly was built between 1818 and 1820 by Joseph Smith, who was a planter, a member of the Virginia legislature, and the operator of nearby Folly Mills. The home remained in Smith's family for several generations. It features a brick serpentine garden wall that "is the only early 19th-century example of this unusual form in the state. Its prototype, Jefferson's walls at the University of Virginia, have been [re]built at least twice," according to the description of Folly in the Virginia Landmarks Register. The house itself, built in the Classical Revival style, is similar to those Jefferson designed; it appears that Smith borrowed some of Jefferson's ideas.

The house is also listed on the National Register of Historic Places; it remains a private residence.

pastor, John Craig, with the congregation of Augusta Stone Church at Fort Defiance (see The Harrisonburg to Port Republic Tour, page 133). Craig preached at Tinkling Springs on alternate Sundays.

It is about 9 miles from the Museum of American Frontier Culture to **Waynesboro**. This town is set against a backdrop of the Blue Ridge Mountains; in fact, the Appalachian Trail runs just above Waynesboro. The settlement was first called Teasville, after an early family, but it took the name of Waynesboro in 1797 in honor of Mad Anthony Wayne, a well-loved Revolutionary War general.

Continue straight on U.S. 250—now called Main Street—past several shopping centers. When you reach the intersection with U.S. Route 340 (a McDonald's is on the corner), continue straight through the traffic light to stay on Main Street. After you pass Waynesboro High School, look for the Plumb House at 1012 West Main.

This clapboard-over-log home was built around 1804. In 1820, it was purchased by Francis Plumb, a printer from England. It is the oldest wooden building in the city. Amazingly, it remained in the Plumb family until 1994, when it was purchased by the city. It is being restored and now houses a museum, open only on selected days. For information, call the Waynesboro–Augusta County Chamber of Commerce; the number is in the appendix.

During the Civil War, the Plumb House was in the middle of the Battle of Waynesboro. Union general Sheridan's forces defeated Jubal Early's troops—the last Confederate force left in the Valley—at the town in March 1865, just a month before the war ended. Early was outnumbered; many of his men had been sent to Petersburg to help General Lee.

Before you enter the downtown area, you'll pass the Shenandoah Valley Art Center, located on the right at 600 West Main. This nonprofit center, an affiliate of the Virginia Museum of Fine Arts, features exhibit galleries, a library, classrooms, and studios. It is open daily except Monday.

Another gallery, the Association of Virginia Artisans Fine Craft Gallery, is located at 327 West Main in the downtown area. It is open Tuesday through Saturday.

The Waynesboro Heritage Museum, housed in an old bank building on the corner of Main and Wayne Streets, offers a look at life in Waynesboro over the past two centuries. It is open daily except Monday and can provide visitors with a map and a walking-tour guide to the city.

Not much is left of Waynesboro's early days, the result of a devastating fire in 1861. The town's location at the junction of two railroads spurred its growth after the Civil War, and it became an industrial boom town in the 1890s. It has remained an industrial and agricultural center ever since.

A curious bit of local history concerns Basic City, located less than a mile from Waynesboro and now taken over by it. Basic City rocketed into existence in 1890, growing from a couple of buildings in January of that year to a town of 1,200 people eight months later. Plans were for the town to include a car works, a paper mill, a hardware factory, a match factory, a lumber and cola company, a brick works, an iron furnace, a large resort hotel, and other businesses. "Basic City will certainly absorb Waynesboro, and by so doing will surely bring them into one city in a short time," predicted one Valley historian a little too enthusiastically in 1891. He added that Waynesboro had "donned a garb of material growth . . . that caused the older people to wonder what the world was coming to."

Note that if you were to continue east on U.S. 250, you would reach I-64 east of town at Rockfish Gap, the main route over the Blue Ridge to Charlottesville, Richmond, and the Tidewater area. Rockfish Gap also marks the end of Skyline Drive and the beginning of the Blue Ridge Parkway.

To continue the tour, turn around at the end of the downtown area and go back up Main Street the way you came into town. In 1 mile, turn left at the traffic light on to U.S. 340, following the signs for U.S. 340 South and I-64. In about 1.2 miles, you'll pass a state historical marker for Walnut Grove, on the right. The old brick house just beyond the marker was the birthplace, in 1757, of Judge Archibald Stuart, the prominent Virginia judge who built Stuart House in Staunton, visited earlier in this tour. Walnut Grove belonged to Judge Stuart's grandfather.

About 1 mile from the marker, you'll cross I-64 and pass a factory outlet mall and the P. Buckley Moss Museum, on the left. Patricia Buckley Moss is a nationally known folk artist famous for her watercolor renditions of Valley life, in particular its rural scenes and Mennonite people.

About 1 mile past the I-64 interchange is a sign pointing left to Sherando Lake, a National Forest Service recreation area that offers boating, fishing, camping, and

Walnut Grove, Waynesboro

*picnicking. Continue south on U.S. 340 for 5 miles to the town of **Stuarts Draft**. About 6 miles past Stuarts Draft, U.S. 340 intersects I-81/I-64/U.S. 11. Turn right at the stop sign on to U.S. 11 North, following the signs toward Staunton. In 0.7 mile, turn left just before the high school on to Route 701 (Howardsville Road), following the sign to Middlebrook.*

This hilly road curves gently through a scenic area seldom traveled by tourists. It soon passes Bethel Church, on the right. The original Bethel Church, one of the early Presbyterian churches in the area, was built as a result of the efforts of Colonel Robert Doak around 1772. Like the members of the Tinkling Spring Presbyterian Church, mentioned earlier, many of the men who belonged to the Bethel congregation fought in the Revolutionary War. The Bethel Church men were commanded by Captain James Tate—one of the church's elders—in the Battles of Cowpens and Guilford Courthouse in 1781. Twenty-three soldiers from that war are buried in the graveyard here. The present church building was completed in 1888.

Across the road from the church is Bethel Green, a beautiful old red-brick farm home listed on the Virginia Landmarks Register. Bethel Green was built on land owned by the first settler in this area, Christian Bumgardner, who arrived in 1772. His grandson, James Bumgardner, a farmer and distillery owner, built this house in 1857. It is quite striking architecturally, with its unusual Jacobean-style enclosed chimneys and Gothic-style porches.

When you reach the stop sign at the intersection with Route 252, turn left and head 1.3 miles south to Middlebrook. Route 252 is one of the prettiest drives in the entire Shenandoah Valley. It passes rolling horse and dairy farms without a hint of modern civilization to mar the natural beauty and timeless feel of the landscape. This area was settled by Scots-Irish immigrants in the 1790s.

The town of **Middlebrook** seems preserved in time. It looks as it must have a century ago, when what is now Route 252 ceased to be a major road from Staunton to Lexington. The entire town has been designated a historic district in the Virginia Landmarks Register, which describes it as "one of the oldest rural villages in the region. . . . The rows of closely spaced dwellings and stores lining the main road maintain the character and scale of the village as it appeared during the height of its prosperity in the 1880s."

About 7 miles from Middlebrook, you will pass through another quaint 19th-century village, **Newport**, and then begin to wind through the hills, following the path of Moffatt's Creek. In 4 miles, look to the right for New Providence Presbyterian Church. This church was established in 1746. Its cemetery contains many interesting old headstones. The sign in front of the church notes that this was the birthplace of the Presbyterian synod of Virginia in 1788 and the location of one of the nation's first Sunday schools.

Old Mill near Newport

About 0.9 mile after the church, turn left on to Route 606 (Raphine Road). This road passes historic Wade's Mill, a restored, operating gristmill that sells its products to the public. The road then winds through the woods and past one of the Valley's well-regarded vineyards, Rockbridge Winery.

Continue 0.5 mile past the winery to the town of **Raphine**.

Wade's Mill

This village was named for the farm of James E. A. Gibbs, who was born near here. In 1856, Gibbs invented the chain-stitch sewing machine. Unlike the lock-stitch machine invented by Elias Howe, Gibbs's machine used only a single thread, which he believed created a stronger stitch. He went into partnership with a Philadelphia businessman named James Wilcox, who improved the machine and named it the Wilcox-Gibbs. Wilcox began to manufacture and sell the machine in 1859.

When the Civil War began two years later, Gibbs became an active supporter of the Confederate cause and paid little attention to his business venture up north. After the war, he found himself short of funds, so he returned to Philadelphia to see how Wilcox was doing. The story goes that Wilcox turned over $10,000—Gibbs's share of the earnings to that time, a huge amount in those days. One Rockbridge County historian reported that more than a million Wilcox-Gibbs sewing machines had been sold by the early 1900s.

After receiving his money, Gibbs returned to the Shenandoah Valley and improved his home, which he called Raphine, from the Greek word *raphis*, meaning "needle." A self-educated man, he used the money to build an impressive library and travel all over the world.

Leaving Raphine, mentally prepare yourself for a cold blast of reality as you approach the major truck stops surrounding the I-81 exit just ahead. Continue straight under I-81, staying on Route 606 East toward Steeles Tavern. In 0.5 mile, look for a sign on the left for the McCormick Farm; it says "Virginia Tech

Shenandoah Valley Agricultural Research and Extension Center, McCormick Farm." Turn left at this sign on to Route 937 (McCormick Farm Road). Drive past the old house and the farm buildings to the parking lot on the right behind the split-rail fence.

Walnut Grove, McCormick Farm

Cyrus Hall McCormick was born in 1809. He grew up in the brick house on this property, called Walnut Grove; the house is now used as offices by Virginia Tech. Cyrus's father, Robert, tried for years to invent an automatic reaping machine but never succeeded. Cyrus picked up the challenge as a young man. Working in a shop on the farm, he developed a prototype that he first publicly demonstrated—rather unsuccessfully—on a farm near Steeles Tavern, just up the road, in 1831. Eight years later, he was back with an improved model, which he demonstrated on a farm at Folly, south of Staunton.

In those days, farmers everywhere were still harvesting wheat and other grains using scythes and sickles, centuries-old tools. It was time-consuming, backbreaking work. The reaper that McCormick developed could cut and stack crops five times faster, a huge improvement that eventually made large-scale farming possible. Most historians agree that the full potential of the American Midwest—which was being settled at the time—could not have been realized without McCormick's "Virginia Reaper."

His first attempts to sell the reaper were discouraging. The biggest demand was from farms farther west—meaning across the Alleghenies—which made shipping a huge problem. In 1848, he decided to relocate his business to Chicago, then just a small town. McCormick proved to be a creative businessman. He was one of the first to extend credit to farmers and to use advertising to spread the word about his product. His company eventually grew to become International Harvester.

News of his labor-saving device spread throughout the world. McCormick's reaper won top honors at the Crystal Palace Exhibition in London in 1851; he was later awarded the Legion of Honor by Napoleon and similar recognition from the emperor of Austria. He was even elected to the French Academy. Historians cite the reaper as being important in providing Union troops with a supply of wheat from the Midwest during the Civil War. But in a broader sense, the reaper represented the first real breakthrough in agriculture since its beginnings 10,000 years earlier. Ultimately, it freed millions of people from life on the farm and allowed business and industry to develop at a more rapid pace.

McCormick Farm is a National Historic Landmark. Three buildings are open for view—a museum containing scale models of McCormick's reapers and audio recordings describing his life and inventions, a gristmill, and a blacksmith shop, all dating back to McCormick's days here. The farm is open daily; picnic tables and rest rooms are available.

The tour ends here. Return to Route 606 and turn right to reach Exit 205 off I-81; this exit is about 20 miles south of Staunton, where the tour began.

Cyrus McCormick farm

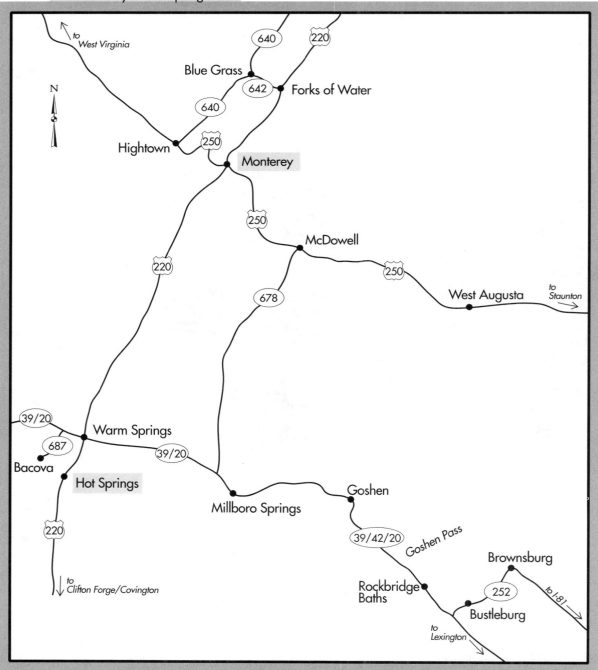

The Monterey to Hot Springs Tour

The Monterey to Hot Springs Tour

*The tour begins at Exit 225 off I-81 at **Staunton**, marked "Route 275 West/ Woodrow Wilson Parkway/Monterey." At the end of the exit ramp, go straight on Route 275 West. After 5.5 miles, turn right on to U.S. 250 West (Churchville Avenue) toward Monterey.*

About 3 miles down the road is a state historical marker. It notes that the last Indian raid in Augusta County took place near here in 1764, when a settler named John Tremble was killed.

*Continue on U.S. 250 West. It is about 1.5 miles to the town of **Churchville**, then about 2 miles to the small settlement of **Lone Fountain**. About 3.6 miles after passing Lone Fountain, the road enters George Washington National Forest and starts to climb over Jennings Gap. In another mile, look for the historic Buckhorn Inn on the right.* This building was once the well-known Buckhorn Tavern, known even earlier as the Dudley House. It dates to around 1811 and was a popular stop for visitors heading to the mineral springs resorts in Bath County.

Two of the tavern's guests in 1854 were Thomas J. Jackson, a professor at the Virginia Military Institute in Lexington, and his first wife, Elinor. Eight years later, Jackson passed by the Buckhorn Tavern again, but this time he was known as General Stonewall Jackson. He was leading his troops toward Mount Solon after their victory at the Battle of McDowell (described later in this tour). During the Civil War, the Buckhorn Tavern became a makeshift hospital; it later reopened as a tavern. Today, nearly 200 years after it

This tour ventures into some of the most beautiful and sparsely populated parts of the Shenandoah Valley. It is concentrated in two western counties—Highland and Bath, each of which has its own claim to a rural lifestyle. Bath County, home of famous mineral springs resorts, including the Homestead, has not a single traffic light—not even a blinking one, as its chamber of commerce proudly asserts. And Highland County is the least populous county east of the Mississippi, having many more sheep than people. The tour ends north of Lexington after passing through a dramatic mountain gorge at Goshen Pass.

Although lengthy in mileage, the tour can be completed in a day. For travelers who want to spend additional time in this mountainous and remote part of the Valley, several side trips to nature preserves and recreation areas are included.

Total mileage: Approximately 154 miles

Buckhorn Inn

began, the Buckhorn Inn offers food and lodging to travelers passing through the area.

U.S. 250 was originally the Staunton-Parkersburg Turnpike, the dream of a young surveyor named James Campbell, who did the preliminary work for its construction in 1822. The toll road was completed in 1838 by Claude Crozet, a French engineer and the first president of V.M.I.'s board of visitors. Crozet was also the mastermind behind the first railroad tunnels through the Blue Ridge, at Rockfish Gap.

After crossing two mountains and descending into the Highland County towns of McDowell and Monterey, U.S. 250 continues into West Virginia, where it traverses four more Allegheny ranges.

It is about 3.9 miles from the Buckhorn Inn to the hamlet of **West Augusta**. *About 4.4 miles past West Augusta, you'll see Mountain House Recreation Area on the right.* This is an entrance point to one of the most popular hiking and nature areas in this part of the Valley—Ramsey's Draft Wilderness Area. The wilderness area encompasses 6,500 acres, most of which is old-growth forest, a rarity in the eastern United States. Especially notable are its stands of virgin hemlocks, some of which are 1,000 years old. These can be seen about 4 miles into a 6-mile trail that runs to the peak of Hardscrabble Knob, which measures 4,282 feet in elevation.

After passing the recreation area, the road begins to climb Shenandoah Mountain (3,760 feet). The scenic overlook at the top of the mountain is worth a stop to take panoramic pictures of the scenery below and visit the ruins of Fort Edward Johnson. Confederate general Edward "Allegheny Ed" Johnson and his men built these fortifications in 1862 to discourage Union troops from invading the Shenandoah Valley from the west. A short loop trail—at points steep and rocky—takes visitors to the ruins; signs along the path tell the story of the fort's construction.

From here, the road descends into Highland County. It crosses the Cowpasture River and then climbs once more, this time over Bullpasture Mountain (3,240 feet). These names were already in use when the first deeds were applied for in the 1720s, and no one is sure of their origin. One story says that when drovers brought their cattle to the mountains for summer grazing, the calves needed to stop and rest at what was called the Calfpasture, the cows could make it to the Cowpasture before stopping, and the bulls

could go nonstop to the Bullpasture River. But it seems unlikely that any living thing could make it over two mountains to the Bullpasture River without resting. A more plausible theory suggests that the bulls, cows, and calves referred to were instead the original populations of woodland buffalo in the area.

The road then quickly descends into a valley, passing cottages and cabins tucked into the forest. Called "Virginia's Switzerland" by the local chamber of commerce, Highland County was formed in 1847 after the Staunton-Parkersburg Turnpike opened up the area. But even today, the highway has not spoiled what is still mostly farm country and wilderness. Three of the state's best trout-fishing rivers are in Highland County: the Cowpasture, the Bullpasture, and the Jackson. Three major Virginia rivers have their headwaters here: the James, the Jackson, and the south branch of the Potomac. And many hiking trails that cross scenic mountain streams are in George Washington National Forest, which occupies much of the county.

It is hard to believe that a county of only 3,000 people is just a morning's drive from the major population centers of the Mid-Atlantic region. More people lived in Highland County in the 1800s (about 4,000) than do today. That figure translates to a population density of about seven people per square mile. (In contrast, Washington, D.C., has about 9,000 people per square mile.) Highland County also has the highest mean elevation of any county east of the Mississippi River. There is no industry to speak of. The

McDowell store

main enterprise here is cattle and sheep production—there are more sheep than people—with a little maple syrup on the side.

The population grows dramatically for two weekends in mid-March each year, when Highland County's Maple Festival, held since 1958, draws folks from all around to watch maple syrup being made at the area's several sugar camps. Maple doughnuts (be prepared to wait in line for these) and pancake breakfasts are especially popular. The same trees that are tapped for syrup in the spring provide a blaze of yellow, red, and orange in mid-October, when the county holds its Hands and Heart Festival.

Continue on U.S. 250 West. It is 8.8 miles from the county line to **McDowell** *on the Bullpasture River, the first town you'll come to after descending Bullpasture Mountain.* This valley was settled around 1727, but the first land deeds were not recorded until the mid-1740s. In 1757, when the French and Indian War threatened area residents, they built the 80-foot-square Fort George on the Bullpasture River about 6 miles south of here on Route 678. It was never attacked by Indians, although a few arrows were shot in its direction.

As you enter McDowell, you'll see the red-brick Presbyterian church. Follow the road to the left of the church (Route 678) past the old school building that now houses the Stonewall Ruritan Club. The large field on your left is where the Battle of McDowell took place.

McDowell is best known for the Civil War battle fought here on May 8 and 9, 1862. After consulting with Robert E. Lee, General Stonewall Jackson received reinforcements from General Ewell and General Edward Johnson to try to keep the Union forces of Generals Frémont and Banks from joining up and threatening the Valley.

This battle, the second in the Valley Campaign, came after Jackson's only battlefield defeat, at Kernstown (near Winchester) in late March. Jackson left General Ewell behind in Elkton (then called Conrad's Store) and took his men to Staunton on a roundabout route to fool Union spies. There, he joined up with Johnson's troops. They crossed the mountains on May 5 and headed to McDowell the next day. Union general Milroy and about 6,000 men—a smaller force than the Confederates had—took the offensive, but Jackson prevailed, finally chasing Milroy across the mountains toward Franklin, West Virginia.

Turn around, return to U.S. 250 West, and turn left to continue into

McDowell. The town was named in 1860 for a governor of Virginia who often visited the area; it had previously been known as Crab Run and Sugar Tree Grove. Early settlers were primarily Scots-Irish, English, and German.

Continue about 9 miles down U.S. 250 to the county seat, **Monterey**. There was only one cabin here when Monterey was named the county seat of newly created Highland County in 1847; that cabin was promptly made the temporary courthouse. The town's population virtually exploded to 313 by 1861; today's population is 222. In the years after the Civil War, Monterey began to draw summer visitors seeking relief from city heat. By the early 1900s, it had three hotels.

Monterey

One of those hotels is still popular with city people today—the Highland Inn, a two-story white frame Victorian structure with long porches on both levels. You'll see it on your right as you enter town on Main Street. It was built in 1904 and has gone through a few major renovations since. The inn offers a restaurant and 17 guest rooms.

The town was named after Monterrey, Mexico, the site of a famous victory in 1846 by General Zachary Taylor. A popular hero of the Mexican War, Taylor was elected United States president in 1848. The town founders also liked the fact that *Monterey* means "kingly mountain" or "royal mountain" in Spanish, which seemed to fit this western Virginia setting.

Highland Inn

The Landmark House—the cabin that served as the county's temporary courthouse—is still standing on Main Street. The building also served as the village tavern.

Across the street from the Landmark House is the county courthouse. The first courthouse here burned down in 1947.

From the flashing traffic light at the town's main intersection, turn south on to

Blue Grass Valley Side Trip

Lovers of wildlife who have extra time to spend in this area's mountainous terrain might consider this scenic loop out of Monterey through the unspoiled landscape of the Blue Grass Valley. *Drive west on U.S. 250 out of Monterey and turn right at the intersection with Route 640 in Hightown. Follow Route 640 to Blue Grass, then take Route 642 to Forks of the Water. From there, follow U.S. 220 South to return to Monterey.*

Route 220, heading toward Warm Springs. In 0.3 mile, look on the left for the old log cabin that houses the Highland Maple Museum. This open-air structure gives visitors an idea of how maple syrup is made.

Across the road from the museum is a large hill known as Trimble's Knob, one of two extinct volcanoes in Virginia (the other is Mole Hill near Dayton, covered in The Harrisonburg to Port Republic Tour). Trimble's Knob blew its top about 50 million years ago.

*It's about a 40-minute drive through pastoral countryside to **Warm Springs**, the next stop on the tour.* Warm Springs is the seat of Bath County, which was formed in 1790 by dividing Augusta, Greenbrier, and Botetourt Counties. Named for its wealth of mineral springs baths, the major economic force here since the mid-1700s, Bath County has just 5,000 residents and proudly claims to have not a single traffic light—not even a flashing one.

Bath County's history is centered on its springs resorts. Today, only one of the many large-scale resort hotels that once thrived here still operates in

Highland Maple Museum

Laurel Fork Side Trip

Laurel Fork is a remote 10,000-acre special management area managed by the United States Forest Service. It contains a variety of plants and wildlife not usually found in Virginia, including 25 species that occur in the state only in this preserve. The wildflowers here are especially beautiful and profuse.

To reach Laurel Fork, take U.S. 250 West from Monterey to Hightown, then follow Route 640 to Blue Grass. At the intersection with Route 642 at Blue Grass, turn left. Drive 9 miles to Forest Road 457 and turn right. This route takes you over the mountains to the southern part of the special management area.

One of the Laurel Fork's 13 blazed trails, Buck Run, features cranberry bogs similar to those in Canada, as well as several beaver ponds. Most of the 28 miles of hiking trails run along the railroad tramlines loggers once used.

This area was the scene of intensive logging operations until the United States Forest Service purchased the land in 1922. The hardwood forests at Laurel Fork reach elevations of 4,000 feet and consist primarily of birch, cherry, maple, and beech.

Camping and picnic areas are available at Locust Springs Recreation Area in the northern part of Laurel Fork. Contact the Warm Springs Ranger District for more information; see the appendix.

a big way—the Homestead in Hot Springs, just 5 miles down the road from Warm Springs. (The other *grande dame* of area resorts, the Greenbrier—originally called White Sulphur Springs—is across the state line in West Virginia.)

Although many of the area's early residents played key roles in the Valley's beginnings and the nation's history, they fought their military battles elsewhere; no Revolutionary War or Civil War conflicts took place in Bath County. Even today, almost 90 percent of the county is covered by forests; more than half its land lies within George Washington National Forest.

The first person to own land here was John Lewis, who is considered the founder of Staunton. It is thought that his grandfather was a French Protestant who fled to Ireland in the 1600s to escape religious persecution. John Lewis came to America from Ireland in 1729, the story goes, for the not-so-lofty reason of avoiding arrest on a murder charge. Fifty years old at the time, he left Ireland in a hurry because he had killed his landlord in self-defense in a dispute over subleasing farmland. His tombstone in Staunton reads that he murdered his "Irish lord."

Lewis's Scottish-born wife, Margaret Lynn, and their children joined him in Lancaster County, Pennsylvania, three years later. Lewis then heard about the promise of fertile land in the Shenandoah Valley. In 1732, they began a journey south to start a new life.

Lewis bought about 2,000 acres in Augusta County and built his home, Bellefonte, in what is now Staunton. He was a leader in that county's affairs in the early days. After he died in 1761, his four sons—Thomas, Andrew, William, and Charles—continued to play important roles in shaping the history of the Shenandoah Valley.

Thomas Lewis, the oldest son, was a surveyor. With Peter Jefferson (the president's father), he created some of the early maps of Virginia. Together, they surveyed the Fairfax Line, an important task because it determined the southern reaches of Lord Fairfax's massive landholdings. In the late 1730s, Thomas, his brother Andrew, and three men in eastern Virginia were granted 30,000 acres to survey and sell in the Cowpasture Valley, most of which lies in what is now Bath County. Thomas Lewis went on to become Augusta County's first official surveyor and one of its original magistrates. He later became an important figure in Rockingham County and built a home that

Shenandoah Valley history is full of stories—perhaps embroidered over the years, perhaps not—of tough times and tough women. One of these stories describes a surprise Indian attack on a farmer as he worked outside his log cabin near Fort Lewis in the 1750s. As he ran for the safety of his home, a flying tomahawk struck his head. His wife pulled him into the house and put him to bed.

When the attacking Indians tried to enter the cabin, the woman quickly bolted the door and threatened them with a gun. Like the wolf in the story of the three little pigs, the Indians decided to come down the chimney. The woman quickly pulled the straw mattress from beneath her husband and threw it on the smoldering fire. The resulting clouds of smoke confused the Indians in their descent, whereupon the brave woman—the story goes—tomahawked them as they fell to the floor.

still stands near Port Republic (see The Harrisonburg to Port Republic Tour, pages 161–62). He called that home Lynnwood, after his mother.

Andrew Lewis was also a surveyor. In the process of surveying Bath County, he selected for himself the land that included Hot Springs and Warm Springs. For a while, he served in the Virginia House of Burgesses, representing the newly created Botetourt County, but he soon became involved in fighting Indians. In 1774, he led the American forces to victory at the Battle of Point Pleasant, considered by some historians to be the first battle of the American Revolution. Later, during the Revolution, he was credited with driving the despised Lord Dunmore—Virginia's Royal governor—out to sea.

The third Lewis brother, William, developed a tract of land in the Sweet Springs area (south of Covington) beginning in 1792.

The youngest brother, Charles—the only Lewis son born in America—became a captain in the Virginia militia and gained a reputation as a brave and effective Indian fighter. In 1762, he and his wife built a home and began a large farm on the Cowpasture River in Bath County; that tract was the location of a small stockaded fort that Charles had commanded in the 1750s. They called their home Fort Lewis. (Virginia has posted a historical marker for Fort Lewis on Route 220 a little more than halfway between Monterey and Warm Springs; it notes that the fort was located 7 miles to the east.) In a family tragedy, Charles was killed during the opening shots of the Battle of Point Pleasant, while serving under the command of his older brother Andrew; he was 38 years old.

In those dangerous early days, many Valley homes were designed to serve as "forts" for area residents. A house could serve as a fort if, for example, it had few or no windows, had slits cut into its cellar walls through which rifles could be fired, had only one door, and was built near or over springs to guarantee a water supply in case of extended attack. But stockaded forts proved to be more effective, since they allowed the pioneers to defend themselves from all sides. Indians rarely attacked stockades. Instead, they often took a more subtle approach, camping out around the fort and preventing supplies from reaching the occupants in an attempt to starve them out.

After passing an old dairy barn on the left and then the Three Hills Inn, you'll enter Warm Springs. Continue straight on U.S. 220 past the intersection with

Route 39. On the right just beyond the intersection are the Warm Springs Baths, also known as the Jefferson Pools.

Three Hills Inn

It appears that the Indians who traveled through this area knew about these springs and used them for years. Here is what one European visitor had to say about them in 1750: "We visited the hot springs and found six invalids there. The spring is very clear and warmer than new milk." By the 1760s, when the area was relatively safe from Indian attack, well-to-do families from eastern Virginia began spending the summer months in the cool, mosquito-free mountains of the Shenandoah Valley.

Now owned by the Homestead Resort, the bathhouses at Warm Springs—one for men and one for women—are as old, if not older, than they look. The round building on the right was built in 1836 as the women's bathhouse. It's 50 feet across and can hold 60,000 gallons of 96-degree water. The men's bathroom, the building on the right, dates to 1761, making it one of the oldest spa buildings in existence anywhere; it is smaller, at 40 feet in diameter. Both bathhouses are still in use.

Jefferson Pools

Thomas Jefferson wrote about Warm Springs and Hot Springs in his only book, *Notes on the State of Virginia*, published in 1787:

> The Warm spring issues with a very bold stream, sufficient to work a grist-mill, and to keep the waters of its bason . . . at the vital warmth, viz. 96 degrees of Fahrenheit's thermometer. . . . The Hot spring is about six miles from the Warm, is much smaller, and has been so hot as to have boiled an egg. Some believed its degree of heat to be lessened. It raises the mercury in Fahrenheit's thermometer to 112 degrees. . . . It sometimes relieves where the Warm spring fails. . . . These waters are very much resorted to in spite of a total want of accommodation for the sick.

Jefferson enjoyed coming here from Charlottesville in his later years. In 1818, at the age of 75, he stayed for three weeks, taking three baths a day—much to his later regret. In a letter to General James Breckenridge that accompanied Jefferson's architectural drawings of the Botetourt County Courthouse, he mentioned that "the use of the waters of the Warm Springs began to affect me unfavorably. [My] sufferings, aggravated by the torment of the journey home over rocks and mountains I had to pass, had reduced

Warm Springs Inn

me to the lowest state of exhaustion by the time I got back."

Across the street from the bathhouses is the Warm Springs Inn. The original Warm Springs resort buildings—a two-story hotel, cottages, and stables—stood on these grounds. The main building of the present inn served as the county's first courthouse from 1792 until 1907; an annex to that building housed the jail and the sheriff's residence.

This area, dominated by the springs, was the center of social and political life in Warm Springs for more than a century. The original hotel, bought by the Homestead Resort in the 1890s, closed in 1924, but the springs remained open, and several smaller lodging places opened to accommodate summer guests.

One of those inns was the mansion of Mary Johnston, a well-known novelist in her day. When her writing career began to falter—because of her outspoken views on women's rights—she had to start taking paying guests for extra cash. (For more about this interesting woman, see The Fincastle to Buchanan Tour, pages 228.) After her death in 1936, one of her sisters continued to run the inn for several years. Today, it operates as the Three Hills Inn, which offers a beautiful view of the mountains from its front gardens.

The original Warm Springs Hotel—much more rustic than fancy—was run for many years by a genial host named John Fry. It is said he personally greeted arriving guests, entertained them with jokes and anecdotes, helped serve the food at mealtimes, organized dancing after dinner, and in general made everyone feel at home.

To get here, guests had to endure a long ride by stagecoach over rough, steep roads—imagine today's Route 39 and U. S. 220 as unpaved nightmares, especially after a heavy rain. In *The Springs of Virginia, 1775–1900*, Perceval Reniers described the final leg of the journey: "Standing on his high-pillared portico, Colonel John Fry, the happy landlord of the Warm, could see each stagecoach as it appeared in the gap of the mountain up on the sky line. It stopped there to rest the horses, pay toll at the gate, and let the passengers get the view. Then it tipped its weight toward the valley, and with one wheel chain-locked raced down the dizzy, zig-zag mile until it pulled up at Colonel Fry's feet, every passenger dithering from fright."

Reniers wrote that Fry would see off his guests on their traditional tour of the other springs resorts with his favorite bad joke: "Go, said he, and get well charged at the White Sulphur, well salted at the Salt, well sweetened at the Sweet, well boiled at the Hot and then let them return to him and he would Fry them."

After the Civil War, General Robert E. Lee and his wife were frequent guests at Warm Springs. At the time, the Lees lived in Lexington, where the general served as president of Washington College (now Washington and Lee University). Their last surviving child, Mary Custis Lee, who was a great-granddaughter of Martha Washington, also came here but was a more frequent guest at the Homestead, where she died in 1918.

Continue 1 mile past the Warm Springs Baths and turn right on to Route 619, following the signs to the Warm Springs Courthouse. While the Warm Springs resort thrived in the 1800s, the nearby village of Germantown (thought to be settled by former Hessian prisoners of war who remained in America after fighting as mercenaries for the British during the Revolution) was becoming a sort of suburb to the springs. It had a mill, a tavern, stores, and a few log homes.

Bath County Library

Today, that pretty mountain town *is* Warm Springs. The mill has been restored to serve as a restaurant and inn, the classically designed old bank building is the town's library, and the "new" courthouse (built in 1913) sits in the center of town. Most of the old homes have been restored. The Bath County Historical Museum, open weekdays except in winter, is housed in an old cottagelike office building to the right of the courthouse and features a genealogical research library.

Drive past the courthouse and turn right on to Old Mill Road. The mill—now restored and operated as the Inn at Gristmill Square—is on the right at the end of street. Turn right on to Route 692 beyond the mill. You'll pass Anderson Cottage and several other old homes, some of which served as guesthouses (Anderson Cottage still does).

Route 692 intersects Route 39 East. Turn right, go to the stop sign, and turn on to U.S. 220 South, toward Covington. If this road looks familiar, it is; the tour has just completed a circle. The road passes the Garth Newel (Welsh for "new house") Music Center in about 3 miles. The center was started by two musicians as a nonprofit organization offering weekend chamber music concerts.

Inn at Gristmill Square

Bacova/Hidden Valley Side Trip

If time permits, you may want to take a short drive to see the old company town of Bacova and Hidden Valley Recreation Area, located along the Jackson River.

From Route 39 west of Warm Springs, turn left on to Route 687 to reach Bacova. This community began as a company town for a logging company in the early 1900s. The company ceased operations here in 1931. In the 1940s, the owners sold the town to private investors, giving its forestland (or what was left of it) to the United States Forest Service.

Malcolm Hirsh spent his childhood summers nearby. In 1957, he bought the town and began restoring the 42 employee cottages and other buildings. By 1965, he began a cottage industry called Bacova Guild, which produced household items—mailboxes in particular—made of laminated fiberglass and featuring wildlife scenes. (As you drive through Bath County, you'll see these mailboxes at the end of almost every rural driveway.) Hirsh sold the company in 1981. The name Bacova, by the way, was derived from letters in BAth COunty VirginiA.

The road to Hidden Valley—Route 621—is to the right off Route 39 West past the cutoff to Bacova. The 1992 film *Sommersby*, starring Jodie Foster and Richard Gere as a couple in the years after the Civil War, was filmed in the Hidden Valley area and in Lexington. The historic 1851 home featured in the film, Warwickton Mansion, now operates as the Hidden Valley Inn; it is owned by the United States Forest Service but is leased to the inn's operators on a long-term basis.

U.S. 220 enters the Homestead Resort in less than 2 miles. One of the resort's well-known golf courses lines both sides of the road here. The road curves around the back of the main part of the resort, past the village of **Hot Springs**, *and to the resort's main entrance, on the left.*

For more than 100 years, the hotel at Hot Springs was the smallest of the three springs resorts in the area. It was popular among people who were seeking relief from physical ailments. The first hotel on what are now the grounds of the Homestead was erected in 1766 by Thomas Bullitt, on 300 acres of land he owned with Andrew Lewis. Bullitt later died fighting in the American Revolution. The hotel operation hobbled along until the 1830s, when it was bought by a physician, Thomas Goode, who believed strongly in the healing powers of the springs. He built a larger and more modern hotel in 1846 but died eight years later. The next owner added a two-story structure that was 222 feet long and could accommodate 120 guests. During the Civil War, that hotel—like almost every other one in the Valley—was used as a hospital by both sides.

As the economy slowly recovered after the Civil War, mineral springs resorts in Virginia began to increase in popularity, both as places of summer retreat and as social, business, and political gathering spots. Seeing an opportunity to increase traffic on the Chesapeake and Ohio Railroad, M. E. Ingalls, its president, brought together a group of investors in the early 1890s to buy several hundred acres that included Hot Springs, Warm Springs, and Healing Springs (an old resort a few miles south of Hot Springs, now called the Cascade Inn). Their plan was to modernize and enlarge the hotel at Hot Springs, which had been called the Homestead since Thomas Bullitt's time. It was then that today's Homestead was born, patterned after luxurious European spas. And Ingalls made sure the resort was easy to get to—in 1892, the C & O railroad was extended from Covington to Hot Springs.

The Homestead

The Homestead's distinctive main building was built in 1902 after a fire a year earlier destroyed the recently renovated and enlarged wooden hotel building. The tower portion was added in 1929 as part of an ongoing expansion. Some of the resort's earlier structures still stand. The Virginia Hotel, located on U.S. 220 as you wind past the town and toward the main entrance to the resort, houses offices and shops today but was once an elegant turn-of-the-century hotel. The Homestead's shops and a café/bakery, now called Cottage Row, are on the left past the Virginia Hotel. Built as guest cottages in the 1800s, they survived the 1901 fire and were converted to their present use in 1984.

Cascades Golf Course Clubhouse

The Homestead's popularity continued even into the Depression years, but World War II caused some disruptions. For three months in 1942, some 363 members of the Japanese diplomatic corps were detained here while an exchange for United States diplomats was being negotiated. After the war, ski slopes and an airport were added. The resort was owned and operated by the Ingalls family until 1993.

From the Homestead, turn around and head back to Warm Springs on U.S. 220. After 5.6 miles, turn right on to Route 39 East. This road passes a turnoff for Douthat State Park, which offers a 30-acre lake, a restaurant, boating, swimming, picnic areas, and campgrounds.

Continue a few miles down Route 39 (which skirts the Cowpasture River) to Windy Cove Presbyterian Church. This church was organized by Scots-Irish settlers in 1749. The first church here was made of logs and is said to have burned down during an Indian attack in the 1750s. A second church, also log, was built north of the present church in 1766. In 1838, this third structure was built.

Falling Spring Side Trip

Falling Spring—described by Thomas Jefferson as "the only remarkable Cascade in this country"—is about 11 miles south of the Homestead on U.S. 220. The Falling Spring Gorge Scenic Lookout is on the right about 0.3 mile past the intersection with Route 640.

A small bronze plaque memorializing Mad Ann Bailey is mounted on a boulder across the street from the lookout (see The Staunton to Steeles Tavern Tour, page 162, for more about Mad Ann). Falling Spring is a 200-foot waterfall. As Jefferson noted, it can't compare with Niagara Falls in volume, but it is at least 50 to 80 feet higher.

On your way to Falling Spring, you'll pass the Cascade Inn, built sometime before 1856 and originally operated as the Healing Springs resort. It is now owned by the Homestead. The challenging Cascades golf course was developed by the Homestead in the 1920s. Its grand clubhouse was the 1890s home of a former owner of Little Healing Springs.

You'll also pass a state historical marker for Fort Breckenridge, another of George Washington's Indian forts erected along the frontier in the 1750s. Shawnee Indians led by Chief Cornstalk attacked the fort during Pontiac's War in 1763.

The next town is **Millboro Springs**. *Continue straight on Route 39 East toward Goshen. About 3 miles southeast of Millboro Springs was Fort Dickinson, one of the string of Indian forts George Washington was responsible for building in the 1750s.* Named for one of the county's first settlers, Adam Dickinson, it was attacked twice by Indians, once in 1756 and again in 1757. Washington thought this fort had particular importance because it was "directly in the Shawnee path to Ohio, and must be a place of rendezvous if an expedition is conducted against the Ohio Indians below Duquesne." He recommended that 250 men be posted here.

When Washington inspected this and other area forts in 1756, he noted that both settlers and soldiers seemed to be vigilant only when the threat of Indian attack was present. He was concerned that they were not constantly on the alert. ("The militia keep no guard, but just when the enemy is about," he noted.) It appears that on one occasion, several children playing outside the walls of Fort Dickinson were snatched by a group of Indians; fortunately, they were rescued.

Goshen *is the next stop on Route 39. You have your choice of two right turns to stay on Route 39 after you pass the charming building that houses the Goshen Library; you can take either one. Route 39 here is designated a Virginia Byway as it enters Rockbridge County.*

About 5 miles down the road, you'll enter Goshen Pass, a 3-mile-long scenic delight. This gorge, carved out millions of year ago by the Maury River, is one of the most unusual sights in Virginia. The road twists past forests thick with rhododendron, past dramatic rock formations, and past the rocky river below. There are several scenic overlooks along the way. In the summer, the area's swimming holes, hiking trails, and picnic spots make it a family playground.

The Goshen Wayside, on the left about 2 miles into the pass, has a covered picnic pavilion and rest rooms and is a popular weekend spot in the summer. On the road near the wayside is a plaque commemorating Commodore Matthew Fontaine Maury (1806–73), whose last job in a distinguished career was as a professor of meteorology at Virginia Military Academy in Lexington. Maury is considered one of the fathers of oceanography.

Maury began his career as a navy officer, but his seafaring days ended when his legs were injured in a stagecoach accident. He later compiled information on maritime winds and currents that made it possible for ship captains to plan shorter routes. This and other work led to the first international marine conference, held in 1853. He also made charts of the seabeds of the Atlantic, Pacific, and Indian Oceans, which made it possible for telegraph cables to be laid. During the Civil War, he became the head of coast, harbor, and river defenses for the Confederate navy.

He loved the Goshen Pass area so much that he directed that upon his death, his casket be carried through the pass when the rhododendrons were in bloom. He died in Lexington in February 1873, so his burial in Richmond was delayed until May. In later years, the North River was renamed the Maury River in his honor.

As you leave Goshen Pass, look to the right for a white frame residence with a double porch. This home was once part of the Wilson Springs Hotel, which dated to 1775. Visitors came to partake of the sulphur springs here. This was not a fancy resort; in fact, the owner let anyone who wanted to build a cabin on the property. During the Civil War, Confederate soldiers camped here while guarding Goshen Pass.

Continue on Route 39 to **Rockbridge Baths**. People first came here in the 1800s to take the magnesia springs baths—actually two pools that stay a constant 72 degrees Fahrenheit. Now closed to the public, the pools are

Goshen Pass

located behind a wall on the left side of the road beyond the creek and past the Maury General Store. The general store, which houses the local post office, makes for an interesting stop; the right side of the building once served as the resort's dance hall.

This community was originally called Jordan's Springs. In 1857, developers built a hotel here and renamed the place Rockbridge Baths. Robert E. Lee often came here while he was president of Washington College in the late 1860s. Beginning in 1874, a former Confederate army physician, Dr. Samuel Brown Morrison, operated the hotel as a sanitarium; ill health forced him to give up the operation in 1900. Virginia Military Institute used the facilities as a summer school beginning in 1921. The hotel burned down in 1926.

*Continue on Route 39 for 2.5 miles, then turn left on to Route 252 (Brownsburg Turnpike), following the sign toward Staunton. The first town on this old pike, which curves through woods and past farms and charming old homes, is **Bustleburg**.* The town's name supposedly derives from the time "a fashionable young lady lost her composure while trying to ride a horse while wearing a bustle," according to one source.

*The next town is **Brownsburg**.* Designated a historic district by the Virginia Historic Landmarks Commission, the town has changed little over

Brownsburg post office

the past century. It was founded in 1783 and named for John Brown, the first pastor of New Providence Presbyterian Church, located just north of town.

After passing through this quiet town, follow the signs for I-81, turning right on to Sterret Road. Be sure to note the beautiful restored stone-and-brick home on the right after the turn; it dates to 1775. The Blue Ridge will come into view as you head east toward I-81.

The tour ends at I-81's Exit 200, which is between Staunton (22 miles north) and Lexington (9 miles south).

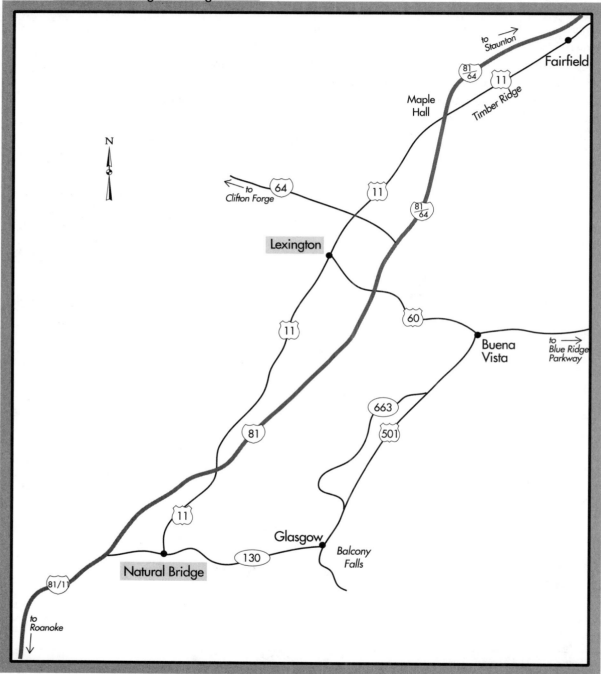

The Natural Bridge to Lexington Tour

The Natural Bridge to Lexington Tour

This tour explores much of Rockbridge County, which was formed in 1777 and named for its famous geological formation—the unusual rock bridge known as Natural Bridge. Most of the county was part of a 92,000-acre land grant made to Benjamin Borden, who came to Virginia from New Jersey in the 1730s. He brought in many Scots-Irish settlers, who eventually formed much of the early population of the southern Shenandoah Valley.

There are two ways to get to Natural Bridge from I-81. If you are coming from the north, take Exit 180, which will put you on U.S. 11 South; follow the signs to the bridge. If you are coming from the south, take Exit 175 and drive U.S. 11 North, following the signs to **Natural Bridge***.*

Natural Bridge really is a bridge. U.S. 11 runs on top of the 90-foot-wide, 215-foot-high stone formation, although drivers are not aware of it as they cross. In fact, the bridge makes it possible for the road to continue through this part of the Valley without having to make a considerable detour.

Natural Bridge was formed millions of years ago after the soft rocks that once formed the roof of a cavern collapsed, leaving the harder rocks standing to form the "bridge." The Monocan Indians are said to have worshiped Natural Bridge long before Europeans discovered it.

One of the first white men to see this amazing natural structure may have been Peter Jefferson, father of the third president and a surveyor who helped create one of the first reliable maps of Virginia. In 1749 or 1750, Jefferson surveyed the area of the Old Indian Trail, which later became the Valley Pike, today's U.S. 11.

This tour begins at Natural Bridge, a wonder of nature that Thomas Jefferson once owned. It then follows backroads to two 1890s boom towns, Glasgow and Buena Vista, both of which were stops along the North River Canal. The tour proceeds to Lexington, which has a well-preserved downtown area full of 1800s buildings, two well-known universities, and the homes and graves of two Virginia heroes, Robert E. Lee and Stonewall Jackson. It then stops along U.S. 11 at Timber Ridge, probably the earliest settlement in Rockbridge County and the birthplace of Sam Houston, the first governor of Texas. The tour ends at Fairfield after passing the historic McDowell family graveyard.

Total mileage: Approximately 46 miles

Natural Bridge

Legend has it that Peter Jefferson had a young assistant named George Washington, who climbed straight up one side of the formation and carved his initials—which can still be seen today—in the rocks 23 feet above Cedar Creek. Some historians question the likelihood of that event, however. Washington spent most of his short career as a surveyor working for Lord Fairfax, whose 5 million acres of land were much farther north; Peter Jefferson worked for the Royal governor of Virginia, not for Lord Fairfax. Washington may have been in this area in 1756 while on an inspection tour of the Indian forts he was responsible for building and overseeing, but no records exist to indicate that he came to the bridge during that time.

In 1774, Thomas Jefferson—completely taken by this phenomenon of nature—asked the Royal governor for, and was granted, a 157-acre tract that included Natural Bridge. He built a two-room cabin for himself and his friends to use when they visited the site. He called Natural Bridge "the most sublime of nature's works" in his *Notes on the State of Virginia*. He wrote, "It is impossible for the emotions, arising from the sublime, to be felt beyond what they are here: so beautiful an arch, so elevated, so light, and springing, as it were, up to heaven, the rapture of the Spectator is really indescribable!"

The bridge had practical value as well. It was used as a "shot drop" during the Revolutionary War; molten lead was dropped from the top into Cedar Creek below, an action that resulted in the rounded balls used for bullets. During the War of 1812, a nearby cave, visible today along the walking trail beyond the bridge, was mined for saltpeter, an ingredient in gunpowder and other explosives.

By the early 1800s, Natural Bridge had become a tourist attraction. Artists' renditions of it became popular as framed prints both here and in Europe. Later in that century, the railroad made a stop here, and the popularity of Natural Bridge continued to grow.

The property has remained privately owned ever since Thomas Jefferson's heirs sold it some years after his death.

From the Natural Bridge parking lot, turn right to drive east on Route 130, following the signs toward Glasgow, located about 4 miles away. This road is a Virginia Byway.

The natural advantages in this area—the James River and the nearby mountains' supply of iron ore and timber—supported several local mills, furnaces, and foundries. In 1851, the North River Navigation Company began building a series of locks and dams on the North River (later renamed the Maury River, after a well-known V.M.I. professor). The locks and dams were designed to connect Lexington with the James River and Kanawha Canal at Balcony Falls near Glasgow.

Glasgow was one of the many Shenandoah Valley boom-to-bust towns of the early 1890s. In 1891, when Glasgow was just 14 months old, it already had 1,200 residents. In those days, land developers swept through the area with grand visions for business and industrial development, often creating planned towns out of the smallest of settlements. But their hopes for Glasgow failed to materialize when the national economy took a dive shortly after the town's founding.

Hints of Glasgow's former promise are still evident in spots. Nothing is left, though, of the grand 200-room Glasgow Inn, constructed here in the early 1890s. The inn had the latest in modern conveniences, including electric lights and elevators. The story goes that the economic bubble burst before the first guest could be tucked in. The grand structure was torn down in the years that followed.

Continue on Route 130, heading east toward the mountains. As you approach the intersection with Route 501, look ahead and to the right for the white farmhouse that sits near the river. This is the Echols Farmhouse, a recent addition to the Virginia Landmarks Register because of its connection to canal history.

The area near the farmhouse was the site of a brutal battle between Indians and settlers in 1742. According to the story, Iroquois Indians were traveling through the Valley when they began to frighten women and children and shoot at horses. A captain in the local militia, John McDowell, led a group of men who intended to "escort" the Indians away from the settlements. The two groups met at the river near here, and the resulting fight left eight Virginians—including McDowell—and 17 Indians dead. The Virginians were buried in the graveyard next to McDowell's home. The graveyard is still there today; see page 208 of this tour.

The Echols Farmhouse was built by Edward Echols in 1855 and is still owned by the Echols family. Here, Edward Echols operated the canal locks and ran a warehouse and a trading post. His mines in the mountains nearby provided the Confederates with a supply of iron ore during the Civil War.

In 1863, the casket carrying General Stonewall Jackson's body passed this way on a flat-bottomed boat en route from his funeral in Richmond to Lexington for burial.

Turn left off Route 130 on to Route 501. Shortly after the turn, you may notice a pair of brick gateposts on the left. The inscription reads, "Willow Grove 1780," suggesting that a historic mansion lies at the end of the drive. Unfortunately, the home burned to the ground years ago.

If you had turned right on Route 501, you would have passed the remains of Balcony Falls Lock and Dam, which are difficult to see from the road. After passing through Balcony Falls, boats carrying cargo to Lynchburg had to negotiate 25 locks and eight dams. To continue on the James River Canal to Richmond, they had to go through 63 more locks and pass six dams and 10 aqueducts. Even though canal travel wasn't speedy, it was still much faster and more efficient than overland travel.

The coming of the railroad in the 1880s put Virginia's canals out of business. In many places, the railroad companies followed the paths of the canals, filling them in with dirt and often using the towpaths as foundations for the rail beds.

What is now Route 501 was built as the Blue Ridge Turnpike by the James River and Kanawha Canal Company. The North River Canal ran alongside the turnpike until curving west at what is now Route 663 (River Road); it then generally followed that road for several miles until it joined back up with the river. The tour now detours slightly to follow that old route.

In 1.4 miles, turn left on to Route 663, which is a Virginia Byway. Stay on Route 663 until in rejoins Route 501 in 6.7 miles. En route, you'll see ruins of the canal locks and other structures on the left.

Route 663 ends at a stop sign at Route 501. Turn left to reach **Buena Vista**. This was another developer-created boom town of the 1890s, although it had been settled for many years before that and had long been supported by its mills and furnaces.

As you enter Buena Vista (pronounced "Byoona Vista"), you'll see a sign on the left at 10th Street for Glen Maury Park. Follow the sign to the park.

This well-maintained city park lies next to railroad tracks that follow the path of the old North River Canal. Several lock and aqueduct ruins are in the vicinity. The park offers picnic shelters, rest rooms, a campground, a swimming pool, tennis courts, hiking trails, and other amenities. The old brick home on the grounds is Paxton Place, built by Elisha Paxton in the 1830s. During the Civil War, Paxton served as a commander of the Stonewall Brigade; he was killed in the Battle of Chancellorsville in 1863. The house is listed on the Virginia Landmarks Register. It is being restored for use as a cultural, historical, and educational center.

Paxton Place

From Glen Maury Park, return to Route 501 and continue through town. There are several interesting old buildings along Route 501 as it passes through Buena Vista, including the renovated former courthouse (now the school board office). The General Store, at 2522 Beech Avenue, one block off Route 501, has been in almost continuous operation since it opened in 1891. And as you leave the village, you'll see Buena Vista's stunning 1890s resort hotel (it seems that every boom town had one) high on a hill at the north end of town. It now serves as the Main Hall for Southern Virginia College, a private institution affiliated with the Latter-day Saints.

Buena Vista school board offices

After passing through Buena Vista on Route 501, follow the signs to Route 60 West. After about 2 miles on Route 60 West, you'll see a sign for the Ben Salem Wayside. This park is the site of the well-preserved ruins of another lock owned by the old North River Navigation Company. The river along here is a popular picnic spot and swimming hole in the summer months.

When the canal was operational, a stone dam located about a mile downstream raised the water level here to nine and a half feet. (The dam no longer exists; people carried away its rocks in later years to build some of the mills in Buena Vista.) The lock allowed operators to raise or lower the water level, permitting boats to go upstream or downstream. The stones of the lock rested on a wooden foundation, which sufficed as long as it could be kept continuously underwater, which prevented it from rotting. Today, in an attempt to preserve those timbers, a stream has been diverted to the lock to keep its foundation wet.

Southern Virginia College

During the 1800s, most goods that left or came into Lexington were shipped by way of flat-bottomed boats called bateaux along the river and this canal. Like the vessels called gundalows farther north in the Valley, these boats were about 90 feet long and were often covered with a canvas awning. They were guided by men who pushed with poles.

Even before the canal was built in the 1850s, the North River was improved for navigation by the addition of sluices, which allowed boats to get through if the water level was high enough—which it often was not. Once the canal to Lexington was completed in 1860, the boats were pulled by mules or horses, which walked a towpath next to the water. In those days, it took 18 hours to make the trip from Lexington to Lynchburg. From Lynchburg, the James River Canal allowed the movement of goods to Richmond. From there, goods were shipped down the James River to Norfolk and out to sea.

Route 60 enters **Lexington** *on the town's eastern edge; continue straight, following the signs for the tourist information center and the downtown historic district. Turn right on Lewis Street and follow the signs to the Lexington Visitor Center, located at 106 East Washington Street at the corner of Randolph Street. Park in the lot at the center to take the brief walking tour that follows.*

DOWNTOWN LEXINGTON

1 Visitor Center
2 The Castle
3 Rockbridge Historical Society Museum
4 Stonewall Jackson House
5 Alexander-Withrow House
6 Rockbridge County Courthouse
7 Lee Chapel

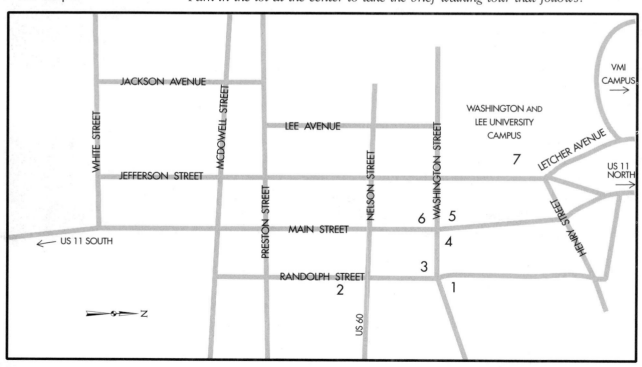

TOURING THE SHENANDOAH VALLEY BACKROADS

The visitor center is open daily. Inviting and well staffed, it offers maps, brochures, a self-guided downtown walking tour, and information about area attractions and history. The staff can also provide a map for the 7-mile Chessie Trail, which runs along the Maury River on the old rail bed between Lexington and Buena Vista.

The downtown area is a enjoyable place to walk, shop, and have lunch or dinner. There are very few 20th-century buildings in the historic area, making it a good filming location for period movies such as *Sommersby*, a Civil War–era story that includes scenes shot here in the early 1990s.

Geography determined that Lexington, located in the center of Rockbridge County, would serve as the county seat. In the mid-1770s, the settlement here was so small that it hardly even qualified as a village. The new county was almost completely rural; its largest settlement was Timber Ridge, a few miles north, visited later in this tour.

The Castle

Lexington was named after the first battle of the Revolutionary War, and the streets were named to honor its heroes. The town that began to grow here consisted mostly of log structures, which were later destroyed by a fire in 1796. The town was soon rebuilt, this time using brick and stone.

From the visitor center, turn left down Randolph Street and walk one block, crossing Nelson Street. Your destination is the stone structure on the left at 6 Randolph Street, one of the oldest structures in Lexington. Known as "The Castle," it was probably built in the 1790s as law offices—and it still houses law offices today.

Retrace your steps to East Washington Street and turn left. You'll pass the Campbell House, which is the home of the Rockbridge County Historical Society Museum; it is located across the street from the visitor center. The museum contains several interesting exhibits of early Lexington history.

Rockbridge County Historical Society Museum

On the right at 8 East Washington is the Stonewall Jackson House, the only home the general ever owned. He moved here in 1859, two years after marrying his second wife, Mary Anna Morrison. They had one daughter, Julia. The house, which later served as a hospital for many years, is open daily for guided tours.

Continue walking up East Washington to Main Street. On the left is the Rockbridge County Courthouse, constructed in 1897; this is the fourth county courthouse in Lexington.

Alexander-Withrow House

One of the most interesting downtown buildings is on the corner at 1 West Washington. The Alexander-Withrow House, which is now home to an arts-and-crafts shop on the ground floor and an inn on the upper floors, features distinctive diamond-pattern brickwork and an unusual hanging roof supported by carved wooden brackets. The home was built around 1789, and its brick construction allowed it to survive the fire of 1796. Over the next 150 years, it housed a post office, printing presses, retail shops, a doctor's office, and a school.

During the 1850s, Main Street was lowered 10 feet as part of a project to remove some of the steep grades in the downtown area. At that time, stone underpinning was installed in the Alexander-Withrow House to create a new lower story—today's ground floor—so that what was once the front door of the building is now surrounded by an iron balcony on the second story.

From the Alexander-Withrow House, continue one block west on West Washington to Jefferson Street. Turn right and walk one block to the campus of Washington and Lee University, on the left.

Lexington has been a college town since 1785, when Liberty Hall Academy, a Presbyterian boys' school, moved here from Timber Ridge after a fire destroyed the school's building there.

Liberty Hall was founded as Augusta Academy in 1749 by Robert Alexander, who was educated at Trinity College in Dublin, Ireland. It occupied several Augusta County locations before it came to Timber Ridge in 1776. A large log cabin was the school's main building. It was located on land donated by two Timber Ridge residents, one of whom was Samuel Houston, a Revolutionary War officer and the father of the first governor of Texas.

With the move to Timber Ridge, the school's name was changed to Liberty Hall, a patriotic and daring statement in 1776. It struggled along for many years during and after the Revolution and was in dire financial condition by the 1790s. Around that time, George Washington was looking for a deserving school to which he could donate his 100 shares of stock in the James River and Kanawha Canal Company; the stock was worth about $50,000, a huge sum in those days. He chose Liberty Hall partly because it was already well established and well respected. In a show of gratitude, the school, which had about 40 students at the time, was renamed Washington Academy in 1798.

The school became Washington College in 1813. In 1871, it was renamed Washington and Lee University in tribute to another famous general, one who helped put the school on more secure financial footing after the Civil War—Robert E. Lee. General Lee served as president of the university for five years, from 1865 until his death in the Lee House on campus in 1870. He started its school of law, as well as classes in business and journalism, and instituted an honor code that is still in force. Today, Washington and Lee, the ninth-oldest college in the nation, has about 2,000 students, more than 300 of whom are in the law school. Interestingly, only about 12 percent of the students are from Virginia.

Over the past two centuries, George Washington's $50,000 gift has been used to help pay the tuition of some 45,000 students. In a fitting gesture of appreciation, the university repaid the gift in 1999—the 200th anniversary of Washington's death—by donating $59,000 to support educational projects at Mount Vernon.

The university's main building—Washington Hall—is an impressive Greek Revival colonnaded structure built in 1824. It was designed by Lexington builder John Jordan, who constructed many other Lexington homes and buildings over a 50-year period. He built his own impressive mansion, Stono, in 1818; it is located on a hill next to the Virginia Military Institute.

Directly across from Washington Hall is Lee Chapel, which was built under General Lee's supervision while he was president of the university; this building also houses a museum. The focal point of the chapel is a beautiful marble sculpture portraying Lee sleeping on the battlefield, carved by 19th-century sculptor Edward Valentine. The museum, downstairs, recently underwent a $2.5 million renovation. It contains a room displaying Lee's office as he left it before his death, Lee family artifacts, and several portraits of the Lee, Custis, and Washington families, including a Charles Wilson Peale portrait of George Washington. (General Lee's wife, Mary Anne Randolph Custis, was a great-granddaughter of Martha Washington.) Many members of the Lee family, including Robert E. Lee and his father, Revolutionary War patriot Henry "Lighthorse Harry" Lee, are buried in a vault

Lee Chapel

behind the museum. The remains of Lee's favorite horse, Traveller, rest in a grave just outside the door. The museum and chapel are open daily year-round; no admission is charged.

Also on the campus is the earlier college president's house, now called the Lee-Jackson House, built in 1842; it is not open to the public. This is where Thomas Jonathan Jackson (later known as "Stonewall") married his first wife, Elinor Junkin, in 1853. She was the daughter of Washington College's president. At the time of his marriage, Jackson was a professor at the other well-known school in Lexington, Virginia Military Institute, located next door to Washington and Lee.

The V.M.I. campus is north of Washington and Lee. To see it, walk up Lechter Avenue (which is what Jefferson Street becomes after the Washington and Lee campus). If you'd prefer, you can reach the campus by car from U.S. 11, which is Main Street in town. Note that the tour passes V.M.I.'s main entrance on the way out of town.

Established as one of several state arsenals in 1816, V.M.I. became a military academy thanks to the suggestion and efforts of one of the town's attorneys in 1839. It is the oldest state-supported military school in the nation.

The school's early programs were influenced by the first president of its board of visitors, Claude Crozet, a respected engineer of the time. Crozet was a French soldier and engineer who served under Napoleon. After emigrating to the United States in 1817, he taught at the United States Military Academy at West Point for seven years. He then came to Virginia, where he spent most of the rest of his life. Probably best known for the railroad tunnel he engineered through Afton Mountain near Rockfish Gap in the Blue Ridge, he also oversaw many other road and tunnel construction projects in the Valley.

Jackson began teaching here in 1851. A West Point graduate, he had served in the army during the war with Mexico, but he was not happy in the peacetime military, so he left the service.

The statue of Jackson that stands in front of the castlelike Barracks Building, built in 1850 and severely bombed by Union general Hunter in 1864, shows him inspecting the battlefield at Chancellorsville, where he was mortally (and accidentally) wounded by one of his own men in 1863, at the age of 39. He reportedly used the two cannons that now sit on either side of the statue when teaching his artillery class.

Jackson, who had been a deacon at Lexington Presbyterian Church (located at the corner of Main and Nelson Streets), was buried two blocks south of the church in what is now called Stonewall Jackson Memorial Cemetery. A statue of Jackson by Edward Valentine stands near his grave.

Six of the 10 V.M.I. cadets who died while fighting in the Battle of New Market were buried on campus behind the statue called *Virginia Mourning Her Dead* at Nichols Engineering Hall.

That building is next door to Jackson Memorial Hall, which houses the V.M.I. Museum, open daily except during late December and early January. This museum has several artifacts of Jackson's, including some of his classroom materials and the raincoat he was wearing the night he was accidentally shot. It also displays his favorite horse, Little Sorrel, whose remains have been preserved since the animal's death in 1886. Other exhibits include an antique firearms collection and displays of the achievements of the school's graduates.

Pendleton-Coles House

The quaint-looking white frame house with peaked gables and a covered porch at the driveway entrance to V.M.I. is the Pendleton-Coles House. It was built in the early 1850s by Colonel Edmund Pendleton, a member of the class of 1842. In this house in 1901, Pendleton's granddaughter married George C. Marshall—perhaps the most famous V.M.I. graduate and later general of the army.

The home serves as the school's admissions office today.

Virginia Mourning Her Dead

Barracks Building, Virginia Military Institute

George C. Marshall Museum

A second museum on campus honors distinguished graduate George C. Marshall (class of 1901), who attained the army's highest rank during World War II, served as United States secretary of state, and won the Nobel Peace Prize for the Marshall Plan, his vision for European economic recovery after the war. The exhibits highlight aspects of 20th-century military and diplomatic history.

Like Washington and Lee University, the V.M.I. campus is a National Historic Landmark.

To continue the tour, retrace your steps to the visitor center parking lot. From the parking lot, drive up East Washington Street to Main Street (U.S. 11) and turn right. This road will take you past the Washington and Lee and V.M.I. campuses. Follow the signs for U.S. 11 North to the stop sign. After crossing the bridge over the Maury River, continue on U.S. 11 for about 5 miles. The highway crosses over I-81 twice. Just after it crosses the second time, look to the left to see the brick mansion known as Maple Hall. Its builder and first owner supposedly designed this impressive Greek Revival home in 1850 in an attempt to outdo his neighbors. It is now operated as an inn and restaurant.

Three Side Trips from Lexington

Lake Robertson is a 581-acre park located 14 miles west of Lexington. It offers camping, a 31-acre fishing lake, a swimming pool, hiking trails, and picnic grounds. It was named for A. Willis Robertson, a United States senator from Lexington and the father of television evangelist Pat Robertson. *To get there, take Route 251 southwest from Lexington to Collierstown, then follow Route 770 to the lake.*

Closer to town is the Theater at Lime Kiln. Since 1983, concerts, plays, and musicals have been performed in this outdoor theater, which is situated on the grounds of an 1896 lime kiln. Each year, the theater puts on a popular musical called *Stonewall Country*, which tells the story of General Stonewall Jackson. *To visit the grounds, follow Nelson Street (U.S. 60) west from Lexington for 1 mile, turn left on to Borden Road, and drive to the entrance.*

Goshen Pass is 12 miles north of Lexington on U.S. 39, which is off U.S. 11 just past the I-64 interchange north of the city. This picturesque and striking mountain gorge is described in The Monterey to Hot Springs Tour, pages 190–91. On the way to Goshen Pass, you'll pass the Virginia Horse Center, which was created by the state in 1985 to provide facilities for shows and competitions.

Less than 0.5 mile down the road from Maple Hall is the Sam Houston Wayside, on the right at Route 716. Turn right into the wayside. The future hero of Texas independence was born in a cabin near here on March 2, 1793. A pink granite boulder brought here from Texas displays a bronze plaque describing Sam Houston's accomplishments.

Houston's father had served with General Daniel Morgan (see The White Post to Millwood to Berryville Tour, pages 59–60) during the American Revolution. After the elder Houston's death, the family moved to live with relatives in Tennessee. Sam was about 13. One of his uncles said of him at the time, "I have no hope for Sam. He is so wild." At the age of 16, he tired of his job in the family's general store and went to live with some Cherokee Indian friends for nearly three years. He joined the army when he was 19 and served in the Creek War in Alabama under General Andrew Jackson. Sam was eventually stationed in Nashville. In 1817, Jackson appointed him to manage the removal of the Cherokees in Tennessee to a reservation in Arkansas. The following year, Houston showed up in Indian clothing at a Washington, D.C., reception for the Cherokees, for which he was reprimanded by his senior officers; he left the army shortly afterward.

Sam Houston Wayside

In the years that followed, he was elected to Congress and became governor of Tennessee. In 1832, Andrew Jackson sent him to Texas, which then belonged to Mexico, to negotiate treaties with the Indians. Houston soon found himself in the middle of a rebellion of settlers against Mexico.

Feisty Frontier Women, Continued

Mary Elizabeth McDowell, daughter of early settler Ephraim McDowell, married a man named Greenlee but was widowed at an early age. She supported herself by operating a tavern near Timber Ridge.

In the early days, Alice Lewis, daughter of John Lewis, the founder of Staunton, was kidnapped by Indians. Mary Greenlee offered John Lewis a deal. She would attempt to rescue the girl if he would provide a horse, saddle, and bridle—but only if she could keep the horse if her mission was successful. The story goes that she tracked down the girl at an Indian camp and brought her safely home.

Years later, when she was 95, she was called to testify in court. When asked to state her age, she reportedly replied, "Why do you ask my age? Do you think I am in my dotage?" She lived another seven years.

Her grandson also lived to a remarkable age, dying in 1915 at age 99.

His strategic defeat of Mexican general Santa Anna at the Battle of San Jacinto, near what is now the city of Houston, resulted in an independent Texas republic. He became its first president.

When Texas became a state in 1845, Houston served as one of its United States senators. But his opposition to secession in the years before the Civil War cost him that office. He was elected governor in 1859, but by 1861, he was deposed from office because he wouldn't swear allegiance to the Confederacy. He died two years later.

Liberty Hall Academy (described earlier in this tour) was also located here in **Timber Ridge**, one of the county's first settlements.

Continue through the wayside and turn right to see Timber Ridge Presbyterian Church, which was founded in 1746. The original part of the present church was built in 1756. Expanded and renovated since then, this is considered the only pre–Revolutionary War Presbyterian church still in use in Rockbridge County.

Behind the church is a house called Church Hill, built in 1866. Historians believe that this house rests partially on the foundation of the log home in which Sam Houston was born.

When you are ready to leave the wayside, return to U.S. 11 and turn right. In 3 miles, look on the left side of the highway for a state historical marker and a walled graveyard a few hundred feet beyond. The marker notes that the cemetery contains the graves of militia captain John McDowell and seven of his companions, who were killed by Indians in 1742 near Balcony Falls (located near what is now the town of Glasgow, described earlier in this tour).

John McDowell's father, Ephraim McDowell, was one of the first settlers in the Lexington area and the patriarch of one of its most distinguished families. Of Scottish descent, he came to America after years of fighting for civil and religious liberty in Ireland. He was in his 60s when he arrived here. He died in 1775 at the age of 104, having outlived both his sons.

John McDowell received 1,000 acres of the original Borden land grant in exchange for his services in surveying the grant. In 1737, he built a house here using peeled logs stained to appear red, which gave the structure its name—the Red House. The house was torn down in 1783 by a later owner and replaced with a structure that became an inn and stagecoach stop.

Dr. Ephraim McDowell Memorial

John McDowell's son, Samuel, fought in the American Revolution and later became a judge in Kentucky. Samuel's son—named Ephraim, after his grandfather—was born in the Red House in 1771 and later became known as "the Father of Abdominal Surgery." In 1809, while practicing medicine in Danville, Virginia, he performed the first successful removal of an ovarian tumor in the United States.

Ephraim's cousin, James McDowell, was born near Lexington and was elected Virginia's governor in 1843. He built a grand home, Col Alto, in Lexington. That home is now part of the Hampton Inn at 401 East Nelson Street.

Continue on U.S. 11 to **Fairfield**, *where the tour ends.* This town has several interesting-looking antique shops and a striking white frame church, Fairfield United Methodist Church, built in 1917.

Follow the signs to return to Exit 200 off I-81, located about 25 miles north of where the tour began.

Fairfield Antique Store

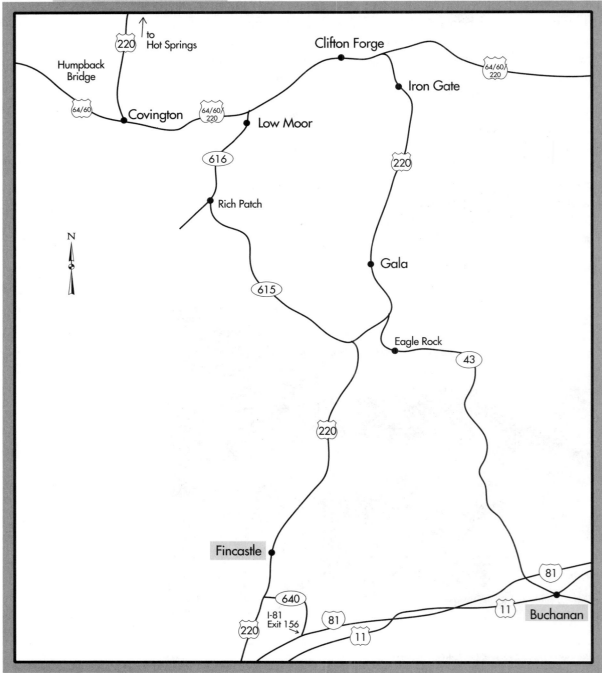

The Fincastle to Buchanan Tour

to Hot Springs
220

Humpback Bridge

Clifton Forge

64/60 220

64/60

Covington

64/60 220

Low Moor

Iron Gate

616

220

Rich Patch

615

Gala

Eagle Rock

43

220

Fincastle

640

81

I-81 Exit 156

220

81

11

11

Buchanan

The Fincastle to Buchanan Tour

The tour begins in **Fincastle**, the county seat of Botetourt County. To get there, take Exit 156 off I-81, marked "Troutville/Route 640." Turn right at the stop sign at the bottom of the ramp; don't go to Troutville. Route 640 veers to the left in 1.5 miles, where it is called Brugh's Mill Road.

Historians generally consider the Fincastle area to be the southern boundary of the Shenandoah Valley. The Valley's tourist bureaus usually place the southern edge at Roanoke, 20 miles southeast of Fincastle. Roanoke, although an interesting city with plenty to see and do, is not covered in this book; however, it makes a good base from which to explore the southern end of the Valley. Roanoke was a late bloomer, developing from the small community of Big Lick to an important railroad hub beginning in the 1880s. But at least a century before Roanoke made it big, Fincastle was the area's most important commercial, governmental, and social center.

Route 640 meets U.S. 220 North in about 2 miles, Turn right to go to Fincastle. In 0.8 mile, look for a state historical marker on the left side of U.S. 220 just before you enter the main part of town. It describes one of the most historically significant homes in the area, Santillane. The house is at the top of a hill a short distance up Route 1211, the first left past the historical marker. Only portions of this private residence can be seen from the road; it's not the white frame home on the hill facing Route 1211, but rather the red-brick mansion at the end of a private drive at the end of the road. This Federal-style house is on the National Register of Historic Places and the Virginia Historic Landmarks Register.

This tour explores the southernmost portion of the Shenandoah Valley, beginning in the charming old town of Fincastle, one of the upper Valley's busiest places in the 1700s. From there, it winds through hilly farmland and across the Rich Patch Mountains into the Alleghany County towns of Covington and Clifton Forge, both important industrial and rail centers in the 1800s and early 1900s. Just outside Covington, it visits the famous Humpback Bridge, the only covered bridge of its kind in the United States. From Clifton Forge, the tour passes through rocky Rainbow Gorge and the towns of Iron Gate, Gala, and Eagle Rock as it heads southeast to Buchanan, once an important port town on the James River and Kanawha Canal.

Total mileage:
Approximately 83 miles

Colonel George Hancock began building Santillane in 1795. Hancock had served as aide-de-camp to Count Pulaski during the Revolutionary War; he later served in Congress. His daughter, Judith, married the explorer William Clark in this house in 1808, two years after he returned from his famous expedition west with Meriwether Lewis. The couple lived in the house for a time, and it was here that Clark wrote his report on that historic journey.

The second owner of Santillane was Henry Bowyer, who fought in the Battle of Point Pleasant in 1774, at the age of 14. He then came to Fincastle to work in his uncle's store but soon went off to fight in the Revolutionary War. Bowyer returned to Fincastle after the war and served as county clerk—an important position in those days—for 43 years. The patriot Patrick Henry is said to have visited his niece, who was Bowyer's wife, at Santillane on several occasions.

To enter Fincastle's historic district, turn right on to Main Street near the state historical marker for the town. The courthouse is just ahead on Main.

The surrounding area long served as hunting grounds for several Indian tribes, including the Catawbas, the Iroquois, the Delawares, the Tuscaroras, the Cherokees, and the Shawnees.

Fincastle is the county seat of Botetourt (pronounced "Bot-e-tot") County, which was formed in 1770. The town was laid out on 45 acres of land donated by a local merchant, Israel Christian, an immigrant who came to the area from Ireland around 1740. It was chartered as a town in 1772. At the time, Botetourt County was huge—it extended to the Mississippi River, encompassing all of what is now Kentucky and much of what are now West Virginia, Ohio, Illinois, and Indiana. It was named after Norborne Berkeley, Lord Botetourt, who was popular because he was the first Royal governor of Virginia to actually live in the colony since 1698; he served from 1768 to 1770.

In 1774, the Battle of Point Pleasant took place in Botetourt County near what is now the town of Lewisburg, West Virginia. There, colonial troops fought the Shawnee Indians, led by Chief Cornstalk, in a successful attempt to open up what is now Kentucky for settlement. That conflict was called "Dunmore's War" by some because they believed it was instigated by Lord Dunmore, Virginia's Royal governor at the time. Dunmore supposedly stirred up the fight with the Indians in an attempt to divert Virginians' attention from their growing problems with the Royal government. Some historians consider the battle to have been the first of the American Revolution.

Most of the county's original settlers were Scots-Irish Presbyterians, also known as Ulster Scots, who began arriving in the Shenandoah Valley in the 1740s. They became strong supporters of the revolutionary cause, thanks in no small part to their dislike of the English government. It wasn't long, though, before German and Swiss immigrants from the northern part of the Shenandoah Valley and Pennsylvania also began to move south. A few English and French families from eastern Virginia also moved to the area. Most of these settlers were farmers. Their most profitable crop was hemp, from which rope was made to satisfy the large demand of British shipping concerns. The settlers also grew wheat and corn.

After the Revolution, the movement of settlers to the south and west picked up considerably. Fincastle became the last place to buy supplies before crossing the mountains. Lewis and Clark stopped here on their way to, and on their way back from, their great exploration of the American frontier.

Many of Fincastle's men fought for the Confederacy in the Civil War, but no battles took place in or near the town. Less than a decade after the war, however, two fires destroyed parts of the central and western parts of town.

In the 1870s, the townspeople began lobbying to bring the railroad to Fincastle, but Roanoke was chosen instead. As a result, by the 1920s, the town's importance as a commercial and resort center began to decline. Since then, its citizens have done a beautiful job of preserving the 19th-century look of the town as a tribute to Fincastle's historic significance.

Fincastle, a virtual museum of American architecture from the late 1700s to the 1900s, is on the National Register of Historic Places. Most of its early houses were of log construction; in later years, they were covered with weatherboarding and painted white. Many old buildings and houses have survived, making this small town a perfect place to get out of the car and walk around. Only 450 people live here today, about half the number who resided here in 1860. When viewed from the local hilltops, the town has a

Fort William

Five miles south of Fincastle on U.S. 220 is a state historical marker for Fort William, one of the string of forts that the young George Washington was put in charge of building along the frontier. The purpose of the forts was to protect area settlers from random Indian raids during the French and Indian War. Constructed sometime before the mid-1750s, Fort William was situated so its guards could see intruders coming across the pass through the Catawba Valley and through two other mountain gaps. Washington specified that 75 men should be stationed here.

In 1755, a group of Indians and their chief visited the fort. The settlers fed them, let them spend the night, and, according to a report by one settler, "endeavored to pay them all deference imaginable."

The mood was not as friendly a few years later, when area residents sought shelter at the fort in 1763 during Pontiac's War.

distinctive "skyline" of five white steeples—one on the courthouse and the others on four of Fincastle's historic churches.

The neighborhood around the courthouse appears to be frozen in the past—the modern automobiles parked at the county office building next to the courthouse seem oddly out of place. All the buildings retain a 19th-century look and feel, and signs of contemporary American commercialism are few.

The handsome brick courthouse is the fourth on this spot. The first was a log building completed in 1773. By 1818, a new structure designed by Thomas Jefferson was under construction. More than two decades later, a third courthouse was built to keep up with growing needs. Apparently, it looked much like the second one, but with a steeple instead of a Jeffersonian dome. Completed in 1848, that building burned down in 1970; it was rebuilt to look like the second building, at least on the exterior. A fireproof vault protected all the old county records during the 1970 fire, which was fortunate; they included the land grants made to George Washington and Thomas Jefferson for property that now lies in West Virginia and Kentucky.

Directly in back of the courthouse is the Museum Building, the oldest part of which was built around 1806 as a county office building. It now houses the Botetourt County Museum, which contains furniture and artifacts dating back to the 1770s. The museum is generally open for a few hours in the middle of the day.

Botetourt County Museum

The brick building to the left of the museum houses county court offices today, but it was once the Western Hotel. The Western Hotel was built to house visiting lawyers; during the 1880s and 1890s, it also served the many visitors to Fincastle Springs, a popular mineral springs resort just a mile from town. Visitors could also stay in another hotel, Hayth's House, which had a ballroom; that hotel was located on Roanoke Street near the courthouse. The springs here attracted people from faraway places like New Orleans, Houston, Galveston, St. Louis, Vicksburg, and Mobile. Virginia's many mineral springs resorts had long been popular summer retreats for people escaping the humid and mosquito-ridden coastal areas.

Next to the courthouse complex is the building that served as the county jail from 1897 to 1966. Its unusual (for Virginia) decorative ironwork has led many to suggest that the town's Southern summer guests—especially those from New Orleans—may have influenced its design. The jail's interior layout was interesting. The first floor served as living quarters for the jailer and his family, the second floor (with room for six) was reserved for women offenders, and the third floor (with room for 16) was for men.

To take a short walking tour of the town, park near the courthouse and head down Main Street to Church Street; turn right. Near the intersection is an old log structure beautifully restored by Historic Fincastle, Inc. It now serves as offices for Fincastle Baptist Church. Known as the Crowder House, it was built around 1791. Like so many other log structures in the Valley, it was covered with clapboards for many years. Note the careful notching of the logs at the corners of the building.

Return to Main Street and continue east to the end of the next block; turn left at Water Street. On the right at the end of the block is a home known as Godwin Cottage. Some think that this unusual-looking house was based on a design of Thomas Jefferson's. It was built sometime before 1880.

Turn right on to Back Street, then left on to Jefferson Street. The house on the corner of Jefferson and Carper Streets is one of the oldest in the area. This is the Peck Cottage, thought to have been built as slave quarters by town founder Israel Christian around 1784. Christian was a member of the Virginia House of Burgesses from 1756 to 1761 and served as one of the county's first justices. The house is log underneath clapboard; two rooms were added later.

Across the street from the Peck Cottage is the town spring, now a park.

Return to Back Street and turn right. This section of Back Street was once known as Jockey Alley. In the 1800s, "Court Day" was held once a month. People from the surrounding area would come to Fincastle to shop, gossip, discuss politics, and conduct business. Horse trading was one of the more popular events of Court Day, so much so that the sheriff was often called in to restore order. Jockey Alley was the official place for buying and selling horses and other animals on those days. A local history book tells about a man who proudly claimed that he made seven trades in one day here and went home with 37 dollars, a watch, a pocketknife—and the same horse he started trading with.

Walk past the park on Back Street to Fincastle Presbyterian Church. Built before the Revolution by the Church of England, this structure was taken

Old jail

Crowder House

Godwin Cottage

Fincastle Presbyterian Church

over by the Presbyterians after the war. The Greek columns and the steeple were added during an enlargement of the church in the 1840s; it underwent another renovation in the 1940s. The unmarked graves on the left side of the church are thought to be those of Revolutionary War soldiers.

Four other churches in town have contributed to Fincastle's history. The congregation of Fincastle Methodist Church was formed in 1789. The well-known traveling Methodist bishop Francis Asbury came to preach here on several occasions in the late 1700s. The current church was built in 1840; the cemetery on the hill above it offers a lovely view of the town and the surrounding countryside. St. Mark's Episcopal Church was built in the 1830s for a congregation that was formed in 1770. First Baptist Church started as First African Baptist Church in 1831. Fincastle Baptist Church is the only church in town with stained-glass windows; it was built in 1896.

Continue past Fincastle Presbyterian Church to Roanoke Street and turn left to return to the courthouse. To continue the tour, drive back to U.S. 220 and turn right (north). After 15.4 miles, turn left on to Route 615 toward Roaring Run just after passing over the Craig Creek bridge. In 2.5 miles, turn right at Route 621 (Roaring Run Road); a white cinder-block general store sits at this corner. Follow the National Forest Service sign to Roaring Run Park, which is on the left about 1 mile down Route 621. This road was once part of the old

Fincastle Methodist Church

TOURING THE SHENANDOAH VALLEY BACKROADS

Fincastle and Covington Pike, which ran along what was probably once an Indian trail. Roaring Run Park is the site of an 1838 iron furnace. Picnicking, camping, and hiking are available.

From the park, continue on Route 621 for 3.3 miles to the stop sign at the intersection with Route 616 (Rich Patch Road); turn right. The white frame Rich Patch Union Church is at this corner up the hill on the right. In 5.5 miles, you'll enter the community of **Low Moor**. The name Rich Patch almost certainly didn't refer to the wealth of the area's residents; legend has it that the name came from the smell of rotting vegetation in a field near Low Moor.

At the next stop sign, turn left on to Route 696. Go under the railroad bridge, following the signs for I-64 West to Covington.

Before you turn on to I-64, look ahead to the access road (Route 1101) that parallels the highway. A short distance to the right down the access road is a state historical marker noting the nearby location of the earliest coke ovens of the Low Moor Iron Company. Those ovens were used to produce coke, a much more efficient fuel for blast furnaces than charcoal. The company, founded in 1873, was a large employer in the area by the 1920s, with 1,600 workers on its payroll. Low Moor was the last of the county's many ironworks towns to survive. The iron company shut down in 1926.

Turn left on to I-64 West. Today's I-64 runs conjunctively with U.S. 60, which had its origins as the Midland Trail, one of the first roads to connect the eastern part of Virginia with the lands across the Alleghenies. Settlers and their wagons traversed this route by the thousands in the 1800s as they headed west. By 1919, the road began to serve another kind of vehicle— automobiles. A travel guide from that era claimed that the Midland Trail was the shortest coast-to-coast motor route.

West of Covington, U.S. 60 crosses the Allegheny divide. In the 1700s, George Washington envisioned a canal in this area that would connect the eastern United States with the Ohio River. Its path would follow the James River and Dunlap Creek. From that point, goods would have to be loaded into wagons and carried across the mountains until the canal could resume along the Greenbrier and finally the Kanawha and Ohio Rivers, in today's western West Virginia and southern Ohio. Washington's dream of canal navigation eventually became a reality, except that the James River and Kanawha canal reached only as far west as Buchanan.

Stay on I-64 past the two exits for Covington, then get off at Exit 10 to follow U.S. 60 East. The Humpback Bridge—the only bridge of its kind in the United States, and the oldest of the eight remaining covered bridges in Virginia—is less than 1 mile down the road.

This picturesque bridge crosses Dunlap Creek at a roadside park, a popular wading and picnic area. The bridge was built of oak timbers in 1857, held together only by pins made of locust wood. The humpback shape allowed the load to be spread evenly over its 100-foot span without the need for a center support. At the center of the bridge, the floor is four feet higher than it is at the ends. The bridge was used to carry traffic until 1929, after which it fell into disrepair until local organizations restored it in 1954.

Three earlier bridges stood here, the first of which was built in the 1820s as part of the James River and Kanawha Turnpike.

From the parking lot at Humpback Bridge, turn right on to U.S. 60 East toward Covington. U.S. 60 is known here as Midland Trail Road and then is renamed Monroe Avenue after it crosses the bridge over the Jackson River into Covington. Turn right at the second block on to Main Street.

Covington is the county seat of Alleghany County, which borders West

The Humpback Bridge

Virginia. Half the county lies within George Washington National Forest.

In 1743, the Royal governor of the Virginia colony granted 30,000 acres in the James River basin to Colonel James Wood, James and Henry Robinson, and Thomas and Andrew Lewis. Part of the tract was in what is now Alleghany County.

Two men from New York, Peter Wright and Joseph Carpenter, were the area's first settlers. They arrived in 1745 or 1746, bought land in what is now the Covington area from the original grant holders, and began farming. Other settlers, primarily Scots-Irish, followed in the next several years.

Beginning in 1754, the settlers, like those in other parts of the Valley, had to deal with the constant fear of surprise Indian attacks. The reason for the attacks was political. The French, during their battle with the British over rights to land in the upper Ohio River Valley, found they had a friend in the Indians, who, after years of mistreatment, were not overly fond of the British. The French and Indian War began in 1754 and ended with the signing of the Treaty of Paris in 1763, in which the French gave up their claim on land east of the Mississippi River to Great Britain.

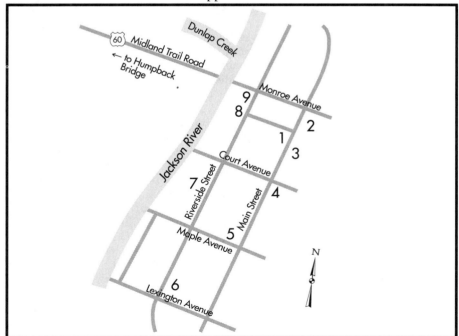

Downtown Covington

1. Courthouse
2. Chamber of Commerce
3. Catholic Church
4. Brugh Building
5. Park's Studio
6. Crawford Residence
7. Pitzer House
8. Child Residence
9. Hawkins Residence

Fort Young, one of the defensive forts George Washington built along the frontier to meet these threats, was erected here in 1756. Washington came to inspect this and nearby Fort Breckenridge later that year. Local residents took shelter, often for days or weeks at a time, behind the stockaded walls of these forts.

There was once a reconstruction of Fort Young in Covington, but it was torn down in the 1990s because of lack of funds to maintain it.

Until 1819, this area was largely farmland, with just a few houses and a gristmill. That year, the town of Covington was laid out. No one is sure how the town got its name. Some say it was named after a descendant of Peter Wright; others claim the name honors a relative of Dr. James Merry, a local physician who bought the Wright property in 1782; and some say it was named after General Leonard Covington, a hero of the War of 1812.

Anne Newport Royall, the Feistiest Frontier Woman of Them All

It was an unlikely match—a well-educated and prosperous, if hermitlike, Revolutionary War patriot, Major William Royall, marries Anne Newport, an uneducated young woman born into a poor family in Baltimore.

Royall met Anne in the late 1700s, when she and her mother were taking the waters for health reasons at Sweet Springs, near Royall's home south of Covington. They were married for 16 years, until Royall's death in 1813. He left Anne almost all of his property, which prompted his nephew to begin a 10-year battle contesting the will. To take her mind off the lawsuit, she left the western Virginia mountains and began to travel throughout the South. She was in Alabama when the lawsuit was decided against her, leaving her penniless.

As a widow of a war officer, Anne figured she was entitled to a pension, so she went to Washington, D.C., in 1824 to collect it. But the wheels of government turned slowly even then. To support herself in the meantime, she began to write a book about her observations of everyday life in America. She managed to convince John Quincy Adams to make a five-dollar advance payment for a copy of the book; Adams took pity on her and tried to help her get her pension. After several weeks of selling advance copies, she had enough money to travel to New England to begin collecting material. The book, *Sketches of History, Life, and Manners in the United States,* was later published in Hartford, Connecticut.

Anne continued her travels. She wrote nine more volumes of sketches of American life. She spoke her mind in those volumes, which earned her many enemies.

By 1831, broke once more, she returned to Washington, where she began to publish a weekly newspaper that she typeset and printed in her rented house near the Library of Congress. She wrote about political corruption, graft, religious groups she viewed as hypocritical, and, last but not least, the bureaucrats who took 36 years to finally give her a widow's pension. By then, she was 80 years old. Sometimes called the first American woman journalist, she published her newspaper, *The Huntress,* until just before her death at age 85 in 1854.

Alleghany County was formed from parts of Bath, Botetourt, and Monroe Counties in 1822, and Covington became the county seat. It remained largely rural until the 1880s, when the economic boom going on elsewhere came to town. Covington grew rapidly from the 1890s to the 1920s, attracting paper and pulp industries, iron furnaces, a silk-making plant, and a tannery.

Without the railroad—which reached Covington in 1867—the town may never have amounted to much. Because the James River and Kanawha Canal never made it this far west, local farmers and merchants had no easy way to get their products to market. But the railroad—which was later extended west to Kentucky, Ohio, and Illinois—put Covington directly on a major east-west route, making it a prime location for industrial development. What began as the Virginia Central Railroad eventually became the great line of the Chesapeake and Ohio by the late 1800s.

One of Covington's most successful industries—the bleached board division of Westvaco Corporation, a New York–based paper and pulp company—has been here since 1898. The plant, located on the outskirts of town, is huge, and the aroma that sometimes wafts into downtown Covington is a reminder of its presence.

Drive south on Main Street to see some of Covington's historic buildings.

The Alleghany Highlands Chamber of Commerce and the local visitor center occupy an interesting old house on Main near the corner of Monroe Avenue (next door to the post office). The house dates back to 1825, when it was built for a man named William Scott. It is best known for an event that took place here during the Civil War. Scott's daughter lived in the house while her husband, a Dr. Hammond, was serving with the Confederate army. Union soldiers under General Averill's command were camped nearby on a cold winter day. One of them came into town, entered the house, and tried to pry Mrs. Hammond's rings from her fingers. Her female servant saw what was happening, grabbed a frozen mop from the outside porch, and proceeded to beat the soldier about the head and shoulders with it. He quickly left, leaving Mrs. Hammond and her rings intact. When the soldier's superior officer heard about the incident, he reportedly gave the woman 200 pounds of sugar and 100 pounds of coffee to make amends for the regrettable incident.

The Alleghany County Courthouse, on the right farther down Main Street, is the third courthouse on this spot. The first structure was built in 1823; this one dates back to 1911. A statue honoring the men from Alleghany County who served in the Civil War stands on the grounds.

On the left at the corner of Main Street and Court Avenue (at 301–303 West Main) is an old house that now houses a restaurant. Known as the Brugh Building or the Oliver Callaghan House, it has survived on this spot without major changes for more than 150 years.

On the right farther down Main Street is Park's Studio. This building was considered the town's skyscraper when People's Bank built it. The Skeen Hotel—the site of one of the county's eight voting places in 1856—formerly occupied the lot.

Continue down Main Street to Lexington Avenue and turn right. Go one block and turn right again, on to West Riverside Street.

The house on the right at 441 West Riverside, near the corner with Lexington Avenue, is probably the oldest home in Covington. It is now referred to as the Crawford residence. Its two front rooms date to 1800 and were built by Dr. James Merry, the merchant who laid out the town. The walnut logs of the original house have been covered with stucco, a common practice in the 1800s.

Continue down West Riverside.

Note the house on the left that is now a design shop and florist's shop. The front portion of this home was built in 1834. A Mr. Pitzer ran an ice business here in the late 1800s; he spent his winters cutting blocks of ice from the river behind the house.

The brick house on the left at 232 West Riverside is known as the Childs Residence or the Burke House. It dates to 1823, when it was built by James Burke, who operated a trading post nearby; the two side wings were later additions. A subsequent owner, John Baker, came to the area from Delaware and was with Stonewall Jackson when he was mortally wounded in 1863. Baker bought this house in 1887. His daughter, Eula, is said to have been the first female justice of the peace in Virginia.

Almost next door to the Burke House, at 212 West Riverside, is the Hawkins residence, built in 1832.

The white stucco house across the street from the Burke House, now

Hawkins residence

occupied by law offices, is the Lawrence House. It was built about 1856.

These are just a few of the interesting old homes in Covington; many lovely residences dating back to the Victorian era line the town's other streets.

Turn right on to North Monroe Avenue and continue straight past Main Street. You are now on U.S. 220 South/U.S. 60 East. Stay on this road through several traffic lights until you see signs for I-64. Get on I-64 heading east. Take Exit 24 to reach Clifton Forge. Turn right at the stop sign at the end of the exit ramp. In 1 mile, you'll begin to enter the downtown area.

Clifton Forge began as a center of mining and forging activities in the early 1800s. The name came from a forge in nearby Rainbow Gorge, visited later on this tour. Its owner named the operation after his father's estate, Clifton, in Rockbridge County.

Like Covington, Clifton Forge owes its continued existence to the railroad. The first one to reach here was the Virginia Central, which completed the line from Staunton to the Jackson River, about a mile from the current station, in 1857. After the Civil War, it was extended west, ultimately connecting with the Covington and Ohio Railroad. Those two lines merged in 1868 to form the Chesapeake and Ohio Railroad.

In 1881, the Richmond and Allegheny Railroad came through town to connect with the C & O. This event put Clifton Forge on the map as an important junction. It is probably no coincidence that Clifton Forge is the headquarters of the C & O Historical Society, which has sizable archives of records and equipment and is one of the largest railroad societies in the nation.

Old C & O Railroad freight depot

As you drive into town on Ridgeway Street, you'll see the rail yards on the right. The main office building, a frame structure, was built in 1906. By the 1920s, the place was buzzing with the sounds and activities of 100 trains a day.

The downtown area begins just past the railroad depot, which is still active. Many visitors come to Clifton Forge to shop at the nonprofit Alleghany Highlands Arts and Crafts Center, just down the street at 437 Ridgeway Street. It features changing exhibits and juried arts and crafts by regional artists. It is open year-round daily except Sundays.

Turn left at the next intersection, Commercial Avenue, then turn right on to

Old Masonic Theatre

Rainbow Gorge

Main Street. On the left at 512 Main Street is a Beaux-Arts brick building originally known as the Masonic Theater, built in 1905. If for no other reason, the theater will be remembered for two animal acts: the time when Roy Rogers appeared on stage with his horse, Trigger, and a pageant that featured 18 sheep on stage. Live performances—presumably humans only—are offered today in its current incarnation as the Stonewall Theater.

On the right at a stoplight farther down Main Street, you'll pass an interesting building that houses Clifton Forge's city hall and police department.

At the second traffic light after the city hall, turn right on to U.S. 220 Business, heading south. (If you were to continue down Main Street past the city hall, you'd reach another railroad-related structure, the old C & O freight depot, which dates to the late 1800s. It has been leased to the C & O Historical Society, which plans to restore the building and turn it into a history center.)

You'll pass over a bridge on U.S. 220 Business; follow the signs for U.S. 220 South. At the next stop sign, turn right to continue on U.S. 220 South, heading toward Iron Gate and Eagle Rock. The state historical marker near here notes the establishment of nearby Douthat State Park in 1936.

As you turn, be sure to note the dramatic rock outcroppings in the mountains across the road. Here, the road enters the gap known as Rainbow Gorge, the site of the iron forge that gave Clifton Forge its name. The Jackson River flows below, on its way to meet up with the Cowpasture River. They merge to form the James River at the southern end of Iron Gate.

*Continue less than 1 mile to **Iron Gate**.* This town was the bustling center of the iron industry in western Virginia in the 1800s.

*In about 7 miles, the road passes the village of **Gala**.* When the Richmond and Allegheny Railway excavated the roadbed for the line through here, the workmen uncovered evidence of an old Indian village.

Just a few miles east of Gala on Route 622 (which was once a busy road to Natural Bridge) is Daggers Springs, a popular mineral springs spa in days gone by. A man named Dagger opened the springs to visitors in 1820. Later in the century, new owners built a hotel that could accommodate 200 people. The springs were the hub of the area's social activities for many years.

Less than 2 miles past Gala, turn left on to Route 43 South (Narrow Passage

Road), a Virginia Byway. The road passes through an area of unusual and varied rock formations on its way to **Eagle Rock**. *In 1.9 miles, look for the ruins of stone furnaces on the right just as you enter the town.*

Eagle Rock was another industrial town that came alive with the boom times of the 1880s. In addition to its iron furnaces, Eagle Rock was known for its lime kilns, which operated until the 1950s. Fires and floods have plagued the town through the years, causing much damage to homes and businesses.

Before 1878, the town went by the more colorful name of Rat Hole. In those days, hobos and peddlers, referred to as "rats," were a common sight in the Valley. Many of them took shelter in an opening in the side of a nearby mountain, giving the town its name. When a post office was established in town in 1878, the locals decided that a better name would be Breckenridge. But it wasn't long before folks complained that this name was too long. The following year, the town was renamed Sheets, after a Civil War veteran. Finally, the picturesque name of Eagle Rock was adopted in 1883, after a bald eagle was killed on nearby Crawford Mountain.

Follow the signs for Route 43 South through Eagle Rock; you'll make several turns. Continue about 5 miles to another old settlement, Mount Carmel. Mount Carmel Presbyterian Church, just off Saltpetre Cave Road, to the right, was

Douthat State Park

Douthat State Park was one of the first six Virginia state parks. It was built with the help of the Civilian Conservation Corps, created by President Franklin Roosevelt to provide jobs to unemployed young men in the 1930s. Some 600 men lived in nearby camps while building the park's structures and dam, clearing hiking trails, and creating campsites and picnic areas. Douthat Lake is a trout-stocked 50-acre lake that features a beach and bathhouse. A visitor center tells the story of the park. During the summer, a restaurant—housed in one of the original CCC facilities—and a camp store are open to the public.

To get to the park, take Exit 27 off I-64 (just east of Clifton Forge) to Route 629 (Douthat Road) and drive 7 miles.

Old house at Mount Carmel

built in 1843. Across the road stands what must have been a grand farm-house for its day, now long abandoned. Saltpetre Cave was mined during the Civil War; saltpeter is an ingredient in gunpowder.

Route 43 follows the James River for a while, then begins to climb through Jefferson National Forest. It passes under I-81 just before reaching the town of **Buchanan**. *Turn right to follow Route 43 South/U.S. 11 South, which is Main Street in town.* (If you were to continue straight on Route 43, you'd join up with the Blue Ridge Parkway in about 3 miles.)

As you enter the town, you'll cross a concrete bridge over the James River; look to the right to see a swinging bridge still used by pedestrians. In 1864, the Confederates, led by General McCausland, attempted to keep General Hunter's Union army at bay by burning an earlier wooden bridge here. The tactic worked in slowing the Yankee advance, but sparks from the fire spread to homes and businesses at this end of town and destroyed many of them.

Buchanan is another old Virginia town, settled around 1738. Here, the Blue Ridge Mountains and the Allegheny Mountains are only 2 miles apart, geographically their closest point. The town was named for Colonel John Buchanan, an early Valley surveyor who married into the Patton family, which settled in the area in the 1740s. Colonel Buchanan formed a militia company here in 1775.

In the 1850s, the coming of the James River and Kanawha Canal to Buchanan defined the town as an important transportation center. From here, merchants and farmers in western Virginia and beyond could ship products to Richmond and other points east and receive products in return. Before the days of railroads, moving goods over water was easier and cheaper than hauling them overland on the few dirt or gravel roads. Surely, no one in those days would have imagined that a century later, road transport would once again be the method of choice, with railroads almost as obsolete as canals.

The canal's coming quickly turned Buchanan into a boom town. The official end of the canal was about 4 miles to the east, but the construction of a dam created a deep, wide lake that allowed the boats to enter the town. Since Buchanan was the major shipping point for the many coal mines and iron forges in the surrounding area, businesses and professions

began to locate here. One letter writer reported in 1852, "Buchanan has got to be a lively place, [with] dancing every night except Sunday."

One busy spot was the 23-room Hotel Botetourt, built in 1851 and still standing. To see it, go one block west off Main Street to Low Street. The Hotel Botetourt claimed Generals Robert E. Lee and Jubal Early among its guests. It was burned during the Civil War by Union troops who thought the Confederates were still in town.

Old Hotel Botetourt

In the next block on the same side of Low Street is a brick building, now a residence, called the Community House. Construction on it was begun, in the true spirit of optimism, around 1840—some 11 years before the canal came to town. The structure's original purpose was to serve as a warehouse for goods transported by canal boats. Many other warehouses and docks were built in town later. The Community House is on the Virginia Landmarks Register.

George Washington pushed the idea of an extensive network of rivers and canals all over America in the years before the Revolution. Already involved in building the C & O Canal in northern Virginia, he proposed a plan to the Virginia General Assembly in 1784 to build a

A popular writer of her time, Mary Johnston was born in Buchanan in 1870 in a house that was torn down years ago to make way for a car dealership. The daughter of a former president of the James River and Kanawha Canal Company, Mary was known as a "delicate" child. As a result, she was schooled at home for all but a few months of her life.

She became a prolific writer of novels, some of which were based on aspects of Virginia history. She published 23 novels in all, the most famous of which was the 1899 bestseller *To Have and To Hold*. In 1911, flush with royalties from her book sales, she and her three sisters built a mountain mansion they called Three Hills in Warm Springs. (See The Monterey to Hot Springs Tour, page 186, for more about this home, which is now an inn.) Her book sales declined when she made no secret of her support for the women's suffrage movement. She died at Three Hills in 1936.

canal "from Tidewater up the James as far as practicable," the ultimate goal being to connect the Atlantic seaboard with the growing settlements across the mountains.

The assembly supported Washington's plan and made him the James River Company's first president. It also gave him 100 shares of stock in the company, which he later gave to the struggling Liberty Hall Academy in Lexington. Officials at the grateful Liberty Hall repaid him by renaming the school for him—Washington College, today's Washington and Lee University (see The Natural Bridge to Lexington Tour, pages 202–4).

The James River Company began constructing the James River and Kanawha Canal in 1786. The goal was to reach across the Alleghenies to the Kanawha and Ohio Rivers. After years of slow progress, the state of Virginia took over the project in 1820. Twenty years later, it completed the first leg, between Richmond and Lynchburg, a distance of more than 156 miles. After many more delays, the 50-mile section from Lynchburg to Buchanan was finally completed in 1851. The canal stopped in Buchanan, never to be extended to Covington and from there to Ohio, as planned. The last lock to be built was at Eagle Rock, at an elevation of 1,000 feet above sea level.

Costing more than $8 million (in mid-1800s dollars), the canal was an engineering feat. It had 90 locks, for a total lift of 728 feet up the mountains. In all, it required 23 dams, 12 aqueducts, 129 culverts, 135 road bridges over it, 20 towpath bridges, and one 100-foot street bridge at Lynchburg. Many of the lock ruins survive. (See The Natural Bridge to Lexington Tour, page 199, for directions to one of the old locks along the North River— now the Maury River—branch of the canal.)

The canal was used for passenger transport as well. Various companies operated "packet" (or passenger) lines that offered a fairly civilized means of travel among points between Buchanan and Richmond. Often, the freight boats took on passengers as well. They measured 75 to 100 feet long and were guided by men wielding long poles; the boats could also be pulled by horses or mules that walked along the towpath next to the canal. The trip from Buchanan to Richmond took one week for freight boats and three days and nights for packet boats.

One woman who traveled from Locust Bottom to Buchanan by freight boat in 1852 wrote an account of her pleasant experience: "Each end of the boat was equipped for cooking and splendid meals were served. We had three dinners on board: fresh fish, bacon, chicken, roast potatoes, biscuits, coffee, and pie. The last was carried in stock and warmed. There was no table; the cook served the plates and we sat on stools and ate."

During the Civil War, the Confederates made good use of the canal to ship iron ore to Richmond, where a large ironworks made heavy artillery for the South.

Although hurt by the war, Buchanan continued to prosper until a terrible flood in 1877 destroyed much of the canal. That tragedy led to the canal's being put up for sale in 1880. It was then abandoned once the railroads extended their lines into western Virginia. Conveniently for the railroads, much of the track could be laid on the 12-foot-wide canal towpaths.

The tour ends in Buchanan. To return to I-81, go back to Main Street (U.S. 11) and drive either south or north, depending on your destination; it joins I-81 in either direction.

Appendix

Federal Agencies, Parks, and Historic Sites

Buena Vista Regional Visitor Center
United States Forest Service
Route 60 East
Buena Vista, VA 24416
540-291-2188

Camp Roosevelt
United States Forest Service
109 Molineau Road
Edinburg, VA 22824
540-984-4101

Deerfield Ranger District
United States Forest Service
Route 6, Box 419
Staunton, VA 24401
540-885-8028

Dry River Ranger District
United States Forest Service
112 North River Road
Bridgewater, VA 22812
540-828-2591

Elizabeth Furnace Recreation Area
United States Forest Service
109 Molineau Road
Edinburg, VA 22824
540-984-4101

The Forest Place
United States Forest Service
Route 1, Box 621
Hot Springs, VA 24445
540-839-5281

Glenwood/Pedlar Ranger Districts (Sherando Lake)
United States Forest Service
P.O. Box 10
Natural Bridge Station, VA 24579
540-291-2188

Harpers Ferry National Historical Park
Harpers Ferry, WV 25425
304-535-6029
www.nps.gov/hafe/home.htm

James River Ranger District (Lake Moomaw)
United States Forest Service
810-A Madison Avenue
Covington, VA 24426
540-962-2214

Laurel Fork (Highland County)
United States Forest Service
Route 2, Box 30
Hot Springs, VA 24445
540-839-2521 or 540-839-5281

Lee Ranger District (northern end of the Shenandoah Valley)
United States Forest Service
109 Molineau Road
Edinburg, VA 22824
540-984-4101

Massanutten Visitor Information Center
United States Forest Service
3220 Lee Highway (U.S. 211)
New Market, VA 22844
540-740-8310

Natural Bridge Visitor Center
United States Forest Service
P.O. Box 10
Natural Bridge Station, VA 24579
540-291-1806

New Castle Ranger District (Roaring Run Furnace)
United States Forest Service
P.O. Box 246
New Castle, VA 24127
540-864-5195

Ramsey's Draft Wilderness/ Mountain House Recreation Area
United States Forest Service
Route 6, Box 419
Staunton, VA 24401
540-885-8028

Roaring Run Recreation Area
United States Forest Service
P.O. Box 246
New Castle, VA 24127
540-864-5195

Shenandoah National Park/
Skyline Drive
3655 U.S. 211 East
Luray, VA 22835
540-999-3500
www.nps.gov/shen/index.htm

Sherando Lake Recreation Area
United States Forest Service
P.O. Box 10
Natural Bridge Station, VA 24579
540-291-2188

Trout Pond Recreation Area
United States Forest Service
109 Molineau Road
Edinburg, VA 22824
540-984-4101

Warm Springs Ranger District
(Laurel Fork, Hidden Valley,
Warwick Plantation)
United States Forest Service
Route 2, Box 30
Hot Springs, VA 24445
540-839-2521 or 540-839-5281

State and Regional Parks

Berkeley Springs State Park
121 South Washington Street
Berkeley Springs, WV 25411
800-CALL-WVA or 304-258-
2711

Douthat State Park
Route 1, Box 212
Millboro, VA 24460
540-862-8100

Grand Caverns Regional Park
P.O. Box 478
Grottoes, VA 24441
540-249-5705

Lost River State Park
Route 2, Box 24
Mathias, WV 26812
800-CALL-WVA or 304-897-
5372

Natural Chimneys Regional Park
94 Natural Chimneys Lane
Mount Solon, VA 22843
540-350-2510

Raymond "Andy" Guest
Shenandoah River State Park
U.S. 340
Front Royal, VA 22630
540-592-3556

State Arboretum of Virginia
Orland E. White Arboretum at
Blandy Experimental Farm
P.O. Box 175
Boyce, VA 22620
540-837-1758

Upper Valley Regional Park
Authority (Natural Chimneys
and Grand Caverns Parks)
P.O. Box 478
Grottoes, VA 24441
540-249-5729

Virginia State Parks
Virginia Department of
Conservation and Recreation
203 Governor Street, Suite 602
Richmond, VA 23219
800-933-PARK or 804-786-1712
www.state.va.us

West Virginia Division of
Tourism and Parks
State Capitol Complex
Charleston, WV 25305
800-CALL-WVA
www.wvparks.com

Chambers of Commerce and Information Centers

Alleghany Highlands
Chamber of Commerce
203 Commercial Avenue
Clifton Forge, VA 24422
540-862-4969

Alleghany Highlands
Chamber of Commerce
241 West Main Street
Covington, VA 24426
540-962-2178

Bath County
Chamber of Commerce
Virginia Building
U.S. 220
P.O. Box 718
Hot Springs, VA 24445
800-628-8092 or 540-839-5409

Berryville/Clarke County
Chamber of Commerce
P.O. Box 365
Berryville, VA 22611
540-955-4200

Botetourt County
Chamber of Commerce
Old Jail Building
Fincastle, VA 24090
540-473-8280 or 540-992-8280

Buena Vista
Chamber of Commerce
2202 Magnolia Avenue
Buena Vista, VA 24416
540-261-2880

Charles Town Main Street
P.O. Box 205
Charles Town, WV 25414
304-535-2627

Edinburg Chamber of Commerce
P.O. Box 85
Edinburg, VA 22824
540-984-8521

Front Royal–Warren County
Chamber of Commerce
414 East Main Street
P.O. Box 568
Front Royal, VA 22630
800-338-2576 or 540-635-3185

Harrisonburg–Rockingham
County Convention and
Visitors Bureau
10 East Gay Street
Harrisonburg, VA 22802
540-434-2319

Highland County
Chamber of Commerce
P.O. Box 223
Monterey, VA 24465
540-468-2550

Jefferson County Visitor and
Convention Bureau
P.O. Box A
Harpers Ferry, WV 25425
304-535-2627

Lexington Visitor Center
106 East Washington Street
Lexington, VA 24450
540-463-3777

Luray–Page County Chamber of
Commerce/Tourism Council
46 East Main Street
Luray, VA 22835
540-743-3915

Martinsburg–Berkeley County
Convention and Visitors
Bureau
208 South Queen Street
Martinsburg, WV 25401
800-498-2386 or 304-264-8801

Mount Jackson Area
Chamber of Commerce
P.O. Box 111
Mount Jackson, VA 22842
540-477-3275

Old Town Welcome Center/
Kurtz Cultural Center/
Shenandoah Valley
Civil War Center
2 North Cameron Street
Winchester, VA 22601
540-722-6367

Roanoke Valley Convention
and Visitors Bureau
114 Market Street
Roanoke, VA 24011
800-635-5535

Shenandoah County Travel
Council
I-81, Exit 283
P.O. Box 802
Woodstock, VA 22664
888-367-3954 or 540-459-2332

Shenandoah Valley Travel
Association
I-81, Exit 264
P.O. Box 1040
New Market, VA 22844
540-740-3132
www.svta.org

Shepherdstown Visitors Center
102 East German Street
Shepherdstown, WV 25443
304-876-2786

Staunton Convention and
Visitors Bureau
P.O. Box 58
Staunton, VA 24401
800-332-5219 or 540-332-3972

Staunton-Augusta Visitors Center
I-81, Exit 222
P.O. Box 810
Staunton, VA 24402
800-332-5219

Strasburg Chamber of Commerce
P.O. Box 42
Strasburg, VA 22657
540-465-9197 or 540-465-3187

Travel Berkeley Springs
304 Fairfax Street
Berkeley Springs, WV 25411
800-447-8797

Waynesboro–Augusta County Chamber of Commerce/ Rockfish Gap Tourist Information Center
I-65, Exit 99
301 West Main Street
Waynesboro, VA 22980
800-471-3109

Winchester–Frederick County Chamber of Commerce and Visitor Center
1360 South Pleasant Valley Road
Winchester, VA 22601
800-662-1360 or 540-662-4135
www.shentel.net/wfcedc/

Woodstock Chamber of Commerce
143 North Main Street
Woodstock, VA 22664
540-459-2542

Museums, Historical Societies, Historical Sites, and Other Attractions

Abram's Delight Museum
1340 South Pleasant Valley Road
Winchester, VA 22601
540-662-6519

Alleghany Highlands Arts and Crafts Center
439 East Ridgeway Street
P.O. Box 273
Clifton Forge, VA 24422
540-862-4447

Association for the Preservation of Civil War Sites, Inc.
11 Public Square, Suite 200
Hagerstown, MD 21740

Augusta Historical Society
P.O. Box 686
Staunton, VA 24402

Bath County Historical Society Museum
P.O. Box 212
Warm Springs, VA 24484
540-839-2543

Belle Boyd House/Berkeley County and Civil War Museums
Berkeley County Historical Society Genealogy and History Archives
126 East Race Street
Martinsburg, WV 25401
304-267-4713

Belle Grove Plantation
P.O. Box 137
Middletown, VA 22645
540-869-2028

Berkeley County Historical Society
P.O. Box 1624
Martinsburg, WV 25401
304-267-4713

Botetourt County Historical Society
P.O. Box 468
Fincastle, VA 24090

Burwell-Morgan Mill
c/o Clarke County Historical Association
104 North Church Street
Berryville, VA 22611
540-955-2600

C & O Historical Society
312 East Ridgeway Street
Clifton Forge, VA 24422
800-453-COHS

Cedar Creek Battlefield Visitors Center
8437 Valley Pike
P.O. Box 229
Middletown, VA 22645
540-869-2064

Clarke County Historical Association
104 North Church Street
Berryville, VA 22611
540-955-2600

Daniel Harrison House
Fort Harrison, Inc.
P.O. Box 366
Dayton, VA 22821
540-879-2280

Edinburg Museum
107 Center Street
Edinburg, VA 22824
540-984-8521

Elkton Historical Society
P.O. Box 1
Elkton, VA 22827

Garth Newel Music Center
P.O. Box 427
Hot Springs, VA 24445
540-839-5018

General Adam Stephen House
309 East John Street
Martinsburg, WV 25401
304-267-4434

George C. Marshall Museum
Virginia Military Institute
Lexington, VA 24450
540-463-7103

George Washington's Office
Museum
Braddock and Cork Streets
Winchester, VA 22601
540-662-4412

Glen Burnie
530 Amherst Street
Winchester, VA 22601
540-662-1473

Glen Maury Park
2039 Sycamore Avenue
Buena Vista, VA 24416
800-555-8845

Hall of Valor Civil War Museum
New Market Battlefield State
Historical Park
P.O. Box 1864
New Market, VA 22844
540-740-3101

Harpers Ferry Historical
Association
P.O. Box 197
Harpers Ferry, WV 25425
304-535-6881

Harrisonburg–Rockingham
County Historical Society
P.O. Box 716
Bowman Road and High Street
Dayton, VA 22821
540-879-2681

Historic Staunton Foundation
120 South Augusta Street
Staunton, VA 24401
540-885-7676

Holy Cross Abbey
Route 2, Box 3870
Berryville, VA 22611
540-955-3124

Ivy Lodge and Belle Boyd
Cottage
101 Chester Street
Front Royal, VA 22630
540-636-1446

Jefferson County Courthouse
Washington and George Streets
Charles Town, WV 25414
304-728-7713

Jefferson County Museum
200 East Washington Street
Charles Town, WV 25414
304-725-8628

Jefferson Pools/The Homestead
Resort
U.S. 220
Warm Springs, VA 24484
540-839-5346

L. Norman Dillon Farm Museum
Route 9
Hedgesville, WV 25427
304-754-3704

Lake Robertson
RFD 2, Box 251
Lexington, VA 24450
540-463-4164

Lee Chapel
Washington and Lee University
Lexington, VA 24450
540-463-8768

Long Branch
P.O. Box 241
Millwood, VA 22646
540-837-1856

Lost River Museum
Lost River, WV 26811
304-897-7264

McCormick Farm/Shenandoah
Valley Agricultural Research
and Extension Center
Virginia Tech
Steeles Tavern, VA 24476
540-377-2255

Morgan Cabin
Bunker Hill, WV 25413
304-229-8946

Mount Hebron Cemetery
East Boscawen Street
Winchester, VA 22601
540-662-4868

Museum of American Frontier
Culture
P.O. Box 810
Staunton, VA 24402
540-332-7850

Museum of American Presidents
130 North Massanutten Street
P.O. Box 40
Strasburg, VA 22657
540-465-5999

Natural Bridge
U.S. 11 and Route 130
P.O. Box 57
Natural Bridge, VA 24578
800-533-1410 or 540-291-2121

New Market Battlefield
Military Museum
P.O. Box 1131
9500 Collins Drive
New Market, VA 22844
540-740-8065

P. Buckley Moss Museum
150 P. Buckley Moss Drive
Waynesboro, VA 22980
540-949-6473

Page County Heritage
Association
P.O. Box 627
Luray, VA 22835

Port Republic Museum/Turner
Ashby House
P.O. Box 82
Port Republic, VA 24471
540-249-5668 or 540-249-5689

Reuel B. Pritchett Museum
P.O. Box 147
Bridgewater College
Bridgewater, VA 22812
540-828-5462 or 540-828-5414

Rockbridge Historical Society
P.O. Box 514
Lexington, VA 24450

The Rumseian Society
P.O. Box 1787
Shepherdstown, WV 25443
304-876-6907

Shenandoah Apple
Blossom Festival
135 North Cameron Street
Winchester, VA 22601
540-662-3863

Shenandoah County Historical
Society
300 Stony Creek Boulevard
Edinburg, VA 22824
540-984-8200

Shenandoah Valley
Art Center, Inc.
600 West Main Street
P.O. Box 907
Waynesboro, VA 22980
540-949-7662

Shenandoah Valley Folk Art
and Heritage Center
P.O. Box 716
382 High Street
Dayton, VA 22821
540-879-2681

Shenandoah Valley
Music Festival
102 North Main Street
Woodstock, VA 22664
800-459-3396 or 540-459-3396

Society of Port Republic
Preservationists, Inc.
P.O. Box 82
Port Republic, VA 24471

Stonewall Jackson House
8 East Washington Street
Lexington, VA 24450
540-463-2552

Stonewall Jackson Museum
at Hupp's Hill
33229 Old Valley Pike
P.O. Box 31
Strasburg, VA 22657
540-465-5884

Stonewall Jackson's
   Headquarters Museum
415 North Braddock Street
Winchester, VA 22601
540-667-3242

Strasburg Museum
King Street
Strasburg, VA 22657
540-465-3175 or 540-465-3428

Theatre at Lime Kiln
14 South Randolph Street
Lexington, VA 24450
540-463-3074

V.M.I. Museum
Jackson Memorial Hall
Virginia Military Institute
Lexington, VA 24450
540-464-7232

Virginia Canals and
   Navigations Society
6826 Rosemount Drive
McLean, VA 22101

Virginia Historical Society
428 North Boulevard
P.O. Box 7311
Richmond, VA 23221
804-358-4901

Virginia Quilt Museum
301 South Main Street
Harrisonburg, VA 22801
540-433-3818

Wade's Mill
55 Kennedy–Wade's Mill Road
Raphine, VA 24472
540-348-1400

Warren Heritage Society
101 Chester Street
Front Royal, VA 22630
540-636-1446

Warren Rifles
   Confederate Museum
95 Chester Street
Front Royal, VA 22630
540-636-6982 or 540-635-2219

Waynesboro Heritage Museum
Main Street and Wayne Avenue
Waynesboro, VA 22980
540-943-3943

Wayside Theatre
Old Valley Pike
Middletown, VA 22645
800-951-1776

Winchester–Frederick County
   Historical Society
1340 South Pleasant Valley Road
Winchester, VA 22601
540-662-6550

Woodrow Wilson Birthplace
   and Museum
18-24 North Coalter Street
Staunton, VA 24401
540-885-0897

Woodstock Museum
137 West Court Street
Woodstock, VA 22664
540-459-5518 or 540-459-3621

Bibliography

Adams, Charles S., ed. *Roadside Markers in West Virginia*. Self-published, 1997.

Bath County Historical Society. *The Bicentennial History of Bath County, Virginia, 1791–1991*. Marceline, MO: Heritage House Publishing, 1991.

Bly, Daniel. *From the Rhine to the Shenandoah*. Baltimore: Gateway Press, 1993.

Boley, Henry. *Lexington in Old Virginia*. 1936. Reprint, Natural Bridge Station, VA: Rockbridge Publishing Company, 1990.

Botetourt County Historical Society. *Botetourt Bicentennial Souvenir Program and History*. Botetourt County Historical Society, 1970.

Branch, Michael P., and Daniel J. Philippon. *The Height of Our Mountains*. Baltimore: Johns Hopkins University Press, 1998.

Bruce, Thomas. *Southwest Virginia and Shenandoah Valley*. 1891. Reprint, Bowie. MD: Heritage Books, 1997.

Cartmell, T. K. *Shenandoah Valley Pioneers and Their Descendants: A History of Frederick County, Virginia*. Winchester, VA: Eddy Press, 1909.

Christian, Frances Archer, and Suzanne Massie. *Homes and Gardens in Old Virginia*. Richmond: Garrett and Massie, 1950.

Clem, Gladys Bauserman. *Stories of the Shenandoah*. Staunton, VA: self-published, 1948.

Clower, J. B., ed. *Glimpses of the Past in Shenandoah County*. Woodstock, VA: Woodstock Museum, 1984.

Cohen, Stan. *Historic Springs of the Virginias: A Pictorial History*. Charleston, WV: Pictorial Histories Publishing Company, 1981.

Comstock, Jim. *Hardesty's West Virginia Counties*. Richwood, WV: 1973.

Couper, William. *History of the Shenandoah Valley*. New York: Lewis Historical Publishing Company, 1952.

Davis, Julia, and Lucian Niemeyer. *Shenandoah: Daughter of the Stars*. Baton Rouge: Louisiana State University Press, 1994.

Dohme, Alvin. *Shenandoah: The Valley Story*. Front Royal, VA: Greatland Publishing Company, 1973.

Dolmetsch, Christopher L. *The German Press of the Shenandoah Valley*. Columbia, SC: Camden House, 1984.

Downs, Janet. *The Mills of Rockingham County*. Self-published, 1997.

Egloff, Keith, and Deborah Woodward. *First People: The Early Indians of Virginia*. Charlottesville: University Press of Virginia, 1992.

Farrar, Emmie Ferguson, and Emilee Hines. *Old Virginia Houses—Shenandoah*. Charlotte, NC: Delmar Publishing Company, 1976.

Flexner, James Thomas. *Washington: The Indispensable Man*. New York: NAL Penguin, 1984.

Foreman, Michael. *Images of the Past: A Photographic Review of Winchester and Frederick County, Virginia*. Winchester, VA: Winchester–Frederick County Historical Society, 1980.

Frye, Keith. *Roadside Geology of Virginia*. Missoula, MT: Mountain Press Publishing Company, 1986.

Fulwiler, Harry, Jr. *Buchanan, Virginia: Gateway to the Southwest*. Self-published, 1980.

Gardner, William M. *Lost Arrowheads and Broken Pottery*. Front Royal, VA: Thunderbird Museum, 1986.

Gilbert, David T. *A Walker's Guide to Harpers Ferry, West Virginia*. 5th ed. Harpers Ferry, WV: Harpers Ferry Historical Association, 1995.

Gurnee, Russell. *The Discovery of Luray Caverns*. Closter, NJ: self-published, 1978.

Hale, Laura Virginia. *Belle Boyd: Southern Spy of the Shenandoah*. Front Royal, VA: Warren Rifles Chapter, United Daughters of the Confederacy.

———. *On Chester Street: Presence of the Past Patterns the Future*. Stephens City, VA: Commercial Press, 1985.

Hart, Freeman H. *The Valley of Virginia in the American Revolution, 1763–1789*. Chapel Hill: University of North Carolina Press, 1942.

Heatwole, John L. *Shenandoah Voices: Folklore, Legends and Traditions of the Valley*. Berryville, VA: Rockbridge Publishing Company, 1995.

Historical Fincastle, Inc. *Around Town: A Pictorial Review of Old Fincastle, Virginia*. Fincastle, VA: Historical Fincastle, 1989.

Ingalls, Fay. *The Valley Road*. New York: World Publishing Company, 1949.

James River Project Committee and the Virginia Academy of Science. *The James River Basin: Past, Present, and Future*. Richmond: Virginia Academy of Science, 1950.

Jefferson, Thomas. *Notes on the State of Virginia*. 1788. Reprint, New York: W. W. Norton and Company, 1954.

Johnston, Wilbur S. *Weaving a Common Thread: A History of the Woolen Industry in the Top of the Shenandoah Valley*. Winchester, VA: Winchester–Frederick County Historical Society, 1990.

Keister, E. E. *Strasburg, Virginia, and the Keister Family*. Self-published, 1972.

Kercheval, Samuel. *A History of the Valley of Virginia*. 1833. Reprint, Harrisonburg, VA: C. J. Carrier Company, 1994.

Kerkhoff, Jennie Ann. *Old Homes of Page County, Virginia*. Luray, VA: Lauck and Company, 1962.

Lambert, Darwin. *The Undying Past of Shenandoah National Park*. Boulder, CO: Roberts Rinehart, Publishers, 1989.

MacMaster, Richard K. *Augusta County History, 1865–1950*. Staunton, VA: Augusta County Historical Society, 1987.

Magin, Irvin D. *Shenandoah County Gazetteer and Historical Geography*. Edinburg, VA: Shenandoah County Library, 1991.

May, C. E. *Life under Four Flags in North River Basin of Virginia*. Verona, VA: McClure Press, 1976.

———. *My Augusta, A Spot of Earth, Not a Woman*. Self-published, 1987.

McCary, Ben C. *Indians in Seventeenth-Century Virginia*. Charlottesville: University Press of Virginia, 1957.

McCue, Elizabeth B. *Staunton, Virginia: A Pictorial History*. Staunton, VA: Historic Staunton Foundation, 1985.

Morton, Oren F. *A Centennial History of Alleghany County*. 1923. Reprint, Harrisonburg, VA: C. J. Carrier Company, 1986.

———. *A History of Highland County, Virginia*. Baltimore: Regional Publishing Company, 1979.

———. *A History of Rockbridge County, Virginia*. Staunton, VA: McClure Company, 1920.

National Park Service, Office of Publications. *John Brown's Raid*. Washington: GPO, 1974.

Niederer, Frances J. *The Town of Fincastle, Virginia*. Charlottesville: University Press of Virginia, 1965.

Norris, J. E. *History of the Lower Shenandoah Valley*. Chicago: A. Warner and Company, Publishers, 1890.

Northern Virginia Daily. *Standing Ground: The Civil War in the Shenandoah Valley*. Strasburg, VA: Shenandoah Publishing House, 1996.

Page: The County of Plenty. Luray, VA: Page County Bicentennial Commission, 1976.

Reeder, Carolyn. *Shenandoah Heritage: The Story of the People before the Park*. Washington: Potomac Appalachian Trail Club, 1978.

Reniers, Perceval. *The Springs of the Virginias: Life, Love, and Death at the Waters*. Chapel Hill: University of North Carolina Press, 1941.

Rothery, Agnes. *New Roads in Old Virginia*. Boston: Houghton Mifflin Company, Riverside Press, 1929.

Rouse, Parker, Jr. *The Great Wagon Road: From Philadelphia to the South*. Richmond, VA: Dietz Press, 1995.

Salmon, Emily J., and Edward D. C. Campbell, Jr. *Hornbook of Virginia History*. 4th ed. Richmond: Library of Virginia, 1994.

Salmon, John S. *A Guidebook to Virginia's Historical Markers*. Charlottesville: University Press of Virginia, 1994.

Shenandoah County Bicentennial Committee. *Dunmore 1772–1778, Shenandoah 1778–1972*. Woodstock, VA: Shenandoah County Bicentennial Committee, 1972.

Stevens, William O. *The Shenandoah and Its Byways*. New York: Dodd, Mead, 1941.

Stoner, Robert Douthat. *A Seed-bed of the Republic: A Study of the Pioneers in the Upper (Southern) Valley of Virginia*. Roanoke, VA: Roanoke Historical Society, 1962.

Strickler, Harry M. *A Short History of Page County, Virginia*. 1952. Reprint, Harrisonburg, VA: C. J. Carrier Company, 1974.

Tennery, Katherine, and Shirley Scott. *Country Roads: Rockbridge County, Virginia*. 2nd ed. Berryville, VA: Rockbridge Publishing Company, 1995.

Terrell, Isaac Long. *Old Houses in Rockingham County*. Verona, VA: McClure Press, 1983.

Trout, W. E., III. *The Maury River Atlas: Historic Sites on the North River Navigation*. Lexington, VA: Virginia Canals and Navigations Society, 1992.

Vaughn, E. Dean. *The Orkney Springs of Virginia*. New York: Carleton Press, 1982.

Virginia Writers Project (Works Progress Administration). *Virginia: A Guide to the Old Dominion*. New York: Oxford University Press, 1940.

Waddell, Joseph A. *Annals of Augusta County, Virginia, from 1726 to 1871*. 2nd ed. Bridgewater, VA: C. J. Carrier Company, 1958.

Wayland, John W. *Historic Harrisonburg*. 1949. Reprint, Harrisonburg, VA: C. J. Carrier Company, 1990.

———. *Historic Homes of Northern Virginia and the Eastern Panhandle of West Virginia*. Staunton, VA: McClure Publishing Company, 1937.

———. *History of Rockingham County, Virginia*. 1912. Reprint, Harrisonburg, VA: C. J. Carrier Company, 1980.

———. *History of Shenandoah County, Virginia*. 1927. Reprint, Baltimore: Regional Publishing Company, 1998.

———. *Scenic and Historical Guide to the Shenandoah Valley*. Dayton, VA: Ruebush, 1923.

———. *Stonewall Jackson's Way*. Staunton, VA: McClure Company, 1940.

———. *Twenty-five Chapters on the Shenandoah Valley*. 1957. Reprint, Harrisonburg, VA: C. J. Carrier Company, 1989.

———. *The Valley Turnpike, Winchester to Staunton, and Other Roads*. Winchester, VA: Winchester–Frederick County Historical Society, 1967.

Williamson, Mary Ann, and Jean Allen Davis. *The History of Edinburg, Virginia*. Stephens City, VA: Edinburg Heritage Foundation, 1995.

Willis, Carrie Hunter, and Etta Belle Walker. *Legends of the Skyline Drive and the Great Valley of Virginia*. Richmond: Dietz Press, 1937.

Wilson, Howard K. *Great Valley Patriots: Western Virginia in the Struggle for Liberty*. Verona, VA: McClure Press, 1976.

Wine, J. Floyd. *Life along Holman's Creek*. Self-published, 1982.

Woodhead, Henry, and Paul Mathless, eds. *Shenandoah 1862: Voices of the Civil War*. Alexandria, VA: Time-Life Books, 1997.

Wust, Klaus. *The Virginia Germans*. Charlottesville: University Press of Virginia, 1969.

Zapton, Steve. *Singers Glen: Portrait of a Village*. Harrisonburg, VA: Harrisonburg–Rockingham County Historical Society, 1979.

Index